ALEXANDER

AND

THE HELLENISTIC WORLD

ALEXANDER

AND THE

HELLENISTIC WORLD

C. BRADFORD WELLES

A. M. HAKKERT LTD.

TORONTO

1970

Set in Aldine Roman
by Ancient and Modern Book Printers
Toronto, Canada
Printed in the United States of America

Standard Book Numbers
Cloth: 88866-501-6
Paper: 88866-502-4

Library of Congress Catalogue Card Number
73-135236

A. M. Hakkert Ltd.
554 Spadina Crescent
Toronto 179, Ontario
Canada

To my students and associates
at Yale, 1960/61, this book is
dedicated in appreciation

Editor's Note

This work is published almost exactly as it was at the time of the author's sudden death. All major editorial decisions had been made; we had selected the illustrations, and had decided upon the nature of the maps and tabular material.

In light of this, we are able to publish this history as the author wanted it to be, with the addition of an index and with the omission of some photographs which were not available. Those who saw the proof suggested a few minor editorial changes, and we have made those changes which I judge would have been accepted by the author. In addition, I have written a very short epilogue which many felt was necessary to provide a suitable ending to the book.

I should like to express my thanks to those who have helped bring this book out under difficult circumstances: to Katharine Peacock, who typed the manuscript first in 1961, and now has typeset and helped to read proof; to Professor Ann Perkins, for editorial suggestions and for a careful reading of the final proof; to Professor Viola Stephens, who also helped with reading the proof; and Jacqueline Nugent, who compiled the index. I appreciate the many suggestions which they and others made, and I myself am responsible for the omission of those that do not appear in the final text.

A.E.S.

Preface

This sketch of the political and cultural history of the Hellenistic World was written during the academic year 1960/61. It is not always easy to write systematically while carrying a full academic load of teaching, and I am grateful to my pupils and associates who furnished me not only moral support but also a degree of compulsion. They would not speak to me until I had completed the day's stint of pages.

There are no beginnings and ends in history. Historians divide it up according to some organizational plan. History is not a congeries of all that happened, still less a collection of the available evidence. Historical writing is close to fiction, in that it must present a sensible and reasoned narrative, but it must be as accurate as possible. In ancient history in general, and in the Hellenistic period particularly, we have, in effect, no facts. We have only evidence, the testimony of ancient historians who operated under the same conditions as we, only with more evidence at their disposal, and the documentary testimony of inscriptions, papyri, and monuments. The latter are true but in need of interpretation; the former represent opinions which are not necessarily true but require critical examination. This is why ancient history is never written definitively, but must always be rewritten in the light of new evidence and new points of view.

In the three hundred years of Hellenism, much happened over a wide front. The career of Alexander the Great is generously documented and presents a unified as well as a romantic theme. Thereafter there are no dominating heroes, but a tangled phantasmagoria of conflicting forces, kings, dynasts, states. There is no obvious theme about which a narrative can be constructed. It has been my attempt to find such a theme, nevertheless, in the growth and consolidation of new political concepts, kingdoms and territorial states, each with its own character but all sharing and developing a common culture, and their gradual absorption in the dynamic and superpowerful Roman Republic. In one sense, this process may be viewed as the rise and fall of the Hellenistic states. It was certainly painful, even sad in many of its aspects. In terms of world history, however, it is not to be viewed as tragic. If Rome had not turned east toward the end of the third century, it would have lacked or acquired much more slowly many of the features of our Western civilization which we associate with, and have inherited from, the later Republic and the Empire. If the nearer parts of the Hellenistic world had not come under Roman domination, they would have lacked the security which Rome provided in the large against the native forces to the north, east, and south. The Iranian revival, notably, constituted a serious threat to Syria and Asia Minor, and while the Arsacid Parthians called themselves "phil-hellene," they were not and could not have been Hellenized as were the Romans. The Parthian king, it is said, sent three magi to Jerusalem to discover if, in fact, as the stars reported, a king had been born in Israel. If it had not been for the Romans, very possibly he would not have had to send envoys but would have been himself master of Palestine, and the Slaughter of the Innocents might have been more effective in preventing the realization of the Kingdom of God.

There are many obligations to acknowledge. I am grateful to the Ullstein Firm in Berlin for having commissioned this history in the first place, and now for having allowed the publication of a revised and augmented English edition. I am grateful to my editor, Professor Alan E. Samuel, for his numerous technical and professional services. I cannot name all of those who, as students or associates, have made corrections and suggestions on the original text. I am indebted to Professor Ann Perkins for advice both as to the section on Hellenistic art and as to the choice and selection of illustrations. And I would thank all of those, scholars or publishers, who have supplied the photographs which are here reproduced; specific acknowledgments are made in each case.

C. Bradford Welles

Eastham, Massachusetts
27 August 1969

Contents

Chapter III Social and Economic Aspects
of the Hellenistic Period

1. Social Aspects

2. Economic Aspects

Chapter IV Hellenistic Culture

1. Philosophy

2. Science

3. Religion

4. Literature

5. Art

Epilogue 225

Bibliography 227

Notes 233

Index 237

Appendix I   The Hellenistic Dynasties

Appendix II   Maps

Illustrations

ALEXANDER

AND

THE HELLENISTIC WORLD

Introduction

Of the four great areas of ancient history, that of the Hellenistic East from the death of Alexander the Great in 323 B.C. to the extinction of the last kingdom with the suicide of Cleopatra VII in 30 B.C. is certainly the least studied as it is, in considerable part, the least known. This is in part due to the uneven and often inadequate sources, part to cultural considerations. The Hellenistic period lacks the literary and artistic monuments which make the study of classical Greece and its antecedents of primary importance. The rivalries and struggles of the Greek city states are of little significance in themselves, but take on a substantial interest in the light of Homer and the lyric poets, Pindar and Bacchylides, and the outstanding achievements of the Attic writers in the fields of drama, history, philosophy, and rhetoric, while classic Greek art has an esthetic and historical value which cannot be overemphasized. Similarly, the Roman Empire, with all its complexity and its bewildering mass of evidence, would have a compelling interest because of the writers of Silver Latin and the Second Sophistic, because of the intellectual ferment which produced Neo-Platonism and Christianity, and because of the wealth of Imperial art through which we see in part also a reflection of great artists of earlier periods whose original works have not survived. As to the Republic, the great writers and outstanding personalities of the Golden Age, together with the intrinsic interest and historical importance of Roman government and law, have made it at all times a popular subject for students and amateurs. But the Hellenistic East, contemporary with the last three centuries of the Republic, is commonly considered only as a part of the Republic's scene and background. This is a period and an area not entirely lacking in cultural interest. The Alexandrian poets, of whom we have learned somewhat more in recent years from finds among the Egyptian papyri, have a considerable importance, although perhaps only Callimachus has any claim to real literary value. Hellenistic science and technology, based in part on age-old observations and techniques derived from earlier Egypt and Babylonia, attained the highest perfection reached in antiquity. Hellenistic philosophy, especially that of the Stoics and Epicureans, provided the standards for the moral behavior of later Western culture. Hellenistic religion and religious thought underlie much of Christianity. And the process of Hellenism, that cross-fertilization of the Greek and Oriental worlds in language and culture which produced the urban society of the Roman eastern provinces, is an exciting study of which we learn much from the non-literary sources, papyri and inscriptions. But the political history of the period is obscure or complex to the point of being bewildering, so that few have undertaken to master or describe the ever-changing nexus of inter-state relations and to view the period as an historical whole. After Benedict Niese at the turn of the century, only Rostovtzeff has been able to do this with some success. My present project is not an attempt to do this, but to provide something of an over-all interpretation and evaluation of Hellenism, to show what it attempted, what means it used and what difficulties it surmounted, and what success it attained.

The geographical and chronological limits of Hellenism have been variously defined. I have omitted the western Greeks from consideration since they do not seem to me to be part of *this* Hellenism. The Hellenization of South Italy and Sicily belongs to an earlier period, and the Hellenization of Rome is best viewed as part of Republican history. The Hellenistic world, then, is the world of Alexander's conquests, extending from the Adriatic to the Indus, from Nubia to the Danube and South Russia. Since this world was, in a political sense, created by Alexander, it seems appropriate to begin with his career. His importance as the founder of Hellenism is attested by the many surviving lives, making him with Jesus of Nazareth one of the best-known and most influential figures in antiquity, if also one of the most controversial. Since the changes in the East produced by progressive Roman involvement and control were subtle if real, and gradual rather than sudden, and since the last century of Hellenism produced the society and culture which underlay the Roman East, it has seemed desirable, in the interest of understanding and continuity, to carry the narrative down to the Battle of Actium and the occupation of Egypt by Augustus. That some periods, some incidents, some processes and phenomena are more largely deployed than others is due either to the nature of our information or to their seeming importance. And an attempt to include everything in a history would be self-defeating.

It is true that the term "Hellenistic" is variously interpreted by art or cultural historians, either in a broader or in a narrower sense geographically or chronologically. In a literal ·as well as an historical sense, it seems to me to be the period when Hellenic culture and language was spread throughout the East by conquest and political association.

The Situation in Greece

This narrative begins with the sudden death of Philip II of Macedon, Alexander's father, an event which brought to power the man who was to bring Hellenism to the East. It may be useful to sketch briefly the background of these events.

Greece of the fifth century had been dominated by two powers, Athens and Sparta, each at the head of a league of states. The result, which the Athenian historian Thucydides thought inevitable, was the clash of the Peloponnesian War, in consequence of which the league headed by Athens was dissolved and the power of Athens was sensibly reduced. In the fourth century, the political scene was more complex, since Sparta was unable to hold an effective hegemony for long. Quarreling with Persia and so losing Persian financial support, Sparta was unable to hire professional soldiers or to buy politicians, and thrown back on its own militia was no longer dominant on the battlefield. This with other factors, such as the rise in education and the general improvement in economic conditions, encouraged the growth of formerly smaller powers, urban and otherwise, to the point that they could compete on not entirely unequal terms with the two greater ones. This was true of Thebes in Boeotia, which at the

Battle of Leuctra in 371 destroyed the myth of Spartan invincibility; it was true, as well, of the unified Thessaly under Jason of
Pherae, of Elis and the newly founded Megalopolis and Messene in
the Peloponnese, of Olynthus and the Chalcidians in the north,
and Aetolia and Phocis in central Greece, and of the tribal states
to the north of Greece proper, such as Illyria, Epirus, and Thrace.
The Anatolian cities were flourishing under the Persian peace,
while such Hellenized satraps as Mausolus in Caria and Artabazus
in Hellespontine Phrygia could support and be supported by Greek
states. The revolt of the Athenian allies, Rhodes, Chios, and
Byzantium, in 357, showed the new direction of affairs. They
were incited by Mausolus, but received very little if any support
from him.

Macedon at the Accession of Philip

This was the political world which Philip of Macedon faced in
the autumn of 359 B.C., when the death of his brother Perdiccas in
a battle with the Illyrians brought him to the regency and then to
the throne. Perdiccas had strengthened Macedon by the incorpor-
ation of the highland cantons, Lyncestis, Orestis, Elimiotis and the
rest, and by the extension of Macedonian control to the east as far
as the mouth of the Strymon and the city of Amphipolis, an
Athenian colony claimed by Athens ever since its defection to the
Spartan Brasidas during the Peloponnesian War. The internal structure of the state had been strengthened by constitutional and
military changes introduced by Alexander I, Archelaus, and
Philip's father Amyntas, so that the kings had a professional as
well as a feudal army, lands and revenues, and a court modelled on
the Persian with feudal nobles and their children (the Royal
Pages), a corps of Friends (military, technical, literary and artistic
associates with whom the king lived, hunted, fought, and feasted),
and a staff of slaves, guards, and attendants. The kings had also a
nexus of relationships with foreign states, tribes, and cities, so that
the foreign policy of Macedon was a personal royal matter. Alliances were contracted between the kings and foreign powers
without regard to other than, on occasion, other members of the
royal family, so that they all lapsed and had to be renegotiated
when a king died. But all of this gave the kings a certain indepen-

dence of the Macedonian people, who nevertheless were the ones who must accept a claimant to the throne and who gave him, probably by acclamation, his royal title. Thus Macedonia in the fifth and fourth centuries was already an established prototype of the absolute monarchy of the Hellenistic period, where to a very large extent the success or failure of the state depended on the skill and personality of the ruler. An infant or an incompetent king might survive if he had guardians of sufficient ability and interest to maintain him, but he would normally be replaced if there were an adult uncle or cousin who was acceptable to the nobles and the army. This made for efficiency, as Demosthenes noted, but also for discontinuity if not a serious crisis when a king died unexpectedly, as frequently happened in so martial a monarchy.

Philip was twenty-two at the death of his brother, and became regent for his young nephew Amyntas. Half of the army had just been defeated with heavy losses, the country was discouraged and in danger of falling apart, while all the apparatus of personal relationships which constituted the state were in abeyance. Rival candidates for the throne existed in the persons of two members of the royal family who had been accepted as kings previously, for short periods. There may have been a safety in numbers. Each was supported by a foreign enemy which had its own interests to advance: Athens on the one hand, which was anxious to win back Amphipolis, and on the other a new Thracian king Berisades, the son of the great king Cotys, who had inherited the westernmost part of the Odrysian kingdom including the coast between Maroneia and Abdera. His territory marched with the eastern conquests of Perdiccas, and he doubtless wished to recover some of the lost territory. This crisis was met diplomatically. Philip made appropriate promises and with their supporters withdrawn, both pretenders ceased to be a threat. The one was captured and killed, the other disappears from history. Philip was fortunate in the occasion. Athens was chiefly concerned with her former possessions in the eastern front, threatened by the other two succession kings of the Odrysians. Neither Athens nor Berisades wished or was prepared for an embroilment with Macedonia, and since they were allies, co-ordinated or concerted action on their part was easily arranged.

The Campaigns of Philip

Philip was fortunate in other ways also. The previous king of
the Odrysians in Thrace, Cotys, father of Berisades, who might
have been a serious threat to the east, was dead, and his three
successors were more concerned with each other than with Macedon. King Agis of Paeonia, to the north, who had been poised for
an invasion, died at the end of 359. Philip had time to get his
troops in order and in a spring campaign of the following year,
King Bardylis of Illyria fell on the field of battle. Olynthus and the
Chalcidians had been at war with Athens as allies of Perdiccas and
did not yet see Philip as a greater menace. Alexander of Pherae in
Thessaly, who had come close to establishing the whole country
under his control but had failed due to Theban opposition, died in
358 leaving a divided Thessaly, with both the north (Larisa) and
the south (Pherae) looking for outside support against each other.
In the following year, Berisades died, leaving his kingdom to a
number of sons, while in the course of the summer Athens was not
only faced by the secession of her eastern allies from Rhodes to
Byzantium, but also lost one of her best commanders, Chabrias, in
a naval battle at Chios. Philip took advantage of the situation to
pick up some cities, Amphipolis, Pydna, and the vitally important
Crenides, which he renamed Philippi, with its control over the gold
and silver mines of Mt. Pangaeus. Olynthus, in alarm, contracted an alliance with Bardylis' successor Grabus, but neither
could help the other. In 356 Grabus, together with Lyppeius in
Paeonia and the sons of Berisades, contracted an alliance with
Athens in which Olynthus also may have been involved. Grabus,
however, was defeated and put out of action by Philip's general
Parmenion, and Athens was fully occupied with operations against
her revolted allies in the Hellespont, where she was not only
unsuccessful but also lost faith in two more of her great generals,
Timotheus and Iphicrates, who were discredited and no longer
entrusted with a command. Philip took advantage of the situation
again and seizing the Athenian dependency of Potidaea, presented
it to the neighboring Olynthus, which became his ally.

In the following year, Athens came to terms with the seces-
sionists and made peace, but was in no mood or no position to
undertake further fighting. Providentially again for Philip, Athens'
allies the Phocians quarreled with the other member of the

Amphictyonic League at Delphi, and occupying the sanctuary, started a sacred war in which her opponents were primarily Thebes and the Locrians. After some successes, Thebes sent her best general Pammenes to Asia to assist the rebel satrap Artabazus, and Philip, escorting him, eliminated the sons of Berisades and occupied the Thracian coast as far east as Maroneia. When Phocian generals entered Thessaly to assist Pherae against Larisa, the latter appealed to Philip, who returned to expel the Phocians and to become master of the whole district, capturing Pherae and Pagasae in the south and only being checked at Thermopylae by an Athenian fleet. Athens had been technically at war with Philip since 356, but had accomplished nothing until then. Now, as the two eastern Thracian kings had become alarmed by Philip's march to the east and were prepared to cede to Athens the Thracian Chersonese, Athens had nothing more to fight for and made peace, or at least accepted an armistice. Philip had leisure to consolidate his conquests and to build up his strength at home. With a plentiful supply of money coming from the mines near Philippi, he could not only establish a brilliant and prestigious court at Pella but make numerous friends abroad. Most of his successes, previously as well as later, were accomplished more by diplomacy and his skill in taking advantage of the international situation than by fighting, although he had accustomed his troops to the latest military techniques as well as to a tradition of victory, and had shown the tough Macedonians that he was a stout fighter as well as a brilliant leader. He had lost an eye in hand-to-hand fighting in the storming of Methone, perhaps in 354.

Starting as regent of a war-torn, disheartened, and divided country, Philip had made himself in eight campaign seasons absolute ruler of a territory which extended from the Thracian coast to the water-shed leading to Illyria, from Thessaly to Paeonia and beyond. He had a large and highly trained army consisting of light and heavy infantry, cavalry, and engineers, an ample supply of money, and supporters or sympathizers throughout the Greek world. He was thirty years old. He had taken advantage of the divisions and distractions of the other powers, but had shown a consummate skill in following the strategy of the limited objective. He had been able to conciliate his new subjects and to grow stronger with his expansion. He was at peace with Athens and the

Chalcidians, his major potential opponents, and the Thebans were his allies. The Phocians had been soundly defeated and compelled to adopt a defensive position at Thermopylae. The two remaining Thracian kings had turned to Athens for support, but Athens, under the reconstruction program of Eubulus, was in no mood for further wars. Possessed of Euboea and much of the Thracian Chersonese and so relatively assured of the grain route to the Black Sea, she wanted only to be let alone to rebuild her economic prosperity. Philip might have stopped here.

The Conquest of Greece

But Philip did not choose to stop. Taking advantage of the lull on the Greek front, he campaigned to the east and to the west. The Illyrians were forced to accept a peace and alliance, and the nearest of the Thracians, Amadocus, became a subject. Then it was the turn of Olynthus, with which hostilities commenced, on what excuse we do not know, in 350. Olynthus turned to Athens for support, but at this critical juncture the Euboean cities revolted; since the revolt was led by Philip's friends, it is hard to think that he had not instigated this. They were sacrificed and Athens recovered the island, but Olynthus was defeated in the field (not without a suspicion of treachery on the part of their generals) and when Athens sent help in the summer of 349 it was too late. The city was invested, and surrendered in the following spring to be destroyed so thoroughly that the site was never again occupied. This was Philip's first use of terror and it was clearly calculated. Philip was not ruthless by nature. He had never even put to death his nephew Amyntas, the legitimate heir to the throne and the instrument of any possible disaffection in Macedonia. But Olynthus was meant as a warning. Athens again began peace negotiations, but before they were concluded in the summer of 346 Philip had eliminated Amadocus and had reduced the remaining Thracian, Cersobleptes, to submission. Then, in a sudden move south, Philip turned the defenses at Thermopylae and overran Phocis, presiding over the Pythian Games at Delphi in the autumn. A stickler for form, Philip asked the Athenians to support his membership in the Delphian Amphictyony.

Again there was peace, and Philip could again campaign in Illyria and tighten his control over Thessaly, but his operations in northwest Greece, where he installed his son-in-law Alexander as king in Epirus (342) and the Macedonian presence in Phocis alarmed the Thebans, and the war-party at Athens with Demosthenes as its spokesman again became active. Demosthenes was charged with gaining new adherents for the revived Athenian League, in the hope of creating a stronger opposition to Philip's further advances, and did succeed in winning over Corinth, Megara, the Achaeans, and some of the northwest Greeks, but there was no money to hire mercenaries even for the fleet, and there was no immediate *casus belli*, or even a specific military objective. Philip's diplomacy was active and he continued to win supporters. During the winter of 343 his envoys were at Athens trying to pursuade the city to join him in a full alliance in place of the existing non-aggression pact. Demosthenes' group opposed this, arguing that Philip could not be trusted, but at the same time the Athenians also rejected a pact with the Persian king, who offered his pecuniary support in return for freedom of operation of his recruiting agents. The result was that Philip and the Persian signed a non-aggression pact and the Persians, picking up mercenaries where they could (principally from Argos, Thebes, and the Anatolian cities) recovered Phoenicia, Egypt, and Cyprus, and perhaps equally importantly, acquired the services of the Rhodian brothers Mentor and Memnon, two of the ablest generals of the period. Athens was again embarrassed by a revolt of Eretria and Oreus in Euboea, while Philip took advantage of the opportunity to eliminate Cersobleptes. Athens recovered Euboea and Philip's friend Hermeias, tyrant of Atarneus, was tricked into surrendering himself to Mentor, and the Persian king began to suspect that Philip's ambitions did not stop with the Hellespont. Thus in 340, when Philip made an abortive attempt to capture Perinthus and Byzantium, the cities were defended both by Athens and by the adjacent Persian satrap. Athens now declared war, but Philip, after a whirlwind winter campaign against the Scythians and Triballi in Thrace, either to punish his troops for their first failures or to secure his rear, burst into central Greece. Athens could only hastily conclude an alliance with the thoroughly alarmed Thebans, summon up her allies, and put an army in the field. After a winter of maneuvering,

Philip overpowered the Locrians on his western flank and turned to face the allied armies at Chaeronea. The decisive battle was fought on the second of August, 338. The Thebans fought well, but Philip's trained army drew the Athenians out of position and his son Alexander with the Thessalian heavy cavalry and mobile units of the phalanx threw himself into the gap in the Greek line and rolled it up. This was the tactic which Alexander used successfully in many later battles, and it ended the war. Thebes was garrisoned, Athens given generous terms (perhaps because her fleet was still in existence and a siege of the city was impractical; but Philip, as Alexander later, always had a sentimental feeling for Athens), and a congress was called at Corinth to lay plans and furnish an organization for a crusade against Persia. Only Sparta and her few allies abstained. Isocrates' dream was realized. Greece was united under an enlightened monarch; and her unemployment, impoverishment, and social unrest were to be ended with the glory, booty, and new territories to be won in Asia. Philip sent an advance force across the Hellespont, and was busy with preparations. Eighteen months later, he was assassinated.

Chapter One

Alexander the Great

1. The Accession of Alexander

The Heir Apparent

Alexander the Great, the son of King Philip II and Olympias, became king of the Macedonians in the month Daesius, May or June, of the year 336 B.C. The circumstances of his succession were unusual and significant.

About 357 B.C., shortly after his accession, Philip had contracted a political marriage with a princess of the Epirot royal house, which claimed descent from Zeus through Achilles as the Argeads did through Heracles, and which had in consequence useful connections with Thessaly. Two children were born of this marriage, a son Alexander in 356 B.C. and a daughter, Cleopatra, about a year later. But monogamy was not an Argead tradition, and Philip soon contracted other marital alliances in Thessaly and in Thrace, probably also for political reasons in part, and other children were born to him. Alexander continued to be his favorite, however, and was brought up as a future king. He was trained for war and was given, under the philosopher Aristotle, the finest of Greek educations. At the Battle of Chaeronea, he commanded the Macedonian left, and (probably under the watchful eye of Philip's general Parmenion) broke the Theban resistance with a charge of his own cavalry brigade, made up probably of Thessalian horse, since the Macedonian Companion Cavalry would have been with Philip on the right. Philip generously held back his own wing to distract the Athenians and to allow Alexander to win credit for the victory.

Thereafter, however, Alexander's position changed for the worse. To improve his relations with the Macedonian nobility, probably in view of his proposed Asiatic campaign, Philip for the first time married a Macedonian, a noble woman named Cleopatra. Her family is unknown, but she was under the guardianship of one Attalus, an experienced general and the husband of a daughter of

Parmenion. This new union was greeted with enthusiasm in Macedonia, where the Epirot Olympias had never been popular, and people dared to express the hope that Philip would now have a legitimate, that is to say, a purely Macedonian heir. Olympias was furious and withdrew to Epirus, doubtless to Philip's relief, but it may have been less welcome that Alexander espoused his mother's cause. He joined her in exile, and it is significant for his attitude that three of the five friends who accompanied him were what the Macedonians called Greek;[1] they were sons of Greek families settled in Amphipolis at Philip's invitation and technically Macedonian, but never accepted as such in Macedonia.

This defection of his only adult and able son just prior to his departure for an ambitious and dangerous campaign overseas placed Philip in an awkward position, and he proposed a reconciliation. On the eve of starting the war, while his forces were mustering and embassies from all his allies and subjects were present to wish him well, he arranged a great festival in honor of the Twelve Gods at the old and holy Macedonian capital Aegae, in the course of which he was himself paraded with them as a thirteenth "god present." Philip had reason to be proud. Olympias had agreed to the marriage of their daughter, Cleopatra, to Alexander the son of Neoptolemus, her brother and the uncle of her two children, and both Alexanders, the Epirot bridegroom and Philip's son, were present in Aegae for the ceremony. Probably the marriage was to be proclaimed at ceremonies in the theater which were to be the high point of the festival. These were to begin at dawn.

The Assassination of Philip

Long before dawn, every seat was filled, and attention was fixed on the entrance. Philip, who normally would have been surrounded by the friends who served him as bodyguards, had been persuaded to make a dramatic gesture of confidence. The friends were ordered to precede Philip into the theater, and Philip followed at a little distance walking between the two Alexanders, his son and his son-in-law. This was the moment when the assassin, Pausanias, sprang forward and stabbed Philip with a concealed dagger.

There was no hesitation. While Philip's friends in consternation crowded about the king, three of Alexander's friends, armed, darted after Pausanias and killed him. His body was crucified, but, it is reported, the head received a golden crown at night, presumably from Olympias.[2] Joined by a third Alexander, the son of Aeropus, prince of Lyncestis, who hastily armed himself, all quickly went to the palace on the citadel, where the Lyncestian Alexander was the first to hail his namesake as king. An investigation was promptly held, and those "implicated" were executed without delay. They included Alexander's cousin Amyntas, for whom Philip had been regent, and who had a strong claim to the throne, his half-brother Caranus, and the two elder brothers of the Lyncestian Alexander. Philip's wife Cleopatra and her infant son were killed by Olympias, and the uncle Attalus, who commanded at the time a Macedonian army operating in Asia Minor, was removed by assassination.

It requires little imagination to visualize the confusion and dismay of the Macedonians. Few can have had real doubt that the killing of Philip had been arranged by Alexander. The alleged grievance of the assassin Pausanias was many years old, and in any case, lay rather against Cleopatra's uncle Attalus than against Philip. Pausanias came from the western mountain district of Orestia, and so did also Perdiccas, one of Pausanias' three slayers. Perdiccas, like his companions Leonnatus and Attalus (not Cleopatra's uncle but the son of Andromenes and Perdiccas' brother-in-law) was then and later one of Alexander's closest friends, and the immediate practical result of their killing Pausanias was to make impossible his questioning under torture. The persons executed were clearly unprepared for Philip's death and unlikely to benefit from it, and one of them was an enemy of Pausanias. The obvious and immediate beneficiary was Alexander and this was his only opportunity. Once on campaign, Philip would be out of reach. It may not be pleasant to think of Alexander encouraging Pausanias to kill his father and then betraying him, but this duplicity is clearly indicated, and the incident is a useful reminder that harmony among the Macedonians was not something to be assumed. Alexander himself on one occasion called them wild beasts, and he knew well that it took more than innocence to be a king of the Macedonians.

Head of Alexander, from Pergamum

With the death of Philip, all of his empire fell to pieces, for its connection was with him personally, not with the Macedonians. Many must have been glad that Alexander had destroyed his rivals to the throne, for there was, at least, no question who would be king. Alexander's own *syntrophoi*, the young nobles brought up with him at court, acted decisively to establish Alexander's control, and they were supported by Antipater, Philip's great general. Parmenion's son Philotas was one of Alexander's friends, and Parmenion himself in Asia Minor allowed or assisted in the assassination of Attalus, his son-in-law, by Alexander's trusted agent Hecataeus. The army was restive, for it had adored Philip, but Alexander quickly put it to work, the surest way to restore discipline.

Alexander Consolidates His Position

The first problem, to be sure, was political, the re-establishment of Philip's position in Macedonia and in Greece. Macedonia had no written constitution and the king's position depended upon his acceptance by the princely families which ruled the clans and by the Macedonian people at large. Their common action took place in the army, with the nobles concentrated in the territorial squadrons of the Companion Cavalry and the people serving in the likewise territorial regiments of heavy infantry, the Foot Companions. Assembled in a mass meeting, they had the traditional right of acclaiming a new king as well as of trying and executing persons accused of plotting against the king. Since the real or supposed assassins were already dead, Alexander had only to state his position and to explain that he would rule so that only Philip's person, and not his policies, were changed. With the previously assured support of the nobles, there was no difficulty. He had no rival in the legitimate line, and he had already given evidence of enough military ability to promise success in the war against Persia, the opportunity for glory and especially profit to which every Macedonian was looking forward.

These activities must have consumed some weeks, giving time for all of Greece to know of Philip's death but not to organize any concerted revolt, and in any case, the Greek envoys who had come to Aegae before Philip's death constituted something like hostages. Except possibly in Thessaly and in Ambracia, where the Macedonian garrison was expelled, Alexander encountered no resistance when he marched south with the army. In Thessaly he was supported by his mother's relatives, the Aleuadae of Larisa, one of whose number, Medius the son of Oxythemis, was a close personal friend. The Thessalians accepted his claim to Greek hegemony and probably elected him president of their League. Their support opened his way to Thermopylae and Delphi, and the Delphic Amphictyons accepted him similarly. Once he was in central Greece, the rest was quickly arranged. Ambracia made its apologies and was forgiven, while Thebes, Athens, and the rest made their submission. A meeting of the League of the Greeks was convened at Corinth, all of the Peloponnesians except Sparta attending. Alexander was named its president and general plenipotentiary for the war against Persia. Plans were made and assessments levied, although Alexander was not yet able to set a date for the invasion. In the sequel, the League was to furnish him seven thousand infantry and nearly a thousand cavalry.

Returning to Macedonia in the autumn of 336, Alexander turned to the military part of his task. To secure the allegiance and support of the Thracians and Illyrians, more than diplomacy was needed. In addition to the normal fierce independence of the tribes, conditions were unsettled because of the recent movement of Celts down to the Danube. The Paeonians had been subject to Macedonia for twenty years, and King Longarus of the Agrianes was Alexander's friend and had joined him with troops, but the Odrysian kingdom had been conquered by Philip only a few years before and was of doubtful loyalty. All of these, as well as the Macedonians themselves, needed a demonstration of Alexander's military ability.

They had not long to wait. Antipater was left as viceroy in Macedonia; Parmenion was with his army in Asia Minor. With only part of the Macedonian army, Alexander marched north at the beginning of the spring of 335, supported by a corps of archers and slingers and by Longarus' Agrianes. It was his first experience with a field force of combined arms, but he demonstrated at once his skill in employing it, as well as the discipline and resourcefulness of the Macedonian heavy infantry and cavalry. The passes over Mt. Haemus were blocked by Triballi intent themselves on migrating southward and made confident by their near-victory over Philip four years earlier. They rolled great wagons down the slope to break the advancing ranks, but the soldiers nimbly let them through or flung themselves to the ground under their shields, and once over the pass, Alexander used his archers to harrass and lure out of their retreat the main body of tribesmen, hiding in a glen by the river. They were helpless before the phalanx, and many were killed. In three days Alexander reached the Danube, where the Triballi had placed their non-combatants in safety on an island, and across the river were Getae in force. An attack on the island with the help of warships from Byzantium was unsuccessful, but Alexander transported horse and foot across the river at night on improvised boats and rafts, and the Getae fled. Isolated, the Triballi surrendered, and envoys came to Alexander from the Celts, proud but impressed. Probably the Odrysians also hastened to make their submission. Alexander had shown his resourcefulness as a commander, and had demonstrated to the Macedonians what was most important to them, that he could win decisive victories without incurring any appreciable loss. And there was ample booty.

Returning westward to the country of the Agrianes, Alexander learned that Cleitus, King of the Illyrians, had formed a coalition against him and had taken the offensive, occupying the Macedonian fortress of Pelium in the valley of the River Erigon. He was supported by Glaucias and the Taulantii to the west and by the Autariatae to the north. Alexander was to be drawn into a trap, and characteristically he accepted and exploited the challenge. Leaving the Agrianes to deal with the Autariatae, he marched up the valley and prepared to assault Pelium, hemmed in by the river on one side and tribesmen on the mountain on the other. It was a situation which might have led to disaster, but discipline and maneuver were successful. The enemy were lured out of the city and down from the mountain. Alexander crossed and recrossed the river under cover of archers and ballistae, the enemy camp was surprised and overrun at night, and Cleitus and Glaucias fled, not only beaten but humiliated. While Alexander had no time to invade their countries, they gave him no further trouble, and he was his soldiers' darling.

It was only just in time. Report had come to Greece that

Alexander was dead, and there was nothing to hold the Hellenic League together. The lead was taken by Thebes, which began an attack on the Macedonian garrison in the Cadmeia, and if time had held, there would have been a Greek army in the field with contingents from Elis, Arcadia, Messene, and perhaps even Sparta from the Peloponnese, as well as the Aetolians and Athens from central Greece. Against Alexander's Hellenic League, Thebes raised the warcry of the King's Peace, promising freedom for the Greeks; and the Persian King was not slow to furnish money. The Athenian Demosthenes was able to buy three hundred talents' worth of arms for Thebes. But Alexander acted too swiftly.

Averaging perhaps twenty miles a day, his combat forces reached Thessaly in seven days and Boeotia in six more, and the allies of Thebes gave her no help. Alexander, on the other hand, had only the troops which had been with him in Thrace, and even with reinforcements from Phocis and Boeotia did not have a large force. The Thebans dared to meet him outside the walls and fought well, but thanks to his fortune, they fought alone. At the height of the engagement Alexander sent his friend Perdiccas with his regiment to force a postern gate on the opposite side of the city; Ptolemy later wrote that Perdiccas acted without orders, but Ptolemy had no love for Perdiccas. With the city captured, there was a general massacre, led by the Phocians and Boeotians who were Thebes' mortal enemies. Six thousand are reported slain and thirty thousand captured, while some escaped, especially to Athens. By vote of the League members present, the city was razed except for the temples and the houses of Pindar and his descendants, and the captives sold as slaves.

The lesson shocked Greece and all defectors hastened to make their peace. Alexander, as usual, knew how to be lenient as well as severe. Athens, notably, was allowed to deal with her own anti-Macedonian leaders. A few fled to Persia, but Demosthenes and others were not harmed, and the Theban exiles were given sanctuary.

2. The Defeat of Darius

Preparations for the Campaign

It was now the autumn of 335, and Alexander had been away

from Macedonia for six months. Without stopping to hold a meeting of the League at Corinth, he informed the Greeks that the Persian War would begin in the following spring, left Greece with his army, and busied himself with preparations. Although urged by Parmenion and Antipater to marry and beget an heir, he refused, either from distaste for marriage or because of the difficulty of finding a politically suitable bride. In spite of the booty from Thrace and from Thebes, his war chest was low; probably much of this had been distributed to the soldiers, to whom Alexander understandably showed himself always generous. Money was raised by the sale of crown properties, but not enough. Then, about April of 334, the army was ready and Alexander marched out of Pella toward the Hellespont. He had very little cash with him, and some said that he was in debt. But he had demonstrated those qualities which were to carry him on to the conquest of the East: ruthlessness and tact, passion and self-control, and above all, a consummate military sense for using combined arms under any conditions of terrain and weather so as to win decisively not only over the bodies of his enemies but over their minds as well. It was certainly in a mood of hope and confidence that the army crossed the Hellespont about the beginning of May.

Parmenion went with Alexander as the second in command, while Antipater remained as viceroy in Macedonia with the mission of keeping Europe quiet and forwarding supplies and men as needed. The Macedonian army was divided, Alexander taking with him the infantry of the upland cantons in six regiments under proven officers, some of whom were personal friends, and the cavalry of new Macedonia, Potidaea and Amphipolis, in six squadrons under officers otherwise largely unknown. In addition he had the Infantry Guards Regiment, the *hypaspists*, under Parmenion's son Nicanor, and the Cavalry Guards, the *ile basilike* or *Agema*, under Cleitus the Black, the brother of Alexander's nurse. Parmenion's second son, Philotas, commanded the entire cavalry brigade. Parmenion himself exercised a battle command over the whole infantry and the left of the line, so that Alexander may well have felt that the influence of his family was excessive. Even one of the regimental commanders, Coenus, was Parmenion's son-in-law; he may have married the widow of Attalus whom Alexander had killed.

The initial Macedonian strength was twelve thousand foot and eighteen hundred horse, and in addition there were allied and mercenary hoplites, Thracian javelin men, archers, and the very useful Agrianes whom Alexander kept ever close to his person. In cavalry the most notable were the eighteen hundred Thessalians, who fought always on the left, but there were allied and mercenary horse also, and Thracian and Paeonian light cavalry. The total force came to less than forty thousand combat troops, including artillerists, and there was a technical staff of engineers as well as the small group of Body Guards in the strict sense, close and proven friends whom Alexander used for special missions and special commands. The trains, which later were to become enormous, must initially have been rather small. With them were the Royal Pages, chamberlains, and slaves, with the literary and scientific and social friends of the King, and the personnel which transported baggage, commissary, and occasionally artillery or siege engines. There were no women, or very few. Alexander sent his newly married soldiers home during the winter of 334/3, and thereafter all who wished acquired wives or concubines as the army advanced. There was also soon to be a prisoner detachment, commanded by Laomedon, one of the three Greeks exiled with Alexander in 337.

The Conquest of Asia Minor

There had been ample warning of Alexander's coming, and a substantial army had been assembled to meet him. All of the Anatolian satraps were present and the army must have been essentially a composite of their satrapal forces, with the addition of some twenty thousand Greek mercenaries under Memnon of Rhodes. There was no single commander, although Memnon had been given the commission in 335 of opposing Alexander's generals Parmenion and Calas, and commanded the only specifically imperial troops engaged. He may have advised withdrawal and wasting the country before Alexander, although this may also be merely a legend following the event, but the Persians had troops enough to win, had they been properly employed. The excellent Iranian cavalry was squandered, and the Greek mercenaries never employed.

The two armies met at the River Granicus about half way between Abydus and Cyzicus, and the battle was rather a meeting engagement than a planned encounter. One account has Alexander storm across the stream at nightfall direct from march column, and fight his way up through the Persian cavalry on the far bank. Another, more reasonably, has Alexander cross at dawn without opposition, but face the Persian attack before the bulk of his forces were over. In any case, the satraps made the blunder of attacking before their infantry was in line. It may be that they hoped merely to kill Alexander and so settle the issue; they may have been simply inept. Alexander advanced in echelon from the right, leading with a mixed force: light horse and javelin men, a regiment of the phalanx and a squadron of the Companions. When this had interrupted the Persian front, Alexander charged obliquely toward the center with his heavy cavalry, and after a sharp fight in which Cleitus saved Alexander's life by cutting off an attacker's arm, the Persian cavalry was routed, and the survivors made their escape. The Greek mercenaries could only surrender, after perhaps a fierce but brief resistance.

So, at the cost of only a few lives, Alexander had won Asia Minor. Statues of the fallen cavalry were erected in Dium, and the prisoners sent back to Macedonia as slaves. Three hundred panoplies were sent to Athens to record that Alexander and the Greeks (other than Lacedaemonians) took spoil from the barbarians of Asia. And marching south to Sardes Alexander staffed the Persian provincial organization with his own officials. The coastal cities surrendered, and thinking a change in government the surest guarantee of their loyalty, Alexander put them in the hands of democracies. Miletus, relying on the Persian fleet, resisted but was taken by storm, and Alexander laid up his own navy temporarily. It was recreated in the following year, but for the moment it served no useful purpose. Halicarnassus was defended by the last Persian land forces in Asia Minor and supported by the fleet, but Alexander's siege engines broke down the walls, and the garrison was evacuated by sea, to take part in Memnon's great naval offensive ended only by his death the following year. Caria was turned over to Ada, the last survivor of the royal house, supported by a small army charged primarily with the capture of the citadels of Halicarnassus. Parmenion with the main body of troops and the trains marched back to Sardes and then on to Gordium, where he wintered, occupied in part with the siege of the satrapal fortress of Celenae.

It was now autumn, and Alexander marched east along the coast, receiving the submission of the cities of Lycia. His boyhood friend, the Greek Nearchus, was left here as satrap to deny the Persian fleet the use of these bases. With the coast in Macedonian hands, the fleet would lose its vital communication with Phoenicia. Then he swung inland through Pamphylia and Pisidia with a purely Macedonian force supported by archers and the Agrianes; it was substantially the same force as he had employed in the Thracian campaign of 335. A winter campaign in the mountains presented difficulties, but Alexander got through successfully without much fighting, although the inhabitants of one hill fortress, who resisted, burned up their families in the Lycian tradition when they saw that Alexander would capture them. Arrived at Gordium late in the winter, Alexander inspected the Gordian Knot, by which the carriage of Midas was fastened to its yoke. The one who untied it, it was said, would be king of the whole world, and so Alexander cut the knot with his sword, according to most reporters. Aristobulus, more literally, wrote that Alexander removed the thole pin and so found the concealed ends, while Ptolemy omitted the incident in his history. Even in his own lifetime, people saw in Alexander what they wished.

Parmenion was an able administrator, and Alexander found everything ready for the march up-country. The newly-married detachment was back from its leave in Macedonia, and with it had come a substantial new levy, chiefly from Macedonia. During Alexander's absence, Parmenion had discovered or invented a plot involving the Lyncestian Alexander, and acting on secret instructions from the King, had arrested him. He was replaced in the important command of the Thessalian cavalry but not brought to trial. Probably the case against him was not strong and Alexander feared public opinion. The satrapy of Phrygia was left in the capable hands of Antigonus, a friend of King Philip, who had commanded the allied infantry of the Hellenic League. He was to play a large role in later history.

Receiving on the way the nominal submission of the Cappadocians, the army got over the passes into Cilicia without difficulty. As always, Alexander led the way with an advance guard consisting normally of the *hypaspistae* or Foot Guards, some or all of the Companion Cavalry, the archers and the Agrianes. Arriving at Tarsus in the early summer of 333, Alexander fell seriously ill, perhaps from the shock of plunging hot and tired into the icy Cydnus River. The situation was alarming, for while word had come of Memnon's death and the progress of Alexander's new fleet commanded by Craterus' brother Amphoterus, there were reports also that the Great King was marching down from Babylon with an enormous army. Alexander demanded from his doctors a drastic remedy, one was administered by Philip the Acarnanian, and Alexander promptly recovered, because of or in spite of the medicine. As part of the later campaign of detraction against Parmenion, it was widely repeated that he warned Alexander by letter against Philip, but Parmenion was with the main body of troops and could not well yet have known of the illness. If he had information against Philip he would not have waited until the cup was at Alexander's lips to present it, and Alexander had shown in the case of the Lyncestian that he was only too ready to act upon suspicion. In any case, Alexander was soon able himself to receive the submission of the Cilician cities and conducted a seven-day campaign against the tribesmen to the west. With the whole southern coast of Anatolia now in his hands, he was free to march south.

The Reduction of the Levant

Parmenion had already been sent ahead with the troops which he would command in battle (the allied and mercenary foot and the Thracian and Thessalian horse) to hold the passes over the Amanus Range and permit the safe passage of the main body down through the coastal plain. He had similarly protected Alexander's marching flank in the Maeander valley in 334, and was to do so again at Damascus, after the battle of Issus. His mission was to fall in behind the column when it had passed, so that the units would be in their battle positions. When he did this, however, the route to the coast was left open, and the result was that the Persians were able to march through the passes and reach the coast at Issus, where they massacred the Macedonians there, sick or wounded in part, and cut Alexander's communications. As soon as he was informed of this, he reversed his march and returned to the Pinarus River, where the Persians had erected field fortifications between the mountains and the sea.

His position was critical, and critics have generally thought that he had blundered. The ancient opinion, however, was that the Persian King had blundered in bringing his large body of troops into a restricted space, and it is more likely that Alexander had trapped Dareius. He had had to sacrifice the soldiers left at Issus, probably garrison troops no longer up to fighting in the field rather than patients in a hospital; but Alexander was not a sentimentalist. He had maneuvered Dareius into a position where he could not fight effectively, and he had placed his own army in a position where it must fight well in order to survive. It was like the admired procedure of Agathocles burning his transports in Africa. Alexander knew that his Macedonians were reliable, but he may well have had doubts about the Greek allies and mercenaries, who had not yet been tested in combat. It is significant that he placed four regiments of the Macedonian phalanx on the left under the command of his most experienced regimental commander, Craterus. They would show the Greeks what was expected of them.

Everything went according to plan. While Parmenion and Craterus contained the Persian heavy infantry, which was made up of Greeks and Iranian Cardaces, Alexander turned the Persian left, in the hills, with his light cavalry supported by the archers, javelin men, and Agrianes, and then launched a decisive attack against the Persian center with the heavy Companion Cavalry and two regiments of the phalanx. It was the same diagonal attack which had worked well at the Granicus, and which was to be employed later at Gaugamela. In danger of being surrounded and driven into the sea, the Persians could only abandon their positions and retire hastily. Alexander with the cavalry pressed the pursuit of Dareius until long after dark, separating him from his surviving forces which retired to the north. Only one force of Greeks, commanded by a Macedonian exile named Amyntas, escaped by breaking through Alexander's lines, and got down to the royal naval station at Tripolis in Phoenicia. There they burned such ships as they could not use, and sailed down to Egypt, which Amyntas undertook to hold as acting satrap; but fortunately for Alexander, the

Egyptians destroyed him and his troops. The Great King could count on no loyalty in that country.

Making their way to Cappadocia, where they were well received and levied additional forces, the other Persian commanders overran most of Asia Minor in two columns, one directed down the Maeander valley and the other, Paphlagonian in composition, against the satrap Calas in Hellespontine Phrygia. The attack was finally halted with the help of the Cilician satrap Balacrus, who recaptured Miletus, and Antigonus, who may have had supreme command, received credit for three great victories. But the campaign must have occupied the spring months of 332.

With the Persian army routed and dispersed, Alexander had not to face any new military challenge for some time. It had taken Xerxes four years to assemble and train the army which he led to Greece, and it was two years before Dareius was able to fight again. In addition, Alexander had captured the hareems of Dareius and the Persian nobles, including Dareius' mother, wife, and three young children. He was in a very strong position to exact favorable terms from the Great King, and Dareius began immediately diplomatic exchanges to see what terms might be obtained, but Alexander would accept no terms. He kept the royal family in honorable confinement, for which he has received high praise in ancient and modern times from those who ignore the fate of the other captured Persian women. Dareius' family had evident value as hostages. Alexander might have marched inland unopposed to Babylon and Susa, but chose rather to go first to Phoenicia and Egypt. This was, of course, tidier. The Persian fleet, based on Cyprus and Phoenicia, was still in existence, and the Levant provinces and Egypt were important as a source of revenue. These could, however, have been occupied by one of his generals while Alexander pressed home his victory and occupied the Persian capitals. Either Alexander did not trust his generals, even Parmenion, or he had compelling reasons, curiosity or religion, to go himself. As it was, he sent Parmenion with a covering force to Damascus, where providentially the Persian field trains were captured intact, and marched south. There was no opposition. The Cypriot and Phoenician princes made their submission and surrendered their ships as soon as they sailed home.

It was now mid-winter, for the battle of Issus had taken place in the late autumn of 333, and reaching Tyre at the time of the great annual festival of Melkart, which took place in connection with the solstice, Alexander asked permission to attend and sacrifice; for Melkart was Heracles, his ancestor. The request looked innocent, but Alexander would not come without an armed escort, and since Tyre was on an island and strongly defended by ships and walls, the city had good hope otherwise of escaping occupation. Again Alexander faced a choice. He was invited to sacrifice in Old Tyre on the mainland, and Tyre was quite ready to become an ally. He can hardly have feared Tyre or been in need of booty. It was only pride and the desire to do the impossible which led him to undertake a siege which proved to last seven months.

Tyre completely occupied its little island. The walls began at the water's edge and the two harbors were also fortified and closed by booms. It could be captured only by building a mole out from the mainland to the distance of a half mile, and this Alexander did; and Tyre became, as it has since remained, a peninsula. This took time, the more so as the Tyrians were able to harrass the workers from their ships until, in the spring of 332, Alexander could put together a fleet and keep the Tyrians bottled up. It seemed also a little impious, and an injured Poseidon sent not only winter storms but a monstrous whale in protest. Prodigies of valor and ingenuity were performed on both sides, and are described at length by our sources. At one point, Alexander became bored and went off on a short campaign against the mountain tribes of the southern Lebanon; he left Perdiccas and Craterus in joint command, for Parmenion was still at Damascus. At another time he became seriously discouraged, and was only brought back to good humor by his friend the regimental commander Amyntas, son of Andromenes, elder brother of that Attalus who had slain Philip's assassin. Even when the mole reached the island Alexander's trouble was not over, for it offered only a narrow point of attack. It was necessary to assault the walls from the sea also, mounting towers and engines precariously on freighters lashed together and this involved technical difficulties in getting the ships near enough to the walls to be effective. There was an exciting brush between divers and their handlers on both sides, trying to place or remove underwater obstacles. Finally, however, the wall was breached at the mole, the marine towers were in position, and the final assault was made by the Macedonian infantry. Alexander stormed across a bridge from tower to wall with a battalion of the *hypaspistae*, the harbors were forced by the Cypriot and Phoenician fleets, and the rest was slaughter. Some who took refuge in the temples were spared, but two thousand surviving soldiers were crucified, thirteen thousand women and children sold into slavery. The city was repopulated and re-established, Apollo "Philalexander" whom the Tyrians had bound with golden chains to keep him from deserting was freed, and Alexander performed his desired sacrifice to Melkart. It had proved very expensive, and was hardly necessary.

Alexander in Egypt

Marching on down toward Egypt, Alexander encountered resistance only at Gaza, the capture of which was less expensive than Tyre and more necessary, since it blocked the road across Sinai. It was fiercely defended by a Persian eunuch named Batis, and standing on a sandy hill, offered difficulty to saps and towers alike. Alexander was seriously wounded by a quarrel, but forced the walls by a combination of artillery and engineering, and the city was converted into a military base. Some believed that Alexander dragged Batis alive behind his chariot, in anger at the time the siege had cost.

It was now early autumn of 332, and Alexander marched into Egypt as the Nile inundation subsided. In some way a satrap had been appointed to replace the one killed at Issus, and he surrendered the country, for he had no combat force. The Egyptians welcomed Alexander and he went to Memphis and performed the royal sacrifice to Apis. He was probably crowned in Egyptian fashion as Pharaoh, and busied himself with administrative and diplomatic affairs. Then, turning these activities over to Parmenion, who had rejoined Alexander at Gaza, Alexander took a small party of friends and a military escort and set out on his real mission, a visit to the oracle of Ammon at the Siwah Oasis. Lying romantically remote in the Libyan Desert, partaking of the wisdom of Egypt without actually being Egyptian, this oracle had an enormous reputation among the Greeks, and was a regular place of consultation in serious matters. As the Pythia at Delphi had been correct thus far in pronouncing Alexander invincible, so

Alexander wished to consult Ammon about his future plans.

It may be that there were other questions, too, which Alexander wished to ask the oracle, for divine begetting was a commonplace in Greek religious thought and Olympias, who was inclined to mysticism and ambitious for her son, had no reason to cherish the memory of Philip. At all events, when Alexander came to the temple, it was generally believed that Ammon addressed him as his son. He assured him also that he would conquer whomever he wished, and Alexander was content. But Ammon's alleged paternity of Alexander, however agreeable to Greek concepts, was to prove embarrassing to Alexander's relations with his Macedonians, who revered Philip and wanted Alexander to remain one of themselves. The whole episode was controversial. There were many versions of the visit to Ammon current in antiquity and there is nothing certain except that it took place. We do not know whom Alexander took with him; perhaps Hephaestion, Leonnatus, Lysimachus, and others of his intimates. Ptolemy, who probably did not go, failed on this occasion to give the composition and command of the accompanying troops. If, as is possible, there were Companion Cavalry under Philotas and Foot Companions under Nicanor or Perdiccas, Ptolemy would have had good reason to suppress their names. For some reason he did state, improbably and in contrast with other reporters, that Alexander returned from Siwah directly across the desert to Memphis, instead of following the coastal route by which he had gone. The approach had been difficult, involving a shortage of water alleviated by a providential rain and other manifestations of divine favor, while the return was without incident.

Either before or after the visit to the oasis, Alexander planned and directed the building of a city west of the Nile Delta between Lake Mareotis and the sea, where there was the ancient and flourishing Egyptian city of Rhacotis with its sanctuary of Oserapis, and where the island of Pharos could be connected with the mainland by a mole to afford, as at Tyre, two good harbors. This Alexandria was the first and most successful of Alexander's name cities, and, built over the next years by Cleomenes, it was to become the capital of the Ptolemies and the greatest city of the Hellenistic East. Connected with the Nile by a canal, it afforded easy communication between Egypt and the Mediterranean, and was equally well adapted for commerce and for administration. Oserapis, the god of the Egyptian town Rhacotis, was hellenized as Serapis and went with Alexander as a god of prophecy, healing, and fertility.

By the late spring of 331 Alexander was ready to march east. His conquests were secure. He had pacified those in Greece who could be pacified, and Agis of Sparta found few adherents when he rose against Macedon a few months later. The satrapies were in the hands of men whom Alexander could trust, provisionally, and Egypt was secured by an elaborate division of command. Two Macedonians divided the command of the occupation troops, a third commanded the fleet, and two others held with garrisons the citadels of Memphis and Pelusium. In addition there were mercenary troops under a Greek from Aetolia and a civil administration under two Greeks and an Egyptian. While Cleomenes of Naucratis proved in the sequel to be most able, and gathered most of the authority into his own hands, it is unlikely that he ever was formally appointed satrap, and all channels of command led directly to Alexander, for he knew that he could really trust no one. Coming to Tyre, he similarly appointed regional directors of finance for Asia Minor and for the Levant, administratively under Alexander's friend Harpalus, the royal treasurer, but reporting directly to Alexander himself. He sacrificed to Melkart-Heracles and received an Athenian delegation, to which he agreed to release the Athenians taken prisoner at the Granicus who had been kept at labor in Macedonia. And then he was ready to meet the Great Persian King.

The Decisive Battle

It was with an army of about forty thousand infantry and seven thousand cavalry that Alexander crossed the Euphrates at Thapsacus in July of 331 and marched unopposed across Mesopotamia. His forces were increased in number since the Granicus, but his battle concept remained the same, based on the co-ordinated employment of combined arms. The King, however, who had staged with a large army at Babylon and then marched north to the wide plains beyond the Lesser Zab east of the Tigris, was preparing something new. At Issus he had hoped to defeat

Alexander with heavy infantry, but had been turned and over-ridden by the Companions. Now he had assembled an enormous cavalry force from the Upper Satrapies, both light and heavy, including the mailed horsemen of the steppe. The battle ground was carefully chosen and prepared. Alexander's phalanx would be contained and disorganized by scythed chariots while his wings would be enveloped by masses of Iranian horse. It was a good plan and it would have worked but for two factors, the difficulties of co-ordinating and controlling large bodies of cavalry in action, and the locally irresistible shock action of Alexander's Companions. Even if it had been feasible, Alexander had no need to attack the Persians at night, as Parmenion suggested, and so steal the victory; and it would have been very dangerous in view of the numbers and mobility of the Persians. Alexander knew that Dareius would be in the center and that he could break through there and drive him from the field. That was all that was necessary, and the rest was maneuver.

On the night of September twentieth, 331, there was a lunar eclipse, judged to be a favorable sign, and indeed, the situation was favorable to Alexander. Dareius had sent out a cavalry screen under Mazaeus, the satrap of Babylon but had not opposed Alexander's fording of the Tigris, and passed up the opportunity to harrass Alexander's advance. He allowed Alexander to reach the battlefield and to fortify a camp, and only formed his troops when Alexander was a few miles away. Mazaeus commanded the cavalry on the right, with the mission of outflanking Parmenion and rolling up the Macedonian line. Bessus, satrap of Bactria, facing Alexander, commanded the cavalry on the left, while Dareius with the foot and horse guards, the Greek mercenaries, and a few elephants, occupied the center. His plan resembled that of Alexander at Issus, but Alexander, while seeming to fall into the trap, actually foiled it.

Instead of advancing straight forward, Alexander inclined to the right, a tricky maneuver which stretched his line dangerously, but which threw Dareius' plan into confusion. To keep the battlefield of his choice, he was compelled to open the engagement on his left, against Alexander's strongest wing, and not with the right as he had planned. A sharp cavalry fight was followed by an attack with the scythed chariots against Alexander's footguards, but this was broken up by skirmishers and did no harm. A gap now appeared between Dareius' left and center, and into this Alexander charged, as at the Granicus, with the Companion Cavalry, the footguards, and four regiments of the phalanx. The weak Persian center could not stand against him, and Dareius had to flee to save his life. This decided the battle, for it did not matter that Alexander's left was in serious trouble.

Simultaneously with Alexander's charge against the king, the Persian horseguards of Dareius' center threw themselves into a gap in Alexander's line and rode straight through it. Alexander being Alexander, it is probable that this was part of his plan, for it removed the best Persian cavalry from his path just when it was most badly needed. At the same time Parmenion was hard pressed by Mazaeus and may have sent Alexander an urgent appeal for help. This was unnecessary. With Dareius in flight, Alexander could, as he had doubtless planned, swing his disciplined column to the left, meeting the returning Persian horseguards who had too late discovered their mistake. There was hard fighting and a number of the Companions were killed or wounded, along with Hephaestion, Coenus, and other officers, but the Persians thought only of escaping. Mazaeus, also, saw that the game was up and ordered a withdrawal before the desperate resistance of Parmenion's troops, especially the Thessalians. The Persian losses were heavy in defeat, but being largely cavalry, many units more or less intact fell back with their king on Arbela, whence, reorganizing, they made their escape over the passes into Media. Mazaeus, however, retired to the south to cover his own satrapy of Babylon and then defected. Alexander rewarded him richly and took him into his service.

Leaving Parmenion to tidy up the battlefield and seize the Great King's field train, Alexander with the cavalry pursued the fleeing Persians as far as Arbela. While Dareius and the army had gone, Alexander captured his war chest, from which he presented a handsome donative to his troops amounting to from two to ten months' pay. Proceeding on to Babylon, which was surrendered by Mazaeus, he rested his army and gave them further proof of the luxury awaiting the conquerors of Asia. Moralists were shocked by the lavishness of their reception and entertainment, but Alexander knew his Macedonians. This was what they fought for, not for an abstraction. Thereafter the army was accompanied by an ever larger baggage train transporting their possessions, women, slaves, and presently children, so that the army's progress resembled that of a people in migration. Alexander encouraged this for other reasons than the troops' pleasure. It made them forget Macedonia and find their home in the camp, and they would raise a new generation with no other loyalties than their own. For Alexander, Babylon was significant in other ways. Mazaeus, the first collaborator among the Persians who was rewarded with the return of his old satrapy, pointed the way to the future administration of Alexander's conquests, and at Babylon Alexander met the Chaldaeans or Magi, whose half-scientific, half-mystical lore satisfied a deep need in his nature. He kept some of them with him thereafter.

The Occupation of Persia

It was now late autumn of 331, and Alexander marched by easy stages down to Susa, being overtaken on the way by reinforcements from Macedonia which Antipater had released before he know that the Spartan Agis would attack him. They were brought by Alexander's friend Amyntas, who resumed his regimental command in the phalanx, and furnished the occasion for a re-organization of the army. While details are lacking, it is clear that new commands were created in the cavalry and light infantry, both to reward deserving officers and to prepare for campaigns in the mountains or on the steppe which were to come. An advance detachment had secured the surrender of Susa, and there was no hurry. At Susa Alexander took over one of the great Persian treasuries, and was rich, giving his friend Menes, appointed finance director for Syria and Mesopotamia, three thousand talents to take down to the coast. Some money was for Antipater, for Alexander did not yet know of his victory over Agis, and some for the recruitment of troops. It was becoming evident that many would be needed, both as battle replacements and especially for garrisons. Abulites, the Persian satrap, was re-appointed, but as in the case of Mazaeus also, he was left a force of troops under a Macedonian officer to ensure his loyalty and keep order.

Susa was the first Persian capital to be occupied, and Alexander for the first time seated himself upon a Persian throne. Here he established the royal prisoners, Dareius' mother and children with many others. Dareius' queen had died before Gaugamela, but the rest were to be taught the Greek language and prepared for their part in the new society which could now be clearly foreseen. Alexander thus was already planning the mixed marriages which took place on his return to Susa from the east seven years later, for he felt himself to be now in fact King of Asia. At Susa he found the statues of Harmodius and Aristogeiton which Xerxes had taken away, and these he sent back to Athens, in gratitude for her support during the war with Agis.

To discharge his obligation to the Hellenic League, however, Alexander must perform the symbolic act of burning the royal palaces at Persepolis, and these lay beyond the snow-covered passes of the Zagros, and his direct route was barred, first by the hill tribesmen of the Uxii, and then by an organized force under Ariobarzanes, the satrap of Persis. Leaving Parmenion to bring up the trains by an easier and unopposed road, he struck into the hills with the Macedonians, supported by the light cavalry, the archers, and the Agrianes, and successfully turned each position. Against the Uxii he sent Craterus ahead to make the envelopment, for Craterus was being developed as a foil for and successor to Parmenion. He had already been trusted with special commands at Issus, at Tyre, and at Gaugamela, and while a staunch Macedonian, he had not been one of Philip's generals and was unquestionably loyal to Alexander. Against Ariobarzanes, however, Craterus was left to furnish a base of maneuver while Alexander led the turning force in a night march over difficult country, and three other regimental commanders, including Coenus, made an even deeper penetration into the Persian rear. Ptolemy was later in his history to claim for himself a special command in the same operation, but this is unlikely, for while one of Alexander's friends, he was still inexperienced, and had not yet become a Bodyguard.

With these obstacles surmounted, Alexander came to Pasargadae and Persepolis, both of which were surrendered to him with their treasuries intact. The former of these he respected because it contained the tomb of Cyrus the Great, but the latter was plundered by the Macedonians as a reward for their services. Greed was motivation enough, but the story was told of the army encountering a band of Greek artisans in the Great King's service who had been maimed and disfigured to prevent their escaping. Alexander promised them rich gifts but the army was angry, venting its wrath on Persepolis. In any case, the burning of the citadel was also a calculated act of symbolism. Probably it was accompanied by a drunken komos or Dionysiac dance, for the Macedonians were fond of celebrating in this way, and doubtless many a Thais was present, for by now the officers were rich enough to afford Greek *hetaerae*. The buildings had been emptied in advance, and Alexander lost nothing of value to him, but it was a sign to the Greek world that the war of revenge was over. In the following spring, the League troops were released to return home, well rewarded. Except for the Thessalian cavalry, they do not seem to have done much hard fighting, and there were probably few who accepted Alexander's offer to continue on as mercenaries.

Persians were appointed as satrap and finance minister, with a Macedonian as garrison commander, according to the now established concept. There was a short campaign in Persis led by Alexander, while Parmenion and Craterus remained behind, and then the whole force moved north on the east side of the Zagros to Ecbatana, the old capital of Media and the greatest communication center of the empire. Here Parmenion was left behind in a somewhat uncertain capacity: not as treasurer, for that was Harpalus in Babylon; not as satrap of Media, for that was a Mede; not as troop commander, for the occupation troops were under several officers responsible directly to Alexander. But Alexander wished to be rid of Parmenion, whose influence was too great and whose attitudes were too old-fashioned. He could not send him back to Macedonia without offense, and there he would find his friend Antipater who also did not approve of much which Alexander did. So he was left here in a dignified but powerless position, and Alexander turned to the pursuit of Dareius.

It was six months after the battle of Gaugamela, but the Great Persian King still had only a handful of troops with him, and these were loyal rather to Bessus and the other eastern satraps than to him, except for the remaining Greek mercenaries. He could only flee, but when Alexander in an even faster pursuit was about to capture him, the satraps slew him and made their escape. They could not let him be taken alive, for then he must surrender the empire. Without him, they could continue the resistance. Alexander probably did not realize the significance of Dareius' death. He ordered that he receive royal burial at Persepolis, and proceeded himself to act as the legitimate king, adopting Persian dress and ceremonial and setting up a Persian court with chamberlains and the traditional hareem, although, says Plutarch, he employed the last only sparingly. But the east did not accept Alexander as Dareius' successor, and it took six more years for the east to be brought, province by province, into submission.

3. The Great Conqueror

The Conquest of the Steppe

In early 330 Alexander marched unopposed through Parthia and Hyrcania to the shore of the Caspian, but encountered sharp resistance from the Mardi to the west. His great horse Bucephalus was captured but released under threats, and tribes of the Caucasus, among whom Greek writers recognized the fabulous Amazons, sent embassies to offer friendship. Proceeding east again across the steppe to Areia and Margiana, the satrap Satibarzanes made his submission and was confirmed in his position, but this was a trap. As Alexander marched on in the direction of Bactria, Satibarzanes rose behind him, expecting Alexander to be attacked simultaneously by Bessus and the Bactrians; but Bessus was late. Alexander divided his forces, leaving Craterus to face Bessus, and with a mobile force of the usual character (the regiments of Coenus and Amyntas, the Companion Cavalry, archers, javelin-men, and Agrianes) turned swiftly against Satibarzanes, who fled with a cavalry escort. Alexander founded a garrison city near Merv to keep order, while he himself, changing direction, marched south into Drangiana, and again founded an Alexandria wherein to maintain a garrison, but it came to be known as Prophthasia, "Anticipation," from events which took place there. And Satibarzanes, attempting again to establish himself in Areia, was slain in a heroic duel by Alexander's boyhood friend, the Greek Erigyius.

At Alexandria Prophthasia, a plot against Alexander's life was "anticipated" which cost the lives of Parmenion and Philotas.

Since Parmenion's other son, Nicanor, had died six months earlier, this ended the old man's dynasty, as only a son-in-law, Coenus, remained alive. Alexander must have complained of Parmenion; many anecdotes were repeated of Parmenion's offering poor advice and being snubbed for it. A proud Macedonian, friend of Philip, the arrogance of Alexander must have been painful to him, and Alexander tolerated no criticism. With Nicanor dead and Parmenion in Ecbatana, Philotas was isolated. A plot was reported involving a group of Macedonians, none of them prominent except the Bodyguard Demetrius, and he was not much known. The plot was, it was charged, reported to Philotas, who discounted it and did not report it to Alexander. When the report reached the king through a royal page, he summoned his friends and immediately made an attack on Philotas and his father. Significantly, the charge was pressed by Philotas' closest friends, Coenus, Hephaestion, Amyntas the son of Andromenes, all trying to protect themselves from suspicion. They demanded and directed torture, taunted Philotas in his suffering and extorted a partial confession, and he was tried and executed by the army, while a messenger, Polydamas, a friend of Parmenion, was sent on the grisly mission of procuring his assassination. All was done quickly, and Alexander was rid of Parmenion and his sons, but many were revolted at the barbarous travesty compounded by the unjustified murder of Alexander of Lyncestis which followed. It was, however, a reminder that Alexander knew how to employ terror.

It was the autumn of 330, and the army moved on up through Arachosia into Paropanisadae, into the frozen winter of the Hindu Kush, where the troops rested in subterranean houses under the snow. As soon as the ground could be worked in the spring, a garrison city was founded, peopled by some Macedonians and Greeks who could march no farther, and a mass of natives. Security was provided by a small body of troops under a Macedonian commander, to watch the Iranian satrap. And when the passes were open, the army marched north into Bactria, occupied its cities without opposition, and crossed the Oxus River into Sogdiana. Bessus and his forces retired before Alexander. Stasanor, a Cypriot prince from Soloi who had joined Alexander at Tyre, was sent back to take over the satrapy of Areia, important for the communcations to the west.

In Sogdiana, Alexander was faced with a difficult problem. It was a country of vast plains rimmed by desert and mountain. The population was nomadic in part, in part concentrated in fortified cities in the river valleys. Control lay in the hands of tribal barons, proud and independent, whose strength was cavalry and impregnable mountain strongholds. Beyond the Jaxartes, to the north, were Scythian tribes never subject to Persia, who only looked for an excuse to cross the frontier in search of plunder. To pacify this region and secure its resources was not easy. Alexander had received reinforcements and was strong in cavalry, but the bulk of his army still marched on foot. The campaign lasted from the spring of 329 to that of 327, and called for all his ingenuity.

The operations opened with deceptive ease. Bessus had assumed the royal title and shown himself overbearing, and the Sogdian barons Spitamenes and Oxyartes surrendered him to Alexander to punish as the murderer of Dareius, although Ptolemy later claimed credit for his capture. They thought to make peace in return for a nominal submission, but Alexander's movements frightened them. He marched north and occupied Maracanda, then advanced to the Jaxartes and stormed its cities, and crossing the river, inflicted a defeat on the Scythians, perhaps his most brilliant military feat, which he had prepared for by his attack on the Getae north of the Danube. Another Alexandria was founded here, called the Farthest. Everything looked well, but suddenly the news came that Spitamenes, reinforced by Scythians, was attacking Maracanda, and Alexander made his only mistake. Inexplicably he sent to its relief an inadequate force under a divided command, and this was trapped and annihilated. The Macedonian reputation for invincibility was shattered, and it did no good for Alexander to ravage the Polytimetus valley. When he retired to Zariaspa-Bactra for winter quarters in the autumn of 329, he left Sogdiana seething with revolt.

It must have been a difficult winter for Alexander. Substantial reinforcements arrived from Macedonia and western Asia, recruited in part by the former satraps of Ionia and Lycia, Asander and Nearchus. The former, Parmenion's cousin, is not heard of again, but the latter, Alexander's boyhood friend, was to play an important role later. Other satraps were called in for an accounting and some were punished. Bessus was executed in barbaric fashion.

Both Iranians and Macedonians were worried and nervous, and it is little wonder that a drunken quarrel broke out between Alexander and Cleitus the Black, the brother of Alexander's nurse; Cleitus, along with Alexander's very close friend Hephaistion, was commander of the royal squadron of the Companions at the time of the quarrel. Insults from one so high may well have made the king nervous, for he called out that he was being betrayed in the course of the melee. Alexander ran him through with a spear and did penance for it, but it was one more warning to the Macedonians that their king was no longer merely one of themselves.

And Alexander was facing a vital decision. He knew that his position as king, both of the Macedonians and of Asia, depended solely on his military prestige. Neither affection nor constitutionality counted for much and there was really no one of importance whom he could trust except possibly Craterus. And Craterus, although he had joined in the attack on Philotas, was too much a Macedonian to like Alexander's Asianizing policies. For this reason, Alexander had kept combat command in his own hands. He had won every victory himself, and this fear of a rival may have led him to send the group of incompetents against Spitamenes. Now he must take the risk. The nomad cavalry could not be run down. It must be met by a number of mobile task forces, securely based and ably led. Their composition might vary, but the core of each would consist of a regiment of the Foot Companions. The original six of these were now increased to eight or nine, and the multiplicity of command would be a safeguard.

When Alexander crossed into Sogdiana in the spring of 328, he left five such task forces behind in Bactria, and the system proved its worth in the summer, when Spitamenes, supported by the Scythian Massagetae, attempted a raid on Zariaspa, and was routed by Craterus. Alexander advanced in five columns, three of which, based on the regiment of Perdiccas, were under his operational control. They overran the country, destroying local centers of resistance, while Hephaestion was given the mission of building forts and fortified cities to maintain order. Coenus was left with Meleager, who had marched up from Bactria with his force, to watch the Scythians over-winter, while Alexander retired to Nautaca in southern Sogdiana. Early in the spring of 327, Spitamenes and the Scythians encountered them and were so decisively defeated that Spitamenes' allies murdered him and fled to return no more. With the capture of Oxyartes' mountain fortress at about the same time by Alexander's light troops, and a great victory of Craterus over hillsmen in the Pamirs, the reduction of the region was complete.

In his winter quarters at Nautaca, Alexander had good reason to be confident. With the support of some of his friends, notably Hephaestion, he attempted to introduce among the Macedonians the Persian court practice of *proskynesis*, prostrating oneself before the King, but did not press this when it encountered opposition. Polyperchon, notably, who ridiculed it, was arrested briefly, but continued in his regimental command. A real or invented plot among the Royal Pages served as an excuse to imprison Aristotle's nephew Callisthenes the historian, but he survived for two years to die in India. The capture of Oxyartes' family made it possible to cement relations with the Sogdian nobility by marrying his daughter Roxane, probably still a child since she did not become pregnant until four years later. Large numbers of Iranian troops, especially cavalry, were taken into service for the Indian campaign.

The Indian Campaign

It was with an army of perhaps seventy thousand foot and ten thousand horse that Alexander crossed the Hindu Kush and invaded India in the late spring of 327. The Macedonians, who had made up nearly one half of the army at the Granicus, now came to hardly more than a quarter of the total, for while we hear of eleven regiments of Foot Companions in addition to the guards and four or possibly five cavalry regiments, it is unlikely that these were still exclusively Macedonian. Reinforcements of the following year raised the grand total to one hundred and twenty-five thousand, but this force certainly never acted as a unit, much of its strength being given to garrison or satrapal duties. While Alexander had drastically reduced the trains, nevertheless the achievement of bringing so large an army over the passes and into the Indus valley was a logistical feat of the first order, and there was, it would seem, little necessity for it. Alexander had conquered the Persian empire and India was only allied or independent territory, which only Cyrus the Great was supposed to have traversed. But India was rich, strange, and adjacent, and Alexander probably never thought of not going forward, driven by that insatiable ambition or curiosity which the historian Arrian calls *pothos*.

The campaign occupied three years, and is obscure in many respects. The relatively sober account of our sources gives way to all sorts of wonderful things, not necessarily untrue: monkeys, snakes, huge banyan trees, Brahmans and gymnosophists, vast rivers and the monsoon rains, the ocean tides, huge armies of cavalry and war elephants deployed on vast plains. Alexander's return route through Gedrosia and along the coast brought parched deserts, savages who lived solely on fish, schools of whales which resembled fleets of warships. There was much fighting, progressively more murderous and aimless, against tribes and cities of which no Greek had ever heard speaking languages which no one knew. Casualties were heavy and on one occasion Alexander, often wounded before, was very nearly killed, being saved only by the shield of Achilles from Ilium borne by a young friend Peucastas. The slaughter and the booty were immense. Communication with the rest of the empire was partial and irregular, and many of the satraps must have felt that Alexander would never return, but on the other hand, there must have been a stream of scientific reports and specimens sent back to Aristotle in Athens, and such writers as Onesicritus, Cleitarchus, and Nearchus provided stories which were the basis of later Greek knowledge of India. These were fabulous and fantastic years, of importance principally for the emergence of that group of men who held the reins of power after Alexander's death. These included the original regimental commanders Perdiccas, Craterus, and Meleager, with the later arrivals Polyperchon, Antigenes, and Perdiccas' brother Alcetas and his brother-in-law Attalus. They included also Alexander's boyhood friends who were now acquiring military experience, Hephaestion, Leonnatus, Ptolemy, and Nearchus, although the latter two are more suspect because their own histories are the primary sources for their own responsibilities and achievements. Seleucus may have held a command in the great battle against Porus, but the post is otherwise assigned to Leonnatus. The Bodyguards Lysimachus, Aristonus, and Peithon the son of Cra teras were certainly present, but held no military command.

For Alexander was still cautiously experimenting with his generals. Craterus and Coenus had won victories in Sogdiana, and were never again to hold independent combat commands. Instead, for the movement down the Kabul valley, Alexander entrusted the main body to Perdiccas and Hephaestion with orders to clear the main road and secure it with fortresses, while he himself with the usual light force of Macedonians protected the left flank by operations against tribesmen in the hills. Craterus was given the inglorious command of the trains. This operation occupied the rest of 327 and the early months of 326, and was climaxed by the capture of the impregnable citadel of Aornus, where Heracles had failed. Coming finally to the Indus River, Alexander found a bridge prepared by Perdiccas and Hephaestion and the entire force crossed into the territory of King Taxiles, who was friendly. Continuing east to the Hydaspes River, Alexander found the next king, Porus, defending the crossing with a large army.

It was now mid-summer of 326, and the river was not yet full. Coenus was sent back to bring up boats from the Indus, and Alexander began daily maneuvers and cavalry movements to disguise the real attack when it should come. When all was ready, he marched up-stream at night, leaving Craterus in camp and three regimental task forces evenly spaced along the bank. This was to extend Porus' defense, but once Alexander had established a beach-head, they were to follow him. The battle which followed was marked by complicated cavalry maneuvers in which Coenus played an important but not very clear part. He commanded cavalry as well as his own infantry regiment, and may have effected an ambush against Porus' cavalry. Against Porus' elephants Alexander employed light and then heavy infantry, and the victory was not difficult, although Porus himself, a huge man on a huge elephant, performed prodigies of valor. Craterus was left to build two cities, one named for the horse Bucephalus who died in the battle, while Alexander continued on east past the Acesines to the Hyphasis, covered by minor operations led by Perdiccas and Hephaestion. This was the first time either of them had held an independent combat command. Hephaestion built a city on the Acesines, and Alexander prepared plans to cross the Hyphasis and march down the Ganges.

The Return to Babylon

But this was too much. The troops refused to go farther, and found a spokesman in Coenus, who had earned the right to speak for the army. Alexander must return to Bucephala and Nicaea for winter quarters, but he did not like to be opposed. Coenus died soon after, whether or not from natural causes, and the dangers and hardships of the next year fully repaid the Macedonians for their disobedience.

A fleet was built, with Alexander's friends acting as trierarchs, and the army moved down stream in the spring of 325. Craterus followed with the trains on the right bank, and Hephaestion with a combat force on the left, while Nearchus was admiral of the fleet, as he was later to report. There was much fighting, especially against the Malli, who occupied the region about the confluence of the Hydaspes and the Acesines, and here Alexander was nearly killed in the assault on a citadel. Further down river, eighty thousand subjects of King Sambus were massacred after a fierce resistance. Perdiccas, Hephaestion, and Ptolemy distinguished themselves in independent commands. From some point below the junction with the Indus, Craterus with the trains was detached and sent back west to Carmania through Arachosia and Drangiana. The Musicani were subdued, Pattala occupied, the delta explored, and Alexander sailed out into the Ocean to sacrifice to Poseidon. He also sacrificed to the gods whom Ammon had designated, as a sign that his mission was accomplished.

Nearchus, with the fleet, waited for the southwest monsoons to end and did not sail until late in September, but Alexander marched west from Pattala in midsummer. His immediate objective was the prosperous tribe of the Oreitae, and the Oreitae were defeated and thoroughly plundered by columns under Alexander, Ptolemy, and Leonnatus, so that the whole region was filled with fire and devastation and great slaughter (as Diodorus reports). Nevertheless, Leonnatus was left there to build a city and supply base for Nearchus, and there was enough fight left in the Oreitae for them promptly to rise against him. Proceeding west again with a small force consisting mostly of Macedonians, Alexander suffered great difficulties from heat and the lack of water and provisions. The region was populated only by small groups of primitive savages along the coast, and the march served no purpose except to show that not even nature at her worst could stop him. Alexander may actually not have known what conditions really were. There were heavy losses among the camp followers and most of the train must have been abandoned, since the pack animals were eaten. Eventually the force got through to Carmania and was joined by Craterus, who had done some fighting but had no serious difficulty, and by the fleet, which, like Alexander's force, had suffered principally from lack of food and water. The reunion was celebrated by a gigantic *komos* in honor of Dionysus, of the sort which the Macedonians liked so well.

It was now early in 324, and Alexander proceeded to take up administrative matters. An accounting was demanded of the satraps and other high officials, and those who had acquired overly large military forces were ordered to disband them. Charges were readily believed as always, and two of Parmenion's executioners who had commanded the garrison in Media were put to death: the Thracian Sitalces and Cleander the brother of Coenus. Harpalus, Alexander's treasurer, fled from Babylon with six thousand mercenaries and five thousand talents but it is not clear what were his offenses, for Alexander would not have objected to mere extravagance. Harpalus reached Greece safely (which suggests that Alexander did not try to apprehend him), and took his troops to the mercenary market at Taenarum and his money to Athens. Both played a part in the Greek uprising of the next year, but Harpalus himself was ignominiously slain in Crete by his lieutenant Thibron.

Army and fleet resumed their movement, Hephaestion leading the trains along the coast while Alexander with a small force crossed the mountains to Persepolis and Pasargadae. There, the acting satrap was put to death and alleged violators of the tomb of Cyrus were discovered and punished. Giving the satrapy to Peucestas, who had learned the native customs and language, Alexander went on to Susa, where fleet and army rejoined. At Susa Alexander executed the Iranian satrap and gave the post to a Macedonian. A victory celebration was held, at which golden crowns were awarded to the eight Body Guards, of whom Peucestas, Leonnatus, and Hephaestion had particularly distinguished themselves, and to Nearchus and Onesicritus, the admiral and the chief pilot (or perhaps the joint admirals) of the fleet. Other officers received large gifts also. The Macedonian rank and file was given a large sum of money, ten or twenty thousand talents, which would have been about a talent each. This was probably not merely in payment of their outstanding debts, for that would have rewarded most the most improvident, and the soldiers, who were well paid and had frequent access to booty, should hardly have been so much in debt. The soldiers' unions with native women were also recognized as legal marriages, and a fund was established to pay for the education of the camp children. As a symbol of the union of the two races, a mass marriage was celebrated in Persian style; Alexander himself married two royal princesses, and eighty of his friends married one noble Iranian woman each. Tradition records the names of Hephaestion, Craterus, Perdiccas, Ptolemy, Nearchus, Seleucus, and the secretary Eumenes. Alexander had been married twice before, once after Issus to the half-Greek Barsine, the daughter of Artabazus, and once to the Sogdian Roxane, but he had as yet no recognized heir.

From Susa must have gone out two important messages to the Greek world, for one of them, at least, was read in the summer of 324 at the Olympic Festival. This was the Exiles Decree, which instructed the Greeks to receive their exiles back, except those who had a religious pollution. It need not have been a contravention of the charter of the Hellenic League if it were phrased as recommended policy: "We think best that you recall your exiles." Alexander may have thought that this measure would be popular, especially if he offered to pay part or all of the cost. But it was not, for these were political exiles, and their home-coming meant the restoration of their property and their influence. In particular, the Athenians and the Aetolians opposed it, and probably little happened before Alexander's death. Curiously, this decree is not mentioned in our most reliable sources, and no Alexander historian mentions the second measure, Alexander's request for a cult in the Greek cities. We know too little to understand what was asked. Possibly Alexander wished to be, like Philip, admitted as the thirteenth with the Twelve Gods, and seen through the eyes of the ancients he would richly seem to have deserved such an honor. Little Greek objection is reported, even though Alexander was not very popular in Greece.

At Susa, also, the Indian gymnosophist Calanus demonstrated to the army his fortitude by burning himself up on a huge pyre, for he was elderly, and feared becoming physically and mentally feeble.

From Susa, fleet and army went up the Tigris to Opis, and there Alexander selected some ten thousand of the Macedonians, the oldest and least battle-worthy, to return to their homes. Their native wives and half-breed children would remain in Asia. Craterus and Polyperchon were in charge of the movement. Craterus was to replace Antipater as viceroy in Europe, and Antipater himself was ordered to come to Alexander with a new levy of the same size. In the meantime, the army would consist of ten thousand Macedonians and thirty thousand Iranians trained in Macedonian fashion, while the four regiments of the Companions would be filled up to strength with Iranians, and a fifth all Iranian regiment would be added. The staff and officer group would also be Iranized. This news was received with anger by the troops, who rioted, but Alexander succeeded in pacifying them. Craterus and Polyperchon set off in leisurely fashion, for a year later they had gotten no further than Cilicia.

Their departure was celebrated by a huge feast, with prayers for harmony between Macedonians and Persians. With the strain of campaign over, everyone turned to the enjoyment of good living, and the first victim was Hephaestion, who succumbed at Ecbatana following a prolonged drinking bout. Alexander was plunged into deep grief, for Hephaestion was his favorite, and probably the one man whom he could trust, especially because he had shown no special skill as a general and was unpopular with the Macedonians. Hephaestion's unfortunate doctor was hanged, a messenger was dispatched to Ammon to ask how he should be worshipped, and the whole army was put into mourning. The sacred fire was extinguished throughout Persia, and the greatest funeral in all history was planned in Babylon. And then, in a winter campaign at the end of the year, the Cossaean country in the Median hills was overrun; they had been the only foes left. Ptolemy commanded one of the two Macedonian columns, while Perdiccas was at Babylon.

In the spring of 323, Alexander came down into Mesopotamia and proceeded slowly toward Babylon. He planned to celebrate

Hephaestion's funeral and then to undertake a campaign into
Arabia, for which some preliminary exploration had already taken
place. Alexander lived only for fighting and adventure, and could
not stop. He sent an expedition to the Caspian Sea and another to
Armenia, and it would not be strange if he thought also of Africa
and western Europe. Had not Ammon promised him the conquest
of the whole world? It was not that Alexander was completely
uninterested in other matters. He was not a destroyer, but like
Heracles and Dionysus a bringer of civilization. He patronized
literature and the arts, learning and science. He built cities, canals,
roads, and harbors. He encouraged good government and pro-
moted what might have become a world citizenship. The grandiose
schemes of the so-called Last Plans brought to light after his death
are probably genuine. But war and exploration were his passion,
and he would go on as long as he could.

He had been warned by the Chaldaeans not to go to Babylon,
but went nevertheless. Hephaestion's funeral was celebrated at vast
cost, and on Ammon's instructions a heroic cult was instituted,
empire-wide but centered in Alexandria, where Cleomenes was
ordered to build a magnificent tomb. Embassies came from all the
known world and were received systematically. Preparations for
the campaign continued, and festivities were constant and protracted. Then suddenly, at a dinner given by his Thessalian friend
Medius, Alexander quaffed a huge goblet of wine in honor of
Heracles (others report simply that he came down with a fever),
and staggered. He was aided back to the palace by his friends, and
there, after an illness of eleven days which seems to exclude the
possibility that he was poisoned, he died early on the evening of
10 June. Characteristically it was only at the last moment that he
gave the signet ring by which his orders were certified to Perdiccas,
the senior and perhaps ablest general. He knew that it would be
futile to name his successor.

Chapter Two

The Hellenistic Kingdoms

1. The Successors of Alexander

The Division of the Empire

Alexander's position was unique, and no one could occupy it. It depended primarily upon his overwhelming and uninterrupted success in war and secondarily upon his skill in handling men, his suspicion, ruthlessness, and fascination. The agency of his success was the Macedonian army, foot and horse, with the auxiliaries whom he almost always led personally, the Agrianes, the archers, and javelin men, Thracians all. Only on three occasions do we hear of his allowing anyone else to command them, and of these, Ptolemy's alleged command at the Persian Gates is probably an invention of his own. Craterus led these troops briefly in 327, and Leonnatus in 325, under what must have been special circumstances. The Thracians were personally loyal as well as skillful fighters. The Macedonians were less loyal to Alexander, but he brought them victories and booty and indulged them in every way except militarily. They always won and their casualties were always few. They were fourteen thousand at the Granicus, twenty thousand at Issus, and perhaps twenty-five thousand in Bactria. Since Antipater in 323 could raise only about fourteen thousand, most of the Macedonians of military age were in Asia, and they were not numerous. When Alexander died, ten thousand of these were in Cilicia and they were the eldest, Philip's veterans who had

The Nativity of Alexander, from Baalbek

never been defeated. The troops in Babylon must have been mainly younger.

Upon these last depended the Macedonian Empire, for the rest of the army did not count for much, politically or militarily. There were perhaps sixty thousand mercenaries, Greek, Anatolian, Asiatic, whose loyalty was to their paymaster, and who were mainly on garrison duty. There was, perhaps, a larger number of Iranians, most of them at Babylon and the rest in satrapal armies, who would be loyal to the King of Asia, but would have no hand in choosing him. In the struggle for power after Alexander's death, they stood aside.

It was for the Macedonians to decide how the empire was to be ruled, and they were not united. The Foot Companions, veterans and young soldiers alike, wanted to elect a Macedonian king, divide up the plunder, and go home. Their champion would have been Craterus, but he was in Cilicia. Meleager and Attalus, regimental commanders, spoke for them, and Alexander's half-brother, Arrhidaeus, was invested with the kingship under the name of Philip. But the Body Guards and Friends of Alexander, supported by the Companion Cavalry, were not ready to give up Asia. They had no candidate for the throne unless Roxane, pregnant, should bear a son; Nearchus proposed Heracles, Barsine's son, but found no support. Ptolemy wanted to put the kingship into commission; that is, to postpone any decision until it should be too late, and this, in effect, was what was done. Meleager and his supporters were betrayed by Perdiccas' brother and brother-in-law, Alcetas and Attalus, and killed. Philip Arrhidaeus remained king and the rights of Roxane's possible son were recognized, but Perdiccas became regent. Of the Body Guards, Aristonus remained with Perdiccas. The others received provinces under the title of satraps, which they would in fact treat as hereditary estates given them by the Macedonians. These were the five most important and most easily defensible areas of the empire. Peucestas retained Persis and Peithon received Media, Ptolemy received Egypt and Lysimachus Thrace, and all proceeded to dig in and make themselves strong and popular. The last two survived to become kings. Only Leonnatus, receiving Hellespontine Phrygia, had no time to rule it. Alexander's boyhood friend Laomedon, brother of Erigyius, received Syria, and the secretary Eumenes obtained

Cappadocia, while the remaining satrapies were left to the satraps who already held them, of whom four, Stasanor of Bactria, Philotas of Cilicia, Asander of Lycia, and Menander of Lydia, were friends of Alexander and present in Babylon at his death. Antigonus remained, aloof and undisturbed, in his Phrygian castle at Celenae. Nearchus, the one-time admiral, was passed over and is barely mentioned thereafter. He may have retained a naval command at court as Seleucus was given the command of the Companion Cavalry. A previously unmentioned but evidently prominent Arrhidaeus was charged with the burial of Alexander at the Ammonium, according to his wish.

All these events and decisions occupied a week or a little longer, and then the satraps rode off posthaste to their governments, taking with them as many friends, as much money, and as many soldiers, especially Macedonian, as they could. Perdiccas was left with the royal family and a much reduced staff and army. He had won the regency, but was in danger of losing the empire. His first necessity was to gain the support of Craterus and Antipater, but for the moment he sent Peithon to quell a mutiny among the Greek garrisons in the upper satrapies.

The Lamian War

Craterus' position is uncertain; we do not know whether he was expected to assist Perdiccas in Asia or Antipater in Europe. In neither case had he any reason for moving, and for the rest of 323 he cautiously remained in Cilicia. Antipater, on the other hand, was faced immediately with an uprising of the Greek world under the leadership of the Athenians, Aetolians, and Thessalians. He marched south with a small force to put down the revolt and was promptly besieged in Lamia, a town in Thessaly, by the Athenian general Leosthenes. The Greeks had little unity and little skill in siege operations, and soon suffered a loss in the death of their general, but the situation was serious. Cleitus the White, the former regimental commander homeward bound with Craterus, was sent to take command of the Hellespontine fleet, while early in the spring of 322, Leonnatus led his satrapal army into Europe. Lysimachus was immobilized by a revolt of the vassal Thracian king Seuthes, and Leonnatus was defeated and killed, but Cleitus annihilated the Athenian fleet at Amorgus, and Craterus, leaving Antigenes with the Foot Guards to guard the treasury at Cyinda, brought up his army to take part in the decisive battle of Crannon, in July. The Greek coalition dissolved and Athens surrendered, accepting an oligarchic government. Good feeling prevailed.

Probably in the late summer of 323, Alexander's Sogdian wife Roxane was delivered of a son who received the name Alexander. Subsequently, the literary sources refer to the "kings," but officially Philip was recognized as ruler until his death in the autumn of 317. Thereafter protocol referred to Alexander IV as king until about 305, long after his death in 310 or the following year.

Craterus married one daughter of Antipater and Perdiccas another, and the regent seemed to have attained his goal. His only presumed enemy, Ptolemy, was occupied with the acquisition of Cyrene, where his intervention had been invited in consequence of trouble stirred up by Harpalus' assassin, Thibron.

The Rise of Antigonus

In the autumn of 322, this harmony was shattered. Olympias, Alexander's mother, entered negotiations with the Aetolians, hard pressed by Antipater and Craterus, and sent her daughter Cleopatra to Asia Minor. Perdiccas had won victories in Cappadocia and Pisidia, and he was now encouraged by Eumenes to marry Cleopatra and claim the throne. At her instigation he murdered Alexander's aunt Cynane, but the Macedonians mutinied and he was forced to allow the marriage of Cynane's daughter Eurydice to King Philip. Antigonus, a friend of Antipater, who alone of the satraps had avoided coming to Babylon in 323 and who was now called on for a financial and administrative accounting, now thought it prudent to flee from his satrapy to Europe, so Perdiccas had no rival in Asia. But before he could be king, he must, according to Macedonian custom, secure the body of Alexander for burial.

At this point, early in 321, everything began to go wrong. Arrhidaeus, perhaps suborned by Ptolemy, slipped through Perdiccas' hands and got to Egypt with the funeral cortege. Perdiccas was forced to. march south against Ptolemy, but his allies the

Aetolians failed to hold Antipater, who crossed the Hellespont with the assistance of Cleitus and the fleet. Eumenes defeated and killed Craterus but Antipater with the Macedonians advanced inexorably. Perdiccas, blocked on the Nile, was killed by his officers (May 320) and, assembled at Triparadeisus in northern Syria, the army declared Eumenes and Perdiccas' other partisans outlaws. Aroused by Eurydice, the soldiers demanded money, but Antipater succeeded in quieting them, and was designated regent. The opponents of Perdiccas were rewarded, Arrhidaeus receiving the satrapy of Hellespontine Phrygia, Seleucus Babylonia, and Antigenes Susiana, with the mission of bringing silver for the soldiers down to the coast from Susa. Antigonus was given half of the Macedonian royal army with Antipater's son Cassander as cavalry commander, and ordered to make war on Eumenes, Alcetas, and Attalus. Antipater now returned to Macedonia with the kings. Polyperchon, in his absence, had beaten off an attack of the Aetolians. But even Antipater's authority did not stop the activity of the ambitious Macedonian generals.

Antigonus was only carrying out his orders when, in 320, he attacked Eumenes in Cappadocia. Although much superior in force and a better general, Eumenes was betrayed by his troops and fled to the impregnable fortress of Nora. His soldiers took service with Antigonus in what was to be the normal later procedure. The wars were between generals, and the armies were loyal only to themselves, following a commander only so long as he was successful. This easy victory, followed the following spring by similar operations against Alcetas and Attalus, gave Antigonus the largest military potential in existence and awakened in him dreams of further grandeur. Ptolemy, on the other hand, in invading Syria, killing Laomedon, and annexing the territory, was thinking more prudently only of protecting Egypt from invasion.

Antigonus' opportunity came in 319 when Antipater died in Macedonia, leaving Polyperchon as regent and his own son Cassander as cavalry commander. The two were hostile, and Cassander went to Antigonus in Asia, where a division of the empire based on spheres of influence was arranged. Cassander would be enabled to return to Macedonia, Ptolemy and Lysimachus would be confirmed in their holdings, and Antigonus would receive a free hand in Asia. Antigonus now had no difficulty in expelling

Arrhidaeus from Hellespontine Phrygia and Cleitus from Lydia. It was necessary for him to eliminate all of the satraps who had acquired a reputation under Alexander and who would never willingly serve another of their old equals. Eumenes still remained, almost a prisoner but of great ability and wide reputation, and Antigonus offered to take him into his service. It was a hard decision for Eumenes, for at the same time Polyperchon, on the advice of Olympias, wrote to him offering in the name of the kings the supreme command in Asia. Eumenes appears romanticized in history, but his support of Perdiccas in 322 showed that he was both ambitious and unscrupulous. After deliberation, he chose to play for the higher stakes, for if he could overcome the handicap of being a Greek and rally the satraps against Antigonus, he might succeed to Antigonus' position. Their consequent contest makes up the history of Asia for the next two years.

Accepting the appointment from the kings in the winter of 319/8, Eumenes had only a handful of troops and a title, but he had made use of the negotiations with Antigonus to escape from Nora, and could move. Antigonus had an army of sixty thousand foot and ten thousand horse, with a few elephants, but his attention was distracted by events in Greece. There, Polyperchon had issued a dramatic proclamation to the cities, promising them his support in overthrowing the oligarchies introduced by Antipater, and democratic revolutions occurred in many places, notably at Athens. Cassander sailed to the harbor of Athens, the Peiraeus, in the spring, and won control of Athens again when Polyperchon met a reverse before Megalopolis; for the cities wanted mainly to be on the winning side. But in support of Cassander, Antigonus had to fight a close but finally successful naval battle with Cleitus, who again commanded the royal fleet. And this gave Eumenes the chance to get through the mountains to Cilicia, where Antigenes and the veteran Foot Guards (the *Argyraspids* or Silver Shields) accepted the royal mandate and provided funds from the treasury at Cyinda to enable Eumenes to recruit an army. And they accompanied him as he moved south into northern Syria and then, at the end of the summer, blocked by Ptolemy and threatened by Antigonus, on east to Babylonia (317/6) where he hoped for support from loyal satraps. But he was rejected by Peithon in Media and repulsed by Seleucus in

Babylon, and wintered in Antigenes' satrapy of Susiana, while Antigonus followed deliberately on his trail, recruiting and engaging in diplomatic activity but avoiding battle, where he would be at a disadvantage against the skill of Eumenes and the prestige of Alexander's last remaining veteran regiment.

But expediency triumphed over legitimacy both in Europe and in Asia, and with good reason, for Eumenes could not really command Macedonians and the royal family was neither united nor capable of ruling. Eumenes could only try to persuade his generals, meeting in Alexander's tent before Alexander's empty throne, and could not give orders, and in Macedonia in 317 the hostility of Olympias and Eurydice resulted in the death of them both as well as of King Philip III. There remained the little Alexander IV, the son of Roxane, but Cassander, married to the royal princess Thessalonice, was king of Macedonia in all but name. And the royal cause was extinguished late in the same year on the plains east of the Zagrus. Eumenes, supported by Peucestas and the eastern satraps, was undefeated in the field, but Antigonus, with ample cavalry supplied by Peithon, managed to capture his camp with the families and property of the *Argyraspids*. This was their real loyalty, and they surrendered Eumenes to recover it, but they were punished by being dispersed permanently among the frontier garrisons. Antigonus, with apparently some reluctance, put Eumenes to death, and executed Antigenes with torture. Master of Asia, he allowed the more remote satraps to continue in their posts, but assassinated Peithon and removed Peucestas, replacing them with his own friends. His only mistake was in allowing a suspicious Seleucus to escape from Babylon and get safely to Ptolemy in Egypt (about July, 316).

The Destruction of Antigonus

As the killing of Meleager had aroused the generals against Perdiccas and the death of Craterus had led to the outlawing of Eumenes, so Antigonus' high-handed action against Antigenes, Peithon, Peucestas, and Seleucus led to concerted action against him by his three allies. All had received their commands from the Macedonians, and fundamentally the attitude of Alexander's friends was the same as that of the common soldiers. They had divided the spoil, and they would oppose anyone who disturbed their enjoyment of it. There was intense diplomatic activity in the winter of 316/5, and in the early spring, in north Syria, Antigonus was presented with a set of demands. As the price of peace, he must return Babylonia to Seleucus and give Ptolemy title to all of Syria. Still more, he must give up the territory in Asia Minor taken from Eumenes and the partisans of Polyperchon, turning over Cappadocia and Lydia to Cassander and Hellespontine Phrygia to Lysimachus. Another demand required Antigonus to divide the thirty-five thousand talents which he had taken from the imperial treasuries. There was a certain equity in all this but Antigonus, as they doubtless expected, refused to negotiate. From Seleucus he had nothing to fear, and against the others he raised the slogan employed by Alexander in the Exiles Decree and again by Philip and Polyperchon in 319. The Greek cities of Asia were already free; that is to say, democratic and ungarrisoned, but Ptolemy, Lysimachus, and Cassander all held Greek cities through oligarchies and garrisons. By demanding that the Greeks should be free, Antigonus won a propaganda victory and announced his plan of campaign. He would not try for additional territory, but attempt to subvert the Greek subjects of his opponents.

The war which followed lasted through five campaign seasons and was ended in a general peace in the autumn of 311. It was fought in Asia Minor, where Antigonus had little trouble in holding the northwest, but had more difficulty with Caria under the independent satrap Asander. Antigonus also had trouble in Lycia, where the Ptolemaic fleet could be brought to bear. The war was fought in Thrace, where Antigonus in 313 brought about a coalition of the Thracian king Seuthes and the Pontic Greek cities, but supported it ineffectually. It was fought in Cyprus, where Ptolemy won and held control. It was fought in Cyrene, which revolted with Antigonus' support in 313 but was subdued again. Most of all it was fought in Greece, where Antigonus' generals had much success and the situation was too confused to give Cassander any rest. In 315, Antigonus was briefly the ally of Polyperchon and his son Alexander, so that Ptolemy could here also raise a demand for Greek freedom. Cassander, hard pressed, appealed for peace in 313, but his allies were not yet ready and Antigonus would make no concessions. But in the early summer of

312, Ptolemy won a decisive victory at Gaza in Palestine. Antigonus had driven him back into Egypt in 315, and had in 314 captured Tyre after a seige of more than a year. He then felt secure enough to leave his son Demetrius in command and go north. Ptolemy's victory over his youthful opponent won time for Seleucus to return to Babylonia, where he was able to establish himself. Antigonus was forced to return hastily to Syria, but when he was unable to secure his southern frontier by a conquest of the Nabataeans or to capture Seleucus, who retired before him into the Upper Satrapies, he was ready to make peace. In all respects but one he had gained, for he had yielded only one point, the return of Seleucus, and it is possible that he did not concede even this in the treaty. One of the letters which he sent to his Greek cities on this occasion has been preserved, and in it he expresses his gratification that their freedom has been formally recognized.[3]

Antigonus had reason to feel confident. Lysimachus was still preoccupied with domestic troubles, apparently, and against Seleucus, Antigonus' general still held the citadel at Babylon. Cassander's attention was drawn to the north by an attack of the Antariatae, and only Ptolemy was in a position to be dangerous. And yet in a few months, by the spring of 310, war had broken out again. Ptolemy charged Antigonus with violating the freedom of the Greek cities of Cilicia Tracheia and sent a fleet there which had some success. That is, he had turned Antigonus' own formula into a *casus belli*. In the meantime, Cassander had successfully subverted Antigonus' last general in Greece, his own nephew Ptolemaeus, and Antigonus could make no retort other than to send to Polyperchon Alexander's last surviving son Heracles; for Alexander IV and his mother had been killed by Cassander a year earlier. But Polyperchon used Heracles only for purposes of bargaining, and killed him in return for Cassander's recognition of his independent position in the Peloponnese. In 308, Ptolemy's generals occupied the coast of Pamphylia and Lycia, and in the same year Ptolemy sailed to Greece and liberated Corinth and Sicyon, which belonged to Polyperchon's sphere of influence. While still proclaiming the freedom of the Greeks, he held "liberated" Corinth and Sicyon with garrisons. He was acting as Cassander's ally but Cassander must have viewed the operation with mixed feelings. About the same time, Seleucus won back

Babylonia, and Antigonus was forced to recognize his position. Ptolemy also won back Cyrene, where his general Ophellas had become independent; but Ophellas became frightened at Ptolemy's growing strength and led an expedition to join Agathocles before Carthage, only to be put to death by his ally.

It was necessary for Antigonus to react strongly, and in the spring of 307 he sent his son Demetrius with a fleet to Athens, where he was mistaken for Ptolemy and got possession of the Peiraeus without difficulty. In a rapid campaign Demetrius secured Munychium and Megara and triumphantly entered Athens, restoring the democracy and being hailed as a god. Two new tribes were added to the traditional ten and named after Antigonus and Demetrius, and the city became a firm ally and a base for future operations. But better was to come. Returning to Caria in the autumn, Demetrius refitted and in the spring invaded Cyprus, posing once more as a liberator. Ptolemy was forced to act, and sailed to Salamis with his entire fleet, only to be decisively defeated. All of Cyprus became a free ally of Antigonus, and he now took the long-awaited decisive step. He had already founded his name-city Antigonea and now, on the news of the victory, accepted the title of king, designating Demetrius as king also. It was a bold step, for there were few Macedonians with him to give sanction to a title which carried with it the claim to the throne of Macedonia.

It was natural that Antigonus should decide upon an immediate invasion of Egypt, striking while the iron was hot, for Ptolemy had been the stoutest foe of any centralizing tendencies since the death of Alexander, and with Ptolemy eliminated and the resources of Egypt in his possession, Antigonus might well hope to receive the submission of his other rivals. Unfortunately for him this invasion was the most difficult of military operations. His fleet was troubled by storms and his army by fortifications and water courses. His troops were short of provisions, and constantly offered bribes to desert. He tried for some months and then, threatened by the spring inundation, was forced to withdraw. Thereupon Ptolemy took the title of king also, followed by Cassander, Lysimachus, and Seleucus. Antigonus no longer had an exclusive claim to the throne of Macedonia.

It would have been a good time to make peace, but Antigonus

was still ambitious and Demetrius restless. An entire year was spent in a spectacular and useless as well as unsuccessful siege of Rhodes, whose only offense was to be neutral. She wished to be friends and to trade with all of the kings, and accordingly, although an ally, had refused to aid Antigonus in the attack on Egypt. It is true that if Rhodian as well as Cypriote harbors could have been closed to Egyptian trade, it would have been a serious blow to the Ptolemaic economy, but the siege cost Antigonus Greek sympathy, and its failure lost him prestige. Nothing daunted, nevertheless, in 303 Demetrius returned to Greece and won many successes in the Peloponnese, was elected general plenipotentiary by a revived League of Corinth, and in the following year marched north and threatened Macedonia. Cassander desperately offered peace, but when this was refused, succeeded in renewing the grand alliance. Lysimachus was now strong enough to invade Asia Minor, and Seleucus, with a huge army well provided with new Indian elephants, marched into Cappadocia. Antigonus' forces had re-occupied Babylon during his absence in the east, apparently in violation of the peace of 306, so he had good reason to co-operate. Demetrius was hastily recalled and the forces were fairly equal, especially as Ptolemy did no more than to invade Palestine and then quickly retire into his impregnable bastion. The issue was joined in 301 on the plains near Ipsus in Phrygia. Demetrius fought magnificently with the cavalry, but Antigonus was defeated and killed, and Demetrius was left with only the remnants of a kingdom. Seleucus and Lysimachus divided Asia, allowing Ptolemy only a putative claim on Syria.

The Rise of Demetrius

Decisive as was the victory of the allies, it did not lead to a period of peace. Unresolved issues remained to cause trouble between them, and Demetrius was still possessed of great power and unrestrained ambition. After the battle he got safely to Ephesus with an army of five thousand foot and four thousand horse, and was prepared to play the role of a sea king. He had a large fleet and an ample treasure, and was securely based on the Phoenician coast, Cyprus, and the seaports of western Asia Minor. Except for Rhodes, most of the islands of the Aegean were in his hands, and in Greece, while Athens declared herself neutral and would not receive him, much of the Peloponnese was held for him by garrisons. He had with him the young Pyrrhus, pretender to the throne of Epirus, whose sister Deidameia he had married as his third wife, while his first wife Phila, still loyal and not divorced, was the sister both of King Cassander and of the wives of Lysimachus and Ptolemy. Of his rivals, only Seleucus was not a connection, but it was Seleucus who gave him his first opportunity.

In the spring of 300, Demetrius left Pyrrhus as his viceroy in Greece and sailed out to resume the war against Lysimachus, probably in Thrace, and met with some success. At the same time, relations between Seleucus and Ptolemy had cooled, each claiming the territory of Hollow Syria which Ptolemy had occupied before Ipsus, and Ptolemy felt it wise to cement friendship with Cassander and Lysimachus by marriages. He gave one daughter, Arsinoe, to Lysimachus, and another, Lysandra, to Cassander's youngest son Alexander. Seleucus, then, felt himself encircled, and impressed with Demetrius' military ability made overtures to him. Seleucus had made, perhaps, the largest contribution to the victory at Ipsus, and yet he had gained very little. Lysimachus had won the real prize: all of Asia Minor down to the Taurus range, while the southern coast from Caria to Cilicia was assigned to Cassander's brother Pleistarchus, apparently as dynast rather than as viceroy. Except for the northern coast of Syria, Seleucus was cut off from the sea and from the Greek world which was the source of his most urgently needed commodity, Greek soldiers, technicians, and businessmen.

Demetrius was delighted by an affiliation with Seleucus, and in the spring of 299 coasted along to Cilicia and, landing, seized the remaining treasure in Cyinda. Pleistarchus fled to Seleucus with loud and legitimate complaints, but was rebuffed, and returning to Caria took thought for his own safety, while doubtless meditating on the perfidy of supposed friends. Seleucus received Demetrius at Rhosus and amid lavish festivities married Demetrius' seventeen-year old daughter Stratonice. Phila was sent back to Macedonia to reassure Cassander, but the worst fears of the allies were fulfilled in the following year when Demetrius and Seleucus together occupied all of Pleistarchus' domain. Again

Ptolemy exercised diplomacy, this time toward Demetrius. Deianeira had died, and Demetrius espoused a young 'daughter of Ptolemy not yet of marriageable age. Pyrrhus went as envoy to Alexandria, where he remained for a year, becoming a favorite of Queen Berenice and receiving in marriage her daughter by a previous marriage, Antigone. It was a good period for Demetrius, although his relations were becoming strained with Seleucus, who suggested as a division of their joint conquests that Demetrius cede to him Cilicia, with Tyre and Sidon.

A new situation was created in 297 by events across the Aegean. On the one hand, a certain Lachares had succeeded in making himself tyrant at Athens, and the exiled democrats invited Demetrius to restore them. Pyrrhus, on the other hand, was restored by Ptolemy to Epirus, and became joint king there with his cousin Neoptolemus, the son of Cleopatra, sister of Alexander the Great. And late in the spring Cassander died of a lingering illness, and after a four-months' reign of his eldest son Philip, Macedonia was divided between his other two sons under the regency of Queen Thessalonice. Demetrius was tempted and sailed over to the Peloponnese and spent the next year in strengthening. his position, while Pyrrhus killed Neoptolemus and became sole king of Epirus. By 295 Demetrius could lay siege to Athens, and starved it into submission after a siege which lasted all winter. In vain Ptolemy's fleet tried to break the blockade, and in vain Ptolemy and Lysimachus attempted to divert Demetrius by attacks on his Asiatic possessions. Lysimachus won over the coastal cities, including Ephesus, and Ptolemy took both Cyprus and the Phoenician ports, Tyre and Sidon, while Seleucus, perhaps as a friendly act, occupied Cilicia to guard it from the others. These seizures may have been accomplished by bribery and treachery rather than by force, and there is no indication that Demetrius exerted himself to prevent them.

Once in Demetrius' hands, Athens was again freed as in 307, and the democracy was restored. Toward this city Demetrius maintained consistently the policy announced by his father in 315. He did, however, maintain garrisons in the Peiraeus and elsewhere, and clearly aimed at a Greek empire. In the summer of 294 he invaded Laconia and almost captured Sparta, but then came the opportunity for which he had been waiting. In Macedonia, the two sons of Cassander were unfriendly, as would be expected. Antipater, the elder, killed his mother Thessalonice and tried to expel his brother Alexander, and the latter appealed both to Pyrrhus and to Demetrius for help. Pyrrhus was nearer, ejected Antipater who fled to Lysimachus, and returned to his kingdom. Demetrius did not march north until late autumn, and then came with his army to Macedonia as if on a friendly visit. Alexander entertained him royally, but was justifiedly suspicious, for accompanying Demetrius into Thessaly on his withdrawal he was slain as he came from the banquet. Demetrius was king of the Macedonians.

The Career of Demetrius

Conditions were favorable, for he had bought off his principal rivals by the sacrifice of his Asiatic possessions. Furthermore, although Alexander's widow Lysandra followed Antipater to Lysimachus and married his son Agathocles, Lysimachus was just undertaking a war against the Getae beyond the Danube and was in no position to interfere in Macedonia. In the next two years Demetrius was able to establish his control over most of Greece, which he may have tried to administer like a satrapy, and he transformed the bourgeois court of Macedonia into an Asiatic kingdom, not much to the pleasure of the Macedonians.

But Demetrius was never one to be content, or to decline any possibility of increasing his territory. About 292 he received an offer from Lanessa, daughter of Agathocles and mistress of the island of Corcyra, of her hand and holdings. The reasons for this are obscure. After a spectacular if unsuccessful invasion of Africa in 310-307 and a peace with Carthage a year or two later, Agathocles had assumed the title of king like the Successors in the East, and about 300 received in marriage Theoxane, a daughter of Ptolemy. Soon after, continuing to play the social part of a Hellenistic king, he gave Lanessa as bride to Pyrrhus, his relative by marriage (they had both married daughters of Berenice, queen to Ptolemy I), with Corcyra as her dower. The history of their marriage is completely obscure, but the kings were rarely faithful or loyal husbands, and in a few years Lanessa broke with Pyrrhus, while retaining Corcyra, and turned to Demetrius, the handsomest man of his time. Demetrius accepted, although this brought him no real advantage and led to a little known war with Pyrrhus and his allies, the Aetolians. It was obvious that Pyrrhus would not tolerate his rival's establishment of a base and sphere of influence in western Greece. There was inconclusive but bloody fighting in Epirus, Thessaly, Macedonia, and even Boeotia, which revolted from Demetrius and had to be reconquered. By 289 operations had reached a stalemate, and Demetrius, ever ambitious, laid plans for the recovery of Ionia from Lysimachus.

He was too late. Lysimachus had been long occupied with the war against the Getae with varying success. He or his son Agathocles or both had been captured on occasion, and although the story is told more romantically, he had certainly been compelled to accept peace as the price of his release. Threatened in Asia, he made an alliance with Pyrrhus, and in 288 both invaded Macedonia from opposite directions. The country, burdened and disaffected, revolted, and Demetrius was forced to flee, while Lysimachus and Pyrrhus partitioned Macedonia. To make the situation worse for Demetrius, Athens revolted also, with the support of Ptolemy. When, in the spring of 287, Demetrius sailed for Miletus, leaving his son Antigonus to protect the remains of his Greek empire, he could take only eleven thousand troops with him.

Diplomatically, the campaign was well prepared. Miletus declared for him, and he landed without difficulty. An inscription informs us that the city received a rich offering from Seleucus in 288/7; it was a princely gift, comprising about 65 talents of gold, nearly 200 of silver, and almost twelve of frankincense, myrrh, cassia, cinnamon, and costus. All was for the use of Seleucus' patron god, Apollo of Branchidae, but the gift can only have been the price of or in gratitude for Miletus' defection from Lysimachus.[4] Other cities, notably Sardes, were easily won over, and Demetrius wintered in Miletus with his new bride Ptolemais. Eurydice, the mother of Ptolemais, had abandoned Ptolemy with her daughter, when Ptolemy had promised the succession to the son of another wife, Berenice. It may be that Eurydice's son Ptolemy, called Ceraunus, the Thunderbolt, came with her also. If so, he defected to Lysimachus the following year.

For then Lysimachus struck both against his ally and his

enemy. He sent his son Agathocles against Demetrius, and marched himself against Pyrrhus in western Macedonia, expelling him and driving him back to Epirus. At the same time Ptolemy's fleet seized the Aegean islands, and with his communications cut and facing overwhelming odds, Demetrius could only abandon the coast and retire to the east. His army was astonishingly loyal but met a series of disasters, and when winter came on, Demetrius could only give himself over to Seleucus. Honorably interned in Syria, Demetrius survived for two more years to die at the age of fifty-four in 283. His son Antigonus Gonatas, securely if narrowly based on the "Fetters of Greece," his loyal garrisons in Demetrias, Chalcis, and Corinth, reigned in his stead.

Demetrius was brilliant, if unstable and restless, the most interesting man of his time, but his pre-emption of the historical spotlight is due to his friendship for the one able contemporary historian, Hieronymus of Cardia, whose narrative is the source of Diodorus' *Library of History* and the *Lives* of Demetrius and of Pyrrhus by Plutarch. In contrast, the other leading figures of the period, with the partial exception of Pyrrhus, appear as vague and poorly delineated. In particular, the role of Seleucus is obscure, since he appears in the sources sometimes as the ally and sometimes as the opponent of Demetrius. It is more likely that the basic pattern of alliances established in 299 was maintained. Except for the reported betrothal of Ptolemais to Demetrius in 298, there is nothing to make us assume that Lysimachus and Ptolemy were not consistent opponents of their neighbors and natural rivals, Seleucus and Demetrius. At all events, in 285 when Ptolemy associated Berenice's son with him as co-ruler, he secured for him as wife Arsinoe, the daughter of Lysimachus and Nicaea.

As the sources present Demetrius in a favorable light, so they are unkind to Lysimachus, and yet what is known specifically of him is good. For forty years he protected the Aegean world from the migrating tribes of the Danube, while within three years of his death the Galatae had overrun Macedonia and Greece and were in Asia Minor. Inscriptions show that he benefited and enlarged the coastal cities — Ilium, Smyrna, Ephesus, and Priene[5] — and gave them a large measure of freedom, although he may have favored oligarchies rather than the democracies which supported Demetrius. His administration seems to have been efficient and not burdensome. And yet in the same year in which Demetrius died, which saw also the deaths of Ptolemy and Agathocles, he became involved in a war with Seleucus which was to end in his defeat and death.

The End of the Successors

It is reported that Lysimachus' wife Arsinoe, Berenice's daughter and the sister of the new king Ptolemy, plotted against Lysimachus' able son and presumptive heir, Agathocles, in favor of her own children. Agathocles was put to death, and his widow Lysandra, Eurydice's daughter, fled to Seleucus with other members of the royal family, probably including her brother Ptolemy the Thunderbolt. This may have been in 284 or 283. Other defections of a more substantial nature followed, notably Philetaerus, the official in charge of Lysimachus' treasury at Pergamum, motivated, it is said, by disgust and fear. It may be supposed that Seleucus' agents were actively promoting subversion. In any case, it was Seleucus who began the war, and in 282 both kings skirmished in Asia Minor. The issue was finally joined at Corupedium in the Hermus valley north of Smyrna, and Lysimachus fell on the battlefield. Seleucus had time to organize the new administration of Asia Minor and to engage in diplomatic exchanges with the Iranian dynasties of Bithynia and Pontus and with the group of Greek cities around Heracleia Pontica, before crossing the Hellespont in August of 281. A few days later he was slain by his protege Ptolemy the Thunderbolt, who may have expected or been promised the throne of Macedonia, and with Lysimachus' death, the generation of Alexander's Successors came to an end. The assassin was a grandson of Antipater and nephew of both Cassander and Lysimachus, and as the latter's avenger, he was popular with the army. He was acclaimed king in Europe, while Seleucus' son by the Iranian princess Apama, Antiochus, already a co-ruler, succeeded his father in Asia. Since 294 he had been married to Seleucus' divorced wife, Stratonice, the daughter of Demetrius. This transfer of a wife from father to son seemed strange even to the Macedonians and was presented to the public as a case of inescapable erotic pathology, but was fully justified as a means of perpetuating the alliance with the house of Antigonus.

Stratonice, also, seems to have been a remarkably able woman.

2. The Period of Stability

The Sources

The next sixty years saw the consolidation and development of the system of Hellenistic states under which the Hellenism of the Orient was to be carried forward rapidly, and which were subsequently to be called upon to defend the Greek and Hellenized world against Rome, but conditions immediately following the assassination of King Seleucus were far from stable. These sixty years were of enormous historical importance, but they are very unevenly known. The intellectual and literary life of the period was active, but little history was written which does not properly belong rather to, and concern, the period of the Successors. The great Alexander historians, Cleitarchus of Alexandria, Aristobulus of Cassandreia, and King Ptolemy of Egypt, did their writing at that time, and so also Diyllus of Athens, who described events down to the death of Cassander in 298. Demosthenes' nephew Demochares wrote a contemporary history of Athens down to about 280, and the Athenian Duris, who was once tyrant of Samos, and began his history with the year following the battle of Leuctra, ended his work at the same date.

The ablest and most influential of the historians of the post-Alexander period was Hieronymus of Cardia, the friend and townsman of Alexander's secretary Eumenes. He lived and wrote at the Antigonid court, and brought his history down to the death of Pyrrhus in 272. Pyrrhus himself left memoirs. Timaeus of Tauromenium, writing in Athens, brought his history of the western Greeks down to 264, but did not deal with the east. Nymphis of Heracleia Pontica wrote an account of his city which survives in part as a source of the much later writer Memnon, and an almost entirely unknown Demetrius of Byzantium described the Gallic migration and the reigns of Ptolemy II and Antiochus I, but even if preserved, neither of these histories would carry us much, if at all, beyond the seventies.

Thus far our information, if not good, is fairly adequate, but it bears almost entirely on Greece and Macedonia, and the same is

true of the period after 250, when the interest of Polybius and of
Plutarch has preserved much of the testimony of the memoirs of
Aratus of Sicyon, the architect of the Achaean League, and of the
Athenian Phylarchus, who alone as the continuator of Duris wrote
a history of the third century down to 219. To our great loss most
of Phylarchus' account of the years from 270 to 250 is lost. It
found its way into later universal histories, but none of these has
survived except Justin's brief epitome of Pompeius Trogus. For
much of our knowledge of the formative period of Hellenism we
are dependent upon inscriptions and the papyri from Egypt, which
often throw an intimate and intense light upon the events of the
time, but which are sometimes obscure and usually limited and
local. Problems occur on every hand, and even such a basic
chronological tool as the Attic archon list remains somewhat
uncertain, after the labor of generations of scholars. In consequence, much of the subsequent account will be in some degree
hypothetical, and many events will not receive the treatment
which they deserve.

The Establishment of the Political Structure

THE SELEUCIDS

   In the events which followed the death of Seleucus, the
Helleno-Macedonian character of the Hellenistic world appears
clearly. The Macedonian dynasties in Egypt and in Asia would
have been lost without access to the Aegean countries. Even as the
son of an Iranian mother, Antiochus, Seleucus' son and successor,
could count on little effective support from the Iranian parts of
Asia, and the Semitic and Anatolian peoples were only more or
less docile subjects. The Macedonians and Greeks in his service had
recognized him as king, but they were of unproved loyalty and
inadequate in number. Seleucus had had little access to Greek
recruiting areas, and must have had few Greeks in the army with
which he defeated Lysimachus, except defectors from Lysimachus
and some of Demetrius' veterans. And many of these may have
joined Ptolemy the Thunderbolt together with the remnants of
Lysimachus' forces. It was vital for Antiochus to hold Asia Minor,
and in fact he acted very promptly. He was probably in Babylon

when the news of his father's death reached him, hardly before October of 281, and the same news set off a revolt in the Seleucid heartland of north Syria, supported, perhaps, by an invasion by Ptolemy. Antiochus' first concern was to re-establish his control there, but he was able also to place an army in the field in Asia Minor, constituted from those elements of his father's forces which had not crossed into Europe and which remained loyal. One division was cut to pieces by the Bithynians, but by midsummer of 280 Antiochus was able to march north himself. A Milesian inscription reports that he assumed the position of *stephanophore* there in that autumn.

PTOLEMAIC EGYPT

The same urgency bore upon Ptolemy II, whose father had maintained a consistently philhellenic policy and had shown himself very skillful in attracting both Macedonians and Greeks into his service. These were vital for both the defense and the administration of his kingdom, but he required equally the materials of war which Egypt did not provide, iron, timber and other forest products for ship construction, and silver and copper for currency. Given the opportunity to sell wheat, papyrus, and other Egyptian products, he could afford to be generous, and had not to tax his Greek allies or subjects as the other kings did, but he needed bases for his fleet. Cyprus and Phoenicia supplied many of his needs, but he was not content with the League of the Islanders, centering on Delos, which had been won from Demetrius in 285. Samos was seized from Lysimachus after his defeat and death at Corupedium, and Miletus was won from Antiochus in 279 and rewarded for its changed allegiance by a gift of land. This was not the first or the last time when the cities could convert a king's necessity to their own advantage.

ANTIGONUS GONATAS

In the assassination of Seleucus, Ptolemy the Thunderbolt was not acting rashly. The issue was the throne of Macedonia, and it must have seemed to many intolerable that this should be simply a spoil of war. With the disappearance of Antipater, the son of Cassander, whose mother Thessalonice was a daughter of Philip II, the old ruling house had become extinct, for Neoptolemus, the nephew of Alexander the Great, had been killed by Pyrrhus. This left four rival lines of legitimacy, for Cassander, Demetrius, Pyrrhus, and Lysimachus had all been legally constituted kings. At his death, Lysimachus had reconstituted the kingdom of Philip II, consisting of Macedonia and Thrace, and to many Macedonians this must have seemed the proper situation, foregoing any Asiatic connections. This is what Ptolemy the Thunderbolt proposed, and he was acceptable as a nephew of Cassander and an experienced general about forty years old. To consolidate his position he married his half-sister Arsinoe, the widow of Lysimachus, and adopted her three sons, securing thereby possession of the strong and relatively independent city of Cassandreia, and formally renounced any claim to the throne of Egypt. This hardly mattered to Ptolemy II, whose security did not depend upon a written promise from his half-brother, but did reassure the Macedonians that their king would not, like Demetrius, plan to use Macedonia merely as a base of operations for further conquests. His position was well established, for Pyrrhus, who actually had been king of at least western Macedonia for a time, was preparing for an expedition into Italy and was glad to recognize Ptolemy the Thunderbolt's position in return for military support.

Antigonus, Demetrius' son, had been thwarted earlier. He had borne the title of king since his father's capture in 285, although he was later to date his long reign only from his father's death in 283, and he was about of the same age as Ptolemy and also a nephew of Cassander. His kingdom in 281 consisted only of certain strongholds in Greece, notably Corinth, the Peiraeus, Chalcis and Demetrias, and he had a small fleet and mercenary army. On the news of Seleucus' death he had made for Macedonia to claim the throne but had been intercepted by Ptolemy and defeated in a sea battle, probably in the Pagasaic Gulf, since he fell back on Boeotia. He resumed his unsuccessful attempts to capture Athens, and made no further effort to interfere in his cousin's consolidation of his position.

Ptolemy the Thunderbolt established his mother in Cassandreia under the protection of a certain Apollodorus as garrison commander and moved on to Pella with Arsinoe and her sons when he met with his first setback. The eldest of these sons, also named Ptolemy, escaped to King Monunius of the Illyrian Dar-

danians and presently returned with an army to seize the kingdom
of his father Lysimachus. The attack was repulsed, but the
Thunderbolt realized his danger. He put to death the other two
boys and consequently was abandoned by Arsinoe, who took
refuge in Samothrace, whence she soon made her way to Egypt
and, after a few years, married her full brother King Ptolemy II
and received in consequence the epithet Brother-Loving, Philadelphus, under which she is known to history. For the Thunderbolt, on the other hand, this probably una\ )idable act of
eliminating rivals has given him in the tradition a character of
wanton cruelty. It can hardly have hurt the scruples of the
Macedonians at the time, for they were well used to dynastic
murders.

At all events, Ptolemy Thunderbolt had not much longer to
live. In the spring of the following year, 279, a wave of migrating
Gauls swept into Macedonia under the leadership of a chief named
Belgius. They may have been numerous but they were poorly
armed and undisciplined, and should have been no match for the
Macedonian phalanx. The Dardanians offered help, but Ptolemy
could hardly trust his antagonist of the previous year and declined.

Ptolemy II and Arsinoe (gold tetradrachm)

He took the field against Belgius and was defeated and killed, and for the next eighteen months Macedonia lacked any strong government. A number of princelings competed for the throne, while a general named Sosthenes kept the army together and exercised some restraint on the Gauls' plundering.

Relief came unexpectedly from Asia Minor and from Antigonus, Demetrius' son, who is known to history as Antigonus Gonatas (a nickname of unknown origin). In Asia Minor Antiochus had been conducting a desultory war in support of one faction of Bithynians under King Zipoetas against another faction under his elder brother Nicomedes and the latter's allies Heracleia Pontica, Byzantium, Chalcedon, and the other cities of the so-called Northern League. Probably Philetaerus in Pergamum remained loyal to Antiochus, although his family came from Tieium, a city of the League, but the Egyptian fleet of Ptolemy II kept raiding the coast in Antiochus' rear and must have been a constant annoyance. Nevertheless Antiochus made good headway and by the end of 279, Nicomedes became worried for the freedom which his ancestors had maintained against the Persians, Alexander, and the Successors, and cast about for further allies. Someone, perhaps some member of the Northern League, put him in touch with Antigonus. At all events, Antigonus sailed to Asia Minor in the spring of 278 and engaged in war "for some time" (as Memnon tells us) with his brother-in-law.

The motives which led him to this step are obscure. Only the preceding autumn he and Antiochus, obviously by agreement, had each sent a contingent of five hundred mercenaries to aid in the defense of Thermopylae against a second wave of Gauls under Brennus who wished to sack Delphi. This was the first time that Greeks had encountered Gauls, and their wild appearance and savage behavior made a fearful impression. Their numbers were considerable and were even more exaggerated in later story; they were enough to put a mixed force of about twenty-five thousand Greeks on the defensive. Most of the states north of the Isthmus of Corinth contributed troops, and command was given to the Athenian Callippus. The Thessalians seem to have maintained neutrality and were, in any case, safe behind their walls, for except for the little Aetolian city of Callium, the Gauls sacked no fortified place. There was a short and rather disastrous raid into

Aetolia, intended perhaps as a diversion, and then the main body of Gauls turned the pass and came down into Phocis.

Their march was subjected to constant harrassmènt and when they came to Mount Parnassus, the weather turned against them. There was a violent thunder storm followed by a heavy snow, both taken by the Greeks to be a sign that Apollo was defending his temple, and finally the Gauls gave up. Suffering heavy losses they made their way back to Thermopylae and out of Greece, while the Greeks were elated over their first resounding military success in eighty years. We possess a decree of the island city of Cos, congratulating "the Greeks" on their victory and thanking the god for his epiphany.[6] It was passed in response to a report sent there by persons unnamed but who can only be the Aetolians, for they now could justify their seizure and control of Delphi. And, it is supposed, they established at this time an annual Salvation Festival (Soteria), which thirty years later was made penteteric and generally accepted as equal in dignity with the Pythian and Nemean Games. What part in these events was played by the small contingents from Antigonus and Antiochus is entirely unknown. Neither king received credit for his help from the Greeks, and by early in 278 the troops must have returned to their bases.

It is strange that Antigonus should lead an army into Asia if he was not strong enough to seize Macedonia when it was in a state of anarchy. Perhaps he hoped for help from his allies when the campaign was over, and as a matter of fact, that is how it worked out, although in an unexpected fashion. After some fighting, Antigonus changed sides, and in an arrangement probably worked out by his sister Stratonice, he agreed to marry her daughter and his niece Phila, and to become the ally of Antiochus. He may have recruited new troops, and late in the summer sailed across the Hellespont to Lysimacheia. Attacked by the Gauls, he tricked them in a night engagement and won a decisive victory, and marching on to Macedonia, was accepted as king. In compensation, Nicomedes and the Byzantines ferried over to Asia the remnants of the Gallic bands, armed them, and employed them as allies against Antiochus. Those who remained in Europe established the kingdom of Tylis, and like the revived Odrysian state continued for a hundred years to plague the Greek coastal cities of Thrace and the Black Sea.

THE POLITICAL PATTERN

With the accession of Antigonus Gonatas, less than four years after Corupedium and little more than three from the death of Seleucus, the political pattern of the Hellenistic period was established as it was to remain until the advent of the Romans. The dynasties of the Antigonids, Seleucids, and Ptolemies were to remain secure in Macedonia, Asia, and Egypt. Macedonia exercised a strong but not preponderant influence in Greece, where Athens and Sparta, the Aetolians and later the Achaeans, played important political roles, and even lesser powers, Epirus and Acarnania, Elis, Argos, and Messene, were at times significant. The smaller islands of the Aegean belonged as allies to whatever power controlled the sea, Egypt and then Macedonia, but the larger ones, and notably Crete with its many strong harbor-cities, and the merchant state of Rhodes with its navy, might pursue independent policies. Egypt controlled Cyprus and the coasts of south-western Asia Minor. Cyrene was within the Ptolemaic sphere of influence, although it was independent throughout the reign of Ptolemy II, but Palestine and Phoenicia were held securely. Except for the coastal cities, Thrace was free of Greco-Macedonian control, and so were the northern areas of Asia Minor, Bithynia, Pontus, Cappadocia, and Galatia (the last being the region in eastern Phrygia settled in 277 by the Three Gallic clans of Trocmi, Tolistoagii, and Tectosages). The little principality (and afterwards kingdom) of Pergamum was able to maintain its independent existence among its larger neighbors, wealthy and secure in its strong citadel and expanding or contracting its territory according to the varying fortunes, expecially, of the Seleucid kings. And these, although often plagued by dynastic differences and even civil war, were to preserve their rule in Asia from the Aegean to the Hindu Kush, although the vast distances of central Asia allowed separatist tendencies to flourish after the middle of the century in Bactria and Parthia. In this relatively stable situation there was much constructive achievement and many small wars, fought mostly by professional armies and not very destructive, except at times in Greece. It was a period of cultural advance rather than of political change.

The foreign policies of the larger powers were those determined by the principle enunciated at this time by the Indian political philosopher Kautilya: Your neighbor is your enemy and your neighbor's neighbor is your ally. Rivalry continued between Ptolemies and Seleucids over their border territories in the Levant and in Asia Minor, between Egypt and Macedonia over control of the Aegean and access to the Black Sea. This situation made Antigonids in Macedonia allies of the Seleucids, especially as the two were separated by buffer states in Thrace and in northern Asia Minor, and the Seleucids renounced any aggressive policies in Greece and the Aegean area. Each side supported the enemies or revolted subjects of the other. Thus Magas in Cyrene supported and was aided by his father-in-law Antiochus I in the First Syrian War (about 279-276), and Antigonus established his half-brother Demetrius the Fair there upon the death of Magas in 258. In return, Ptolemy II must have favored and perhaps even supported the smaller states and free Greek cities of Asia Minor against the Seleucids, and in Greece he gave subsidies and occasionally naval support to Pyrrhus of Epirus, to Athens, Boeotia, Sparta, and Achaea, facing the usual embarrassment when they quarreled with each other. When Antigonus' nephew Alexander, the governor of Corinth, revolted in 253 and took the title of king, his independence was recognized by Ptolemy. If our evidence were adequate, it would be possible to write a very interesting diplomatic history of the period.

Greece

Within Greece, the traditional state of war of all against all continued with the usual shifting alliances and intestine-factional strife, but the horrors of war were greatly mitigated by the larger size and the smaller number of the states involved. The individual cities were either normally under the effective control of another power, as Athens and Corinth were controlled by Macedon, or maintained their independence under tyrants, like Elis, Sicyon, Argos, and Megalopolis; these tyrants were commonly friendly to and supported by Macedon. Only Sparta under Cleomenes III (237-222) pursued the type of imperialistic policy practiced by Sparta, Athens, and Thebes in earlier Greece. Sparta had pursued her traditional policy of hostility to tyrants and to Macedon, and this led to a war in Aetolia in 280, for the Aetolians were the allies of Antigonus Gonatas, and to the Chremonidean War of 265-260, when King Areus brought his Peloponnesian allies (Elis and some Arcadian cities) against those who were trying to enslave the Greeks, as a great inscription found at Athens tells us;[7] and Athens and Sparta were joined and encouraged by King Ptolemy II, who was following the policy of his father and his sister in support of Greek freedom. The revolt of Athens was unsuccessful, for Areus was defeated south of Corinth, unable to pass the Macedonian defenses at the Isthmus, and the Egyptian fleet under Patroclus, together with some Ptolemaic troops including probably Gallic mercenaries which established land bases in Attica,[8] could do nothing to affect the course of events on land. Antigonus, who received some support in the form of Gallic mercenaries furnished by his brother-in-law Antiochus,[9] could beat off a diversionary attack by King Alexander of Epirus and reduce Athens by starvation. Sparta was temporarily enfeebled but Athens was not seriously injured, and the total effect of this, the most general Greek war of the first half of our period, was very small.

Rather, the period must be regarded as a constructive one in Greece. Between 275 and 272, it is true, the scene was disturbed by the return from Italy of King Pyrrhus of Epirus, who was a brilliant general but a very bad statesman, for he loved nothing but war. His campaigns in South Italy and Sicily had seen many spectacular victories, but these were of the 'pyrrhic' sort, costing so much as to leave the victor weaker than the vanquished. After five years he was forced to slip out of Tarentum by stealth and return to Epirus with only a few troops, but in the spring of 274 he was able to invade Macedonia, recovering his old kingdom and compelling Antigonus Gonatas to take refuge in the coastal cities. After his Gallic mercenaries had pillaged the royal tombs at Aegae, however, he became unpopular, returned to Epirus, and in the following year was off on a new adventure against Sparta in support of a pretender to the throne named Cleonymus. He almost captured Sparta in 272, but by now all of his enemies were united against him. Antigonus, again in possession of Macedonia, entered the Peloponnese with an army, and a struggle followed for the city of Argos, in the course of which Pyrrhus was killed by a tile thrown by a woman from a roof. His son, Alexander, made peace and returned to Epirus, and except briefly in the Chremonidean

War undertook no martial adventures. Pyrrhus had not significantly affected Greek history.

The most important and the most novel feature of the period was the growth of the two great leagues, for the part played by Macedon, while large, was not preponderant as it had been earlier. Antigonus Gonatas was fortunate in his northern policy. He was able to maintain friendly relations with the Illyrians and Thracians, and Paeonia was subject. In Greece, he was the head of the Thessalian League and held fast to the key fortresses of the east coast, Demetrias, Chalcis, the Peiraeus, and Corinth. When revolts occurred, as of Athens in the Chremonidean War and of Corinth under his nephew Alexander (253-246), he worked only to restore the situation, and no more. This enabled him to keep the peace with Epirus and the Aetolians, and so to give Macedonia itself a chance to recover and rebuild after the strain of the wars of Alexander and the Successors. Probably few Macedonians migrated to Asia or to Egypt during his reign, while the Hellenization of the country continued. Pella, for example, appears in an inscription as a typically autonomous Greek city.[10] Upon his death in 239, he was succeeded by his son Demetrius, a descendant of Antipater on both his father's and his mother's side but inheriting a little Iranian blood through the Seleucids, and his little-known reign was marked by northern invasions and a war against both the Achaean and the Aetolian Leagues simultaneously. It was only under his cousin Antigonus Doson, the regent for his son Philip, that Macedon again played a major role in Greek history, being drawn into Peloponnesian affairs by the Achaeans to offset the rising power of Sparta.

THE AETOLIAN LEAGUE

Of the two leagues, the Aetolians alone had played an important part in earlier Greek history, for the twelve little Achaean cities were insignificant. The Aetolians were villagers and mountaineers, with a general assembly of citizens under arms and an annually elected military commander or general who was the chief administrative official. He was advised by an executive committee of *apokletoi*, who represented the council of one thousand, elected by the Aetolian communities proportionately to their military contribution. Known originally merely as wild

View of Pella, 1965

fighters in their own territory, the Aetolians first assumed a prominent position in 322, when they played an important role in the Lamian War, and subsequently were allies of Perdiccas and Antigonus against Antipater and Cassander. About 300 they began expanding to the east in central Greece, granting membership in the league on equal footing to those cities or tribes which joined them. Gaining effective control of Delphi in the nineties of the third century, they played a major part in the defense of the sanctuary against the Gauls and established a festival, the Soteria, in celebration of their success. Annual at first, this was made penteteric and panhellenic after 250, and in keeping with their patriotic character the Aetolians, through Delphi or directly, actively encouraged the establishment of national festivals (as at Magnesia on the Maeander)[11] and especially the general recognition of cities and sanctuaries as *asyla*, not subject to attack or pillage. Since the Aetolians were known as pirates, such prohibition must have applied against their own privateers and represented a real self-sacrifice. It is in this period, also, that there occur great numbers of manumissions inscribed on the walls of buildings at Delphi, and for this, too, the Aetolians may claim a certain obscure credit. The growth of the league continued until the early twenties of the century, by which time it was the largest territorial state in Greece, including Elis, Messenia, and eastern Arcadia as well as all of central Greece from the Ambraciot Gulf to the Euripus.

The expansion of the Aetolian League and its increasing centralization may be traced through the records of meetings of the Amphictyonic Council, inscribed on stone at Delphi. The Thessalians, Macedonian subjects, do not appear after 278, and the later delegates or *hieromnemones* came only from states friendly to Aetolia, which had itself acquired representation in an unknown manner; for Aetolia had never previously been a member of the Amphictyony. In 277 Aetolia had three delegates, and thirteen others came from seven different areas. By 226 Aetolia had fifteen delegates and only two other states sent any: the Delphians themselves and Chios, to which the Aetolians had granted representation about 258. Chios and the Aetolians had also exchanged citizenship rights by the procedure known as *isopoliteia*. Other former members had either become hostile, like

Athens or Argos, or had been absorbed, like Phocis and the Locrians.

All this was accomplished rather by diplomacy or military pressure than by war. The cornerstone of the Aetolian policy was peace with Macedon, interrupted only briefly about 292 and again twenty years later, when they were caught up in hostilities between Macedonia and Epirus, and became allies of Pyrrhus. In 239, on the other hand, the new king Demetrius II married an Epirote princess Phthia and the Aetolians were forced to seek an alliance with the Achaeans, who had only six years earlier forcibly opposed in vain their conquest of Boeotia, and two years earlier had defeated them at Pellene (241). Demetrius allied himself with Agron, King of the Illyrians, and received assistance not only against the Aetolians but also against the migrating Bastarnae in the north. But the extinction of the Epirote royal family in 235 gave the Aetolians the opportunity to annex the kingdom, and their operations went subsequently so far as an attack on Sparta itself. Nevertheless these warlike activities do not conceal the fact that the Aetolians were not so much conquerors as a growing national state, something which the Greeks had never been able to achieve on this scale before.

THE ACHAEAN LEAGUE

In contrast, the Achaean League appeared later in history and was rather a federation of cities than a state. Except for the original Achaean cities, there was no common citizenship, but there was a representative assembly voting by city, not proportionally, which elected a general and other common officials. Taxes were collected, but the business of the League was foreign policy, that is war, and consistency was difficult because the general had wide powers but any individual could hold the office only every second year. Founded, or refounded, in 280, the League remained insignificant until 251 when Aratus, whose father had been a friend of Antigonus Gonatas and a prominent citizen of Sicyon, won possession of his native city by killing the tyrant Nicocles. Sicyon was coveted both by Antigonus and by Antigonus' rebellious nephew, Alexander of Corinth, and the position of Aratus, a young man of twenty years, was precarious. Entering into negotiations with the Achaeans, he joined Sicyon to them, and from 245, when he became general for the first time, he was the dominant personality in the League and, more than any other, became responsible for guiding its expansion. A poor field commander, but an able strategist and a subtle politician, able and ambitious and little troubled by scruples, he held the position of general almost every other year down to 222, and pursued almost as long a consistent policy of hostility to Macedon and the Macedonian system of tyrants. This brought him into opposition with the Aetolians but it made for peace with Sparta, the policies of which were similar; and it ensured regular monetary subsidies from the Ptolemies in Egypt.

In 243 Aratus took Corinth from Antigonus, who had recovered it only three years before, after the death of Alexander. It was betrayed to him by Syrian soldiers in the service of Antigonus, whose loyalty may have been shaken by Ptolemaic successes against Seleucus II in the Third Syrian War (246-241). This opened the Isthmus route to Megara and Athens, and isolated Antigonus' loyal tyrants in the Peloponnese. An Aetolian raid in 241 as far as Pellene accomplished nothing, for Aratus was able to catch the enemy off their guard and destroy them, but the accession of an energetic king of Sparta, Cleomenes III, in 237 and the consequent entry into the League in 235 of the great anti-Spartan city of Megalopolis with its able tyrant Lydiades gave the League's foreign policy a different direction.

Argos was won in 229, and in the same year Aratus achieved his ambition to free Athens from the Macedonian garrison. Athens declared and maintained a policy of neutrality under a democratic government led by the brothers Eurycleides and Micion, but Aratus' successes led to an alliance between Macedon, the Aetolians, and Sparta. The Aetolians connived at the seizure of their allies or League members, the Arcadian cities of Tegea, Mantineia, and Orchomenus, by Sparta. Then, in 225, Cleomenes introduced a revolutionary program at Sparta, involving cancellation of debts, redistribution of land, and the enrollment of new citizens, and the conservatives everywhere were seriously frightened. The Aetolians, without commitments in the eastern Peloponnese, reverted to neutrality, but the Macedonian king, Antigonus Doson, was persuaded or bribed to become an Achaean ally. Aratus gave up to him the strategically all-important citadel of Acro-Corinth, and

Antigonus occupied Argos, which was betrayed to him by the conservatives. In 223 he was elected general of the Achaean League and won over the Arcadian cities. An occupation and sack of Megalopolis by Cleomenes the following winter was only a diversion for the stout-hearted population simply retired to Messene, and in the summer of 222 the Spartan army was decisively beaten in the Battle of Sellasia. Cleomenes fled to Egypt and Sparta was occupied and became a republic, but Antigonus was recalled hastily home to repel an invasion of the Illyrians, and died fighting.

The Achaean League was all-powerful in the Peloponnese, but Macedonian troops controlled the Isthmus, so that the position of the new young king, Philip V, was essentially the same as that of Antigonus Gonatas fifty years before. With the humbling of Sparta and the neutralization of Athens, there were only three considerable political powers in Greece. Since the Aetolian policy was not hostile to Macedon and since the Achaeans were allies of Macedon, the land might well look forward to a period of peace. The Aetolians had created something like a national state in central Greece, and if the Achaean union was looser, it worked nevertheless to eliminate local hostilities. The historian Polybius three generations later could claim that its objectives were the freedom and harmony of the Peloponnese. Polybius himself was an Achaean from Megalopolis, and explained in this way the fact that all of southern Greece came to be known as Achaea. He is responsible, together with Aratus whose memoirs were also widely known, for the generally favorable picture of the Achaean League in history, even beyond its deserts.

The Early Ptolemies

Of the new monarchies, it was Ptolemaic Egypt which most closely concerned the Greeks during this period. The second and third Ptolemies, Philadelphus (285-246) and Euergetes (246-221), continued the philhellenic policy of Ptolemy Soter, none the less popular and successful because it was expedient. The Ptolemies advocated the freedom of the Greeks, although this meant in practice merely the support of any states which were anti-Macedonian. The Greek sanctuaries were filled with Ptolemaic offerings of an imaginative character. At Thebes, for example, it was probably Ptolemy Philadelphus who inscribed on an altar a hymn to the Libyan Ammon supposedly composed by Pindar. Whether genuine or not, like the idealized history of the Pharaohs written by Hecataeus of Abdera, it was intended to make the Greeks feel that Egypt was an admirable and a congenial land, and in the Panegyric of about 273 Theocritus praised Philadelphus for his power, wealth, and generosity, and Egypt for its peace and luxury. The marriage of Philadelphus with his sister Arsinoe in the previous year was compared to the sacred marriage of Zeus and Hera, and this may well have been its inspiration, for brother-and-sister marriage was not an Egyptian tradition any more than it was Greek. Arsinoe was widely honored and worshipped in her lifetime and later, but we are not told why she was represented in bronze at Helicon riding upon an ostrich, unless she appeared, perhaps, as a tenth Muse, the Muse of Africa. This propaganda was effective, and we find in the papyri the names of many Greeks who took Theocritus' advice to take service with Ptolemy.

And this was the achievement of the Ptolemies. Theocritus called Philadelphus the lord of Phoenicia and Arabia, Syria and Libya and Aethiopia, Pamphylia and Cilicia, Lycia and Caria and the Cyclades, and we find about the same list of foreign possessions ascribed to Euergetes after the Third Syrian War by the Adulis inscription.[12] This adds a few places, Thrace and the Hellespont, for example, and less realistically Euergetes' supposed temporary occupation of Mesopotamia and Babylonia, but these fluctuations were unimportant. In three wars with the Seleucids (about 279-276, 259-253, and 246-241), the Ptolemies made gains or suffered losses of a limited nature. The Island League of the Cyclades was lost to Antigonus Gonatas of Macedonia at the Battle of Cos, either shortly before 261 or shortly before 253, in each of which years the records of Delos report a peace. Probably these islands were recovered at the time of the revolt of Alexander of Corinth, and lost later when the Macedonian fleet won another victory at Andros (perhaps about 244). Later, about 227, Antigonus Doson made a brief and inconsequential expedition against Ptolemaic possessions in Caria. None of this, however, prevented Egypt from continuing to draw Greeks down both from Greece and from Asia Minor, and from proceeding with the building up of

Alexandria as the second city of the Hellenic world and the organization and exploitation of the valley of the Nile.

The cultural aspects of this process are discussed below. Here it need only be noted that the Ptolemies, with the help of such experienced political advisers as Demetrius of Phaleron who prepared their code of laws, built a centralized bureaucratic state based on existing Egyptian patterns, headed by a "Manager" or *Dioecetes* similar to the Pharaonic Grand Vizier, with offices in Alexandria, where were located the departments of state with their thousands of clerks and their vast records. All of the country's economy was under their control. Planting was done according to an approved schedule, and industry was organized on a system of royal concessions or monopolies, under the eye of tax-farmers and officials. Security and justice were the concern of the governors (*strategoi*) of the nomes or local districts, assisted by military settlers (*cleruchs*), police, and judges. The higher posts were held by Greeks or Macedonians, where these were available, and otherwise by Egyptians, especially by reliable members of the old governing class and where a knowledge of the native language was necessary. Other foreigners, especially Jews, were employed both as officials and as soldiers. The laws were strict to protect the royal interest, but enforcement was clearly difficult, and there were many opportunities to make money, legitimately or not. Greeks came in large numbers, especially under Philadelphus, when the great Fayum Oasis southwest of Memphis was opened to cultivation and settlement, and many of them prospered. Many married Egyptian women, and began to create the mixed population which we find in the following century.

The show place of Egypt was Alexandria, with its palaces and other public buildings, the sanctuaries of the royal cult and of Serapis, the Museum and Library, the magnificent harbors and docks, and the island of Pharos with its great lighthouse, joined to the mainland by a mole nearly a mile in length. Practically unassailable by enemies, a deep-water port joined to the Nile by a navigable canal, with an agreeable year-round climate, Alexandria was ideally designed by nature to be a center of commerce and entertainment, and the Ptolemies made it a cultural center as well, building up the finest library in the world and providing generous salaries for scholars and men of literature. Athens retained its

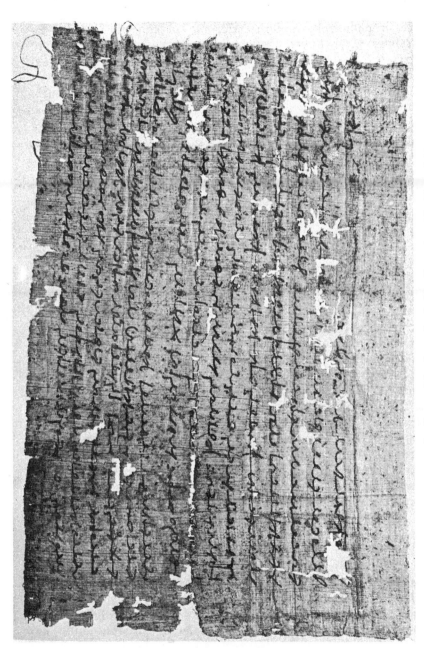

A papyrus dealing with the schedule of sowing (P. Yale 36)

place in philosophy and rhetoric, and so continued to be the university city, but science, learning, and literature came to Alexandria, and perhaps also art, although the problem of Alexandria's contribution to art remains unsolved.

Alexandria, as a royal residence-city, was given little autonomy, although it had a Greek citizen body with the usual ephebic and gymnasial education (in contrast with Egyptians, Jews, and other non-citizen residents), probably a council or *boule* (if so, this disappeared later), and elected or appointed magistrates. The city Ptolemais in upper Egypt, in contrast, founded by Ptolemy I, had a Greek civic constitution of the normal type, and in general the Ptolemies seem to have behaved toward cities under their control without preconceptions. The cities of the Aegean Islands and of the western Anatolian coast retained their own governments, subject sometimes to a Ptolemaic resident (as the king's son Ptolemy in Miletus about 260) and garrison, or the over-all supervision of a royal admiral. On the other hand, Telmessus in Lycia was handed over as a gift-estate (*dorea*) to a royal relative, Ptolemy the son of Lysimachus (possibly the son of King Lysimachus and Arsinoe, who revolted against Ptolemy the Thunderbolt in 280). And Ptolemy I included himself among the magistrates of Cyrene in such a way as to control it constitutionally, and the system may well have continued under Magas and later when Euergetes married Magas' daughter Berenice and united the territories. The cities of Palestine and Syria were sometimes garrisoned, sometimes free. Much of the land was directly administered, almost as in Egypt, but the frontiers were occupied by such friendly native chiefs as the Tobiads of the Ammonitis. In Cyprus, the traditional kings had been eliminated and the cities were in principle free allies, but there was a garrison and a centralized government under a *strategos*.

The Seleucids

The other great Hellenistic monarchy, that of the Seleucids, was somewhat isolated from the Greek world by the fringe of Ptolemaic possessions along the Asiatic coast, for the Seleucids could count only on the Troad and the Ionian port of Smyrna in Asia Minor, and these were lost to Attalus I after 240. The

Ptolemaic allegiance of Miletus and Ephesus was only briefly interrupted between 259 and 245, and this at the price of giving the cities their freedom, an act of generosity which earned Antiochus II his cognomen of Theos (God) but which left the cities able to return when they wished to the Ptolemaic alliance. For these ports, the artificial harbors of the north Syrian coast were no adequate substitute. The only good harbor in Cilicia was the inland, river harbor of Tarsus, and in Syria, Laodicea on the sea like Alexandria, was, without its moles, little more than an open roadstead, while Seleucia in Pieria was seized and converted into a Ptolemaic fortress at the very beginning of the Third Syrian War. With the Hellespont and Bosporus occupied by Bithynia and the cities of the Northern League, and Aeolis dominated by an independent Pergamum, the Seleucids must have seemed to the Greeks rather remote, and it is significant that we hear of very little migration of Greeks into the Seleucid Empire, except from the cities of western Asia Minor which were, like Magnesia on the Maeander, directly controlled by the dynasty.[13]

It is also likely that the Seleucid kings seemed less congenial to the Greeks than did the Ptolemies. Seleucus I, alone of the Successors, kept his Iranian wife. While this undoubtedly helped to retain the good will of his Iranian subjects, it meant that the later kings of the dynasty, while "wanting to be called, as they were, Macedonian" (as Pausanias wrote of Ptolemy I), were nevertheless half-Iranian in blood, and later Seleucids intermarried freely with the Iranian royal families of Pontus and Cappadocia. While our evidence is poor, it seems clear that the Seleucid armies and probably also their officials and friends included a much larger number of Iranians and other Asiatics than Macedonians or Greeks. Like the Ptolemies they attracted the attention of no competent historian, although Phylarchus did describe the war between Antiochus I and Eumenes of Pergamum, a narrative of which not one fragment remains, and unlike the Ptolemies, they dissipated much of their energies in dynastic quarrels.

About 269, Antiochus I put to death for treason his eldest son and co-ruler Seleucus. In 246, Antiochus II was poisoned by his first wife Laodice, the daughter of his uncle Achaeus, because he had six years earlier married in her place Ptolemy's daughter Berenice, and now proposed to designate her son as the heir to the throne. And after Seleucus II had re-established the unity of the kingdom in 241 and freed it from the Ptolemaic army of occupation, the same Laodice set up his brother Antiochus, surnamed Heirax or "The Hawk," as a rival king in Asia Minor, and the resulting War of the Brothers ended in a division of the kingdom into two parts. This was profitable only to Attalus I of Pergamum, who took advantage of the opportunity to attack Hierax (230-229) and to lay hands on the Troad and Ionia.

While most of this territory was afterwards recovered by Seleucus III (226-223) and his brother Antiochus III, the dynasty was seriously weakened, the more so since the frequent changes of ruler made against continuity of policy. The kings came to the throne young and died violent deaths. Antiochus II may have been nearly thirty at his accession but Seleucus II can hardly have been twenty, while Antiochus III was fifteen and Hierax only fourteen. This placed great responsibility in the hands of the king's ministers and undue power in the hands of such dowager queens as Laodice, a serious situation in view of the absolute and undivided nature of the Macedonian monarchy. This was a greater danger for the Seleucids than the vast extent and the heterogeneous character of their kingdom, although these factors also contributed to the gradual disintegration of their holdings. Already Seleucus I had ceded India to Chandragupta in return for an alliance and access to the supply of Indian war elephants. The friendly relations continued under the latter's son Ashoka, a convert to Buddhism, whose devotion to his new faith is attested by an inscription in Greek and Aramaic discovered in Afghanistan.[14] And in the last years of Antiochus II both Parthia and Bactria became independent, the former under an Iranian, the latter under a Greek dynasty. The Parthian era began with the year 248/7, and like the Seleucid era, dating from 312/1, continued in use in the East for centuries.

In Asia Minor also, the basic weakness of the Seleucid kingdom (which recalls that of the Persian Empire a century earlier) made possible the survival and growth of the lesser powers. Pontic Cappadocia and southern Cappadocia were accepted as independent kingdoms and as Seleucid allies against Bithynia and the Gauls. Their kings, Iranian by descent, Mithridates and Ariarathes, married daughters of Antiochus II, just as did also

Diodotus of Bactria, who may have been regarded as an ally against Parthia, and later a daughter of Mithridates married Antiochus III.

These states came gradually under Hellenistic influences, but not as rapidly as Bithynia, which flourished under Nicomedes, who presently founded a name-city, Nicomedeia, at the head of the Gulf of Astacus. It was to have a long and illustrious history. Upon his death, which must have occurred before the middle of the century, the throne was seized by an elder disinherited son Ziaelas, with support from Armenia and the Gallic Tolistoagii. Ptolemy, Antigonus, and the Northern League had been appointed guardians to protect the designated heir, but as soon as Ziaelas had won the throne in a brief campaign, the system of alliances was re-established. In a letter to Cos, Ziaelas refers to Ptolemy as his friend and ally,[15] and the historian Memnon tells without dating it of a naval war of Byzantium and Heracleia against an unidentified Antiochus (probably Antiochus II at the very end of his reign).

Only the Gauls were unpredictable, and raided whomever they pleased. On one occasion they even forced Heracleia and Pontus into joint action against them. Heracleia continued friendly with Ptolemy III, who sent grain and built a temple of Heracles in the city. Sending grain to the Black Sea is paradoxical, in view of the fact that this region was always a rich source of grain to the Greek world, but troubles in Thrace or South Russia may have cut off the usual supply. Byzantium and Calatis fought a trade war, the latter being supported by Istrus,[16] and such disturbances, combined with the growth of powerful new native kingdoms in Thrace and in South Russia, may well have created unfavorable conditions for grain production and sale.

Pergamum

The principal gainer from Seleucid weakness, however, was Pergamum. Secure on his crag in the Caicus Valley, the eunuch Philetaerus, a Hellenized Paphlagonian from Tieium, had guarded one of the treasuries of Lysimachus until he transferred his allegiance to Seleucus about 283. But after Seleucus' death he was, in effect, an independent "dynastes." His strength was his wealth,

Eumenes I of Pergamum (tetradrachm)

for his professed allegiance to Antiochus I did not lead him to surrender the treasure of Lysimachus. Rather he minted this prudently, the coins bearing the image of Seleucus but his own name, and used it not only to maintain a body of mercenaries but as an instrument of foreign policy. He ransomed Seleucus' body and returned it to Antiochus and gave generously to neighboring cities, to Pitane, Aegae, and especially to Cyzicus, where an inscription records donations spread over five successive years (281-276).

Abroad, he made himself favorably known to the Greek world by gifts to Apollo at Delphi and at Delos and to the Muses at Thespiae. Under his rule Pergamum became a Greek city and under his successor Eumenes (263-241) it appears as an autonomous political body apart from the court, a royal residence but not a royal city. There were annually five civic officials called generals (*strategoi*) and a board of treasurers, in whose selection the dynasts must have had a hand but who were formally independent. The dynast with his friends and his soldiers lived in the citadel, and the city sacrificed to him under the titles of Benefactor (Euergetes).

When Eumenes inherited his uncle's position upon the latter's death in 263, he undertook a bolder policy. He defeated Antiochus I in a battle near Sardes, probably instigated by Egypt, which had done badly in the Cremonidean War. This would have been in 261 if, as is possible, the Seleucid king fell in the fighting. In consequence, Eumenes was able to extend his control throughout the whole Caicus valley, founding garrison cities named Philetaereia and Attaleia where he stationed troops. Under unknown circumstances these mutinied, but an inscription reports the agreement reinforced by mutual oaths by which he brought them again under his command.[17]

It was Attalus I, however, nephew and adopted son of Eumenes, who gave the dynasty its place among the Hellenistic kingdoms. His mother was Antiochis, a Seleucid princess and sister of the Laodice who was queen to Antiochus II, so that he had royal blood in his veins, and he took the title of king after opening his reign with a victory over the Gauls. These tribesmen had been defeated in about 277 by Antiochus I in a battle determined by his war elephants, but had nevertheless continued to harass Asia Minor to an extent that not only individual cities but even the Seleucid kings had paid them regular subsidies to escape attack. The victory of Attalus, fought at the sources of the Caicus as inscriptions from Pergamum tell us, must have been defensive, the repulse of a Gallic attack. Nevertheless it won great repute for Attalus, and probably was the occasion for the first of the great monuments of Pergamene sculpture, the figures of wounded or dying Gauls set up in a victory monument at Pergamum and later repeated in a second one in Athens.

Ten years later, supporting his cousin Seleucus II against the latter's brother Antiochus Hierax, Attalus won further victories over Antiochus and his Gallic allies, and succeeded in driving Hierax out of Asia Minor altogether, but his conquest of Ionia and other parts of Seleucid Asia Minor was of brief duration. It had, however, one lasting effect. Either as an ally of the Gauls or in fear of the growing power of Pergamum, Ziaelas of Bithynia had become a friend of Hierax, and thereafter rivalry between Bithynia and Pergamum became a constant feature of Anatolian politics. But Bithynia was weakened by the murder of Ziaelas by some Gallic mercenaries, and at the end of our period Pergamum was the strongest state in Asia Minor.

Gaul killing his wife

Hellenism in the East

It is difficult to estimate the progress of Hellenism in Asia during this period. Inscriptions give us some historical information; thus it is possible to trace the course of Attalus' wars from the remains of his victory monument at Pergamum. We have a good deal of information on the relations of the kings, Seleucids and Attalids, with the old Hellenic cities of the Anatolian seaboard, and an inscription from Samos gives us a picture of how negotiations were carried out.[18] Some mainland properties of Samian citizens had been reclaimed by Antiochus II, and a certain Bulagoras was sent as envoy to recover them. He went first to Ephesus, and then followed the king to Sardes, soliciting favor probably by gifts with the king's friends, for it is not said that he had an audience with the king. In the end he was successful, and secured a letter from Antiochus to Samos and a second to the local troop commander and to the manager (*dioecetes*) of the king's land confirming the Samians' claims. Later Bulagoras went to Alexandria to attend the festival of the Ptolemaia, and so Samos preserved a balance between the dynasties.

In general, even the mainland cities preserved autonomy and often independence. Under Antiochus I a certain Aristodicides of Assus, a royal friend, received a gift of large tracts of crown land in the Troad with permission to attach this to "any city in our friendship and alliance," Ilium and Scepsis being mentioned specially. This evidently gave assurance that the grant would not be revoked by a subsequent king, in contrast with transfers of property not so attached. And even the sale of estates by Antiochus II to his divorced queen Laodice were recorded in several cities, although they did not come under the jurisdiction of any city.[19] The cities commonly showed their loyalty to the dynasty by establishing a civic cult for the royal family. The cult of Stratonice, the sister of Antigonus Gonatas and queen successively of Seleucus I and Antiochus I, was established at Smyrna with especial magnificence, and Antiochus II secured wide recognition for the sanctity (*asylia*) of the city in consequence.

Thus the Hellenistic kings, like the Persians before them, reconciled the sovereignty of the cities with their own superior authority. The effective device was the recognition of the king as king by the city, and this recognition was commonly, perhaps universally, joined with the establishment of a local royal cult. This recognition carried with it the right of the king to receive loyalty and support from the city, and his obligation to benefit and protect the city. The kings were, by definition, Saviors and Benefactors, who could be appealed to in time of trouble.

In general, the kings continued the previously existing organization of their territories in provinces or satrapies which were under military governors (*strategoi*), beside whom stood financial or economic officials (*oikonomoi* or *dioiketai*) and royal judges. The king's land proper, occupied by crown peasants, was administered directly, but otherwise the king's agents dealt with organized tribal leagues (*ethne*) or with local potentates (*dynastai*). So far as possible, local security and local administration was delegated to these as well as to the cities, and it was partly with this end in view that the kings, and particularly the early Seleucids, founded many new cities, giving them dynastic or other Greek names. An inscription of the time of Antiochus III shows how Apollonia in the upper Maeander Valley was responsible for a number of temple villages.[20]

These new cities were of many types. Some were completely new creations on a new location, like the four Seleucid capitals in northern Syria (Antioch, Apamea, Laodicea, Seleuceia), while others were previously existing cities which were re-organized and usually renamed (Pergamum, Sardes, Tarsus). Some had their origins in military colonies. Many had little self-government and few Greek or Macedonian inhabitants at the beginning, and were managed by the garrison commander or by a king's representative (*epistates*), but as time passed the population became more homogeneous and Greek-speaking, and the characteristics of a Greek polis begin to appear: popular assembly, council, and elected and responsible magistrates.

This was the pattern of Hellenism in Asia, and it was only accelerated when it proved possible to import a body of Greeks to constitute a ready-made citizen body. Among the many replies to the appeal of Magnesia on the Maeander at the end of the third century, for general recognition of its sanctuary of Artemis Leucophryene and the games held periodically in her honor, are a number of decrees of cities in the eastern part of the Seleucid kingdom, couched in normal Greek diplomatic form. One of these, the remote Antioch in Persis, recalls that it had, on request, received at one time a substantial group of settlers from Magnesia.[21]

3. The Period of Roman Intervention

The Struggle for Supremacy

It is a truism of history that expansionist powers collide, and also that expansion brings with it ever wider interests and responsibilities which make its further course difficult to limit or to control. If the Hellenistic world of the third century B.C. seemed in many ways to be moving toward a stable concord of states content with their own territories and willing to live at peace with their neighbors, there were still at the end of the 220's unresolved conflicts and ambitions which threatened further conflict.

THE STATE OF AFFAIRS BEFORE ROME

Egypt under Ptolemy III had recovered the Cyrenaica and retained a firm hold of the foreign possessions which were essential to its security: Syria/Palestine, Cyprus, and the coasts of Lycia and Caria, with outlying coastal footholds as far as the Hellespont. Racial and administrative problems existed at home but were not yet acute, and foreign trade flourished with Greece, with the Black Sea, and with the western Mediterranean. Ptolemy IV (221-205) was faced with no pressing problems. In contrast, the Seleucid kingdom under the young king Antiochus III (223-187) could hardly acquiesce in the effectual if not perhaps legal independence of Bactria and Parthia, and needed desperately to recover the lost contact with the Greek west through Asia Minor. This involved conflict with Pergamum in the first instance, secondarily with Egypt, and only remotely with the lesser Anatolian states which were for the time being valuable as allies. And ever since Seleucus I, the dynasty had always kept open its claim to Syria and Palestine, the Ptolemaic possession of which was made the more insulting by their occupation of one of the Seleucid capitals and name-cities, Seleucia in Peiria.

In Asia Minor, Attalus I of Pergamum had occupied the former Seleucid territory and possessed the largest state in the peninsula. He cannot well have thought of expanding further at the moment, but he faced both internal and external problems. In contrast with the Seleucids and the Ptolemies, the Attalids inherited none of the prestige which attached to the dynasties descended from the ·great Macedonian generals, and with all their generosity and the growing magnificence of their capital they were never popular. They ruled by virtue of their wealth and their soldiers, and while Attalus received wide recognition and gratitude for his victories over the Gauls, it was still possible for a poet of Telmessus to refer to his purple robes as weals inflicted on the backs of his subjects. His foreign relations were difficult. Bithynia was his enemy, and since Bithynia was a friend of the Ptolemies, it was not easy for Pergamum to count on much Ptolemaic support, Pontus and Cappadocia were not necessarily friendly to Bithynia, but they were traditional allies of the Seleucids, and the dynasties were interconnected by marriage. There remained only the Gauls, but in addition to the fact that they had only recently been defeated, they were in general quite unpredictable, although often useful as a source of mercenary soldiers.

In Greece, the seemingly definitive settlement based on the battle of Sellasia was thrown into doubt by the death of Antigonus Doson and the accession to the Macedonian throne of the seventeen-year old Philip V (221-179). If on his father's side he inherited the wise moderation of Antigonus Gonatas and the traditional alliance with the Seleucids, from his mother, the Epirote princess Phthia, he inherited something of the blood and traditions of Pyrrhus and Alexander the Great. Sparta had been defeated but not crushed by Antigonus and the Achaeans, and might well be expected not to give up her formerly proud position without a further struggle. The Achaeans were probably surfeited and content as well as made cautious from having to draw upon Macedonian support to win the war just over, but the Aetolians, while not engaged in this contest and so fresh, had bowed to force and surrendered their possessions in the western Peloponnese, while retaining Phigaleia and Elis as bases for future operations.

Throughout the century, the Aetolians had been at peace with Macedon, claiming for themselves a dominant place around the

Maliac Gulf and so controlling the Pylian as well as the Delphian
Amphictyony, but not contesting Macedonian control of Thessaly.
This peace was interrupted only when Macedonia undertook such
a western policy as that of Demetrius I in 292 and Demetrius II in
239, which seemed to the Aetolians to threaten their position on
the coast of the Adriatic. The kingdom of Epirus no longer
existed, but its place in power politics had been taken by the
Illyrians, who, under King Agron, acting as an ally of Macedon,
had defeated the Aetolians at Medeon in Acarnania in 231. Now
the Illyrians themselves were in difficulties, and their weakness
and frustration constituted an invitation to Macedonian intervention and so a threat to the peace of Greece.

ILLYRIA: FIRST ROMAN INTERVENTION

It was in Illyria that the expanding power of Rome first
impinged on the Greek world, but it was not Rome's first contact
with the East. The older legends of the Arcadian Evander and the
Trojan Aeneas are known to be of some antiquity, although, like
the claim of Athenian influence on the Twelve Tables, they are as
incapable of proof as they are reasonable and possible. The rise of
Rome to the first power in Italy in the fourth century must have
attracted some attention, although it has left no trace in contemporary Greek records. Few believed or believe in a Roman
embassy to Alexander the Great in 323, but Polybius reports a
Rhodian tradition in 166 of a hundred and forty years of
collaboration with Rome,[22] under the title of friendship, it is
true, and not of alliance, but the distinction had less meaning in
Roman than in Greek political theory, and the beginnings of the
relationship were dated back to the end of the fourth century.

Certainly Pyrrhus' war in Italy made the name of Rome
known to everyone in the East, and Hieronymus of Cardia wrote
its history and included an "archaeology" or story of Rome's
antiquities. Soon thereafter Timaeus included a history of Rome
in his Sicilian history, the account of which Polybius professed
himself a continuator. At the same time, Rome began to appear in
other forms of Greek literature: Callimachus and Lycophron
wrote poems about Rome. Ptolemy II exchanged embassies with
Rome in 273 and Ptolemaic influence has been seen in the early
Roman coinage, if this does, in fact, go back to 269. Political and
economic contacts continued and became more frequent. The
western commerce of the Ptolemies brought them in touch with
Rome, at least in South Italy, and the Coan embassies of about

240, seeking recognition of their city's inviolability (*asylia*), brought back replies from a Sicilian and an Italian city within the Roman Empire. It was inevitable that political contacts also should in time occur across the Adriatic, and characteristically the earliest alleged instance, some time before 246, was that of a request for assistance against the Aetolians by the Acarnanians. This is doubtful, for no help was sent, and Polybius calls the Romans' first embassy to Greece that sent to the Aetolians in 228. At all events, the Roman involvement in Illyrian affairs was due to the complaints of her Italian allies, whose shipping was being harrassed by privateers of Queen Teuta.

The incident is presented in Polybius as a wanton act of piracy, similar to those which he later credits to the Illyrian Scerdilaidas, Demetrius of Pharos, and the Aetolians. But it must be remembered that, in all antiquity, war included if it did not consist exclusively of plundering an enemy's possessions, and that Polybius, an Achaean, presents an account unfriendly to both the Aetolians and to Philip V of Macedonia, as well as to Philip's allies the Illyrians. It may be that Teuta was only trying to maintain sovereignty and to collect tolls from ships of passage in the lower Adriatic. It is possible also that Roman commerce along the eastern coast of the Adriatic had been molested. In any case, Rome sent an embassy in 230 demanding that the practice cease, and when this was ignored a fleet and army came out in the following year and enforced the demands. The Roman strength was overwhelming and there was little fighting. By the treaty signed in 228 Illyria gave up all of her conquests along the west coast of Greece and otherwise agreed to remain quiet, while Rome took under her protection, i.e., for herself, several islands including Corcyra and a stretch of mainland, centering on Atintania.

Embassies were sent off to the Achaeans and to the Aetolians, perhaps rather to explain and justify the Roman acquisition of Greek territory than, as Polybius writes, to cheer the Greeks with the assurance that the threat of Illyria had been ended. For actually, what Rome took was neither a part of Illyria nor a possession of Illyria but those Greek areas which the Illyrians had been attempting to conquer. No embassy was sent to Macedonia, although Rome now marched with Macedonia on the west, but diplomatic relations were established both with Athens and with

Corinth, which latter city, a member of the Achaean League, recognized the Romans as Hellenes and admitted them to the Isthmian Games. In 228, then, Rome became a Greek state, however the legal situation may have been conceived in Roman terms. Rome could, in any case, only regard her relationship with these new subjects, allies, or friends as permanent and involving clear obligations on both sides, and Rome possessed a military power far greater than any or all of the Greeks, based on abundant manpower, strict discipline, and advanced tactics and weapons, while the ruling oligarchy at Rome was patient, pertinacious, and inflexible. The contest which now began was uneven.

For the next eight years, preoccupied with the Gauls in northern Italy and with the Carthaginian advance in Spain, the Romans paid little attention to their commitments in Greece, and Illyria continued and increased her close relations with Macedonia. King Agron's brother Scerdilaidas and Demetrius of Pharos, in control of the halves of a divided kingdom, were able to cooperate, and Demetrius supported Antigonus Doson of Macedonia by sea in his Carian campaign and on land in the Peloponnese. It is natural that when Philip V came to the throne of Macedonia, the first aggressive act of his reign should have been struck by Demetrius, who in 220 attempted to seize the Messenian port of Pylos. This attempt at expansion to the south was in violation of the treaty with Rome, but perhaps Demetrius thought that as Rome's ally in the First Illyrian War, the prohibition against sailing out of the Adriatic would not apply to him. At all events, it was the Aetolian commander in Phigaleia who came to the rescue. Demetrius was repulsed, but the Achaeans regarded the Aetolian move as unfriendly, attacked their army and were defeated at Caphyae in Arcadia, whereupon they appealed to Philip. The Hellenic League, at his request, declared war and ordered the Aetolian League dissolved.

It is hard to think that the Aetolians did not communicate all this to Rome, for in the following year a Roman expedition (the Second Illyrian War) drove Demetrius into exile, destroying his fortresses of Dimale and Pharos. At the same time, the Aetolians marched into Macedonia and burned Dium, and Philip, now joined by Demetrius, was distracted by an invasion threat of the Dardanii. But the Aetolian relief, won rather by their allies than by their own arms, was short lived. In 218 Philip, with Illyrian assistance, operated in Cephallenia, invaded Aetolia from the west and sacked the capital Thermum, and marching into the Peloponnese compelled Sparta to accept a friendly government. In 217 he conducted a successful campaign against the Dardanii and returned to expel the Aetolians from Phthiotic Thebes. He had gained enough to accept the peace for which the Aetolians were appealing through friends and neutrals, Chios, Rhodes, Byzantium, and Egypt. At the Congress of Naupactus, which arranged a settlement on the basis of *uti possidetis*, the Aetolian Agelaus reminded the king of the Roman danger, and while this came strangely from the side which had employed Roman aid only two years previously it accorded well with Philip's thinking. He had heard of Hannibal's victory at Lake Trasimene, and saw the opportunity to re-establish his ally Demetrius or to gain possession of Illyria for himself, since he was no longer friendly with Scerdilaidas.

THE FIRST MACEDONIAN WAR

In the autumn of 217, Philip invaded Illyria, and the next four years were occupied with operations in this area. At first he avoided involving the Romans, but after the Roman defeat at the Battle of Cannae, negotiations led to an alliance with Hannibal in 215, and Philip clashed with Rome at Oricus and Apollonia, and got possession of Atintania. The Achaeans, Philip's allies, took no part in the war and even quarreled with Philip over Messenia, where he thought to establish himself at Ithome, and relations between them were cool when Aratus died in 213. Philip was not accomplishing much, either for himself or in the cause of removing Roman influence, and the results were precisely the reverse of those contemplated by Agelaus. Rome was fully occupied in Italy, Sicily, and Spain, but in 212 was able to persuade the reluctant Aetolians to implement the alliance and come to their rescue. In the following winter the alliance was extended to include Sparta, Attalus of Pergamum, and King Pleuratus in Illyria, and this brought in the Achaeans on Philip's side.

When Prusias of Bithynia joined Philip out of hostility to Attalus, the war had assumed extensive proportions, and it was unusually destructive. Livy gives the substance of the agreement between Rome and Aetolia, and this account is substantiated by

the discovery of a fragment of the original text in an inscription
from Acarnania:[23] of cities taken jointly the Aetolians would
receive the land and buildings, the Romans everything movable.
The arrangement was extended to the other allies, and so when the
Roman and Pergamene fleets captured Aegina in 210, Attalus
received the island, paying the Aetolians thirty talents for their
interest in it, and it remained a Pergamene base in Greek waters to
the end of the dynasty. The Romans took property and people,
and their commander only reluctantly allowed Aeginetans to
ransom themselves in place of being sold as slaves.

Fortunately, Rome took little part in the war. Philip showed
great energy, and had the best of it, in spite of attacks by Illyrians
and Dardanii in 208. Acarnania was detached from Aetolia, and
when Attalus was called home to repulse a raid by Prusias and (in
207) Sparta was decisively beaten by the Achaeans under their
able general Philopoemen, the allies had had enough and made
peace in 206. Then the Romans arrived in force, angry that their
allies should propose a separate peace, and a general conference
took place at Phoenice (205). A settlement based generally on the
status quo was reached, and signed by almost all of the Greek
states. The signatories were, on Philip's side, the Thessalians,
Boeotians, Acarnanians, Epirotes, Achaeans, and Prusias; on the
side of the Romans, the Spartans, Eleans, Messenians, Athenians,
Ilians, Attalus, and Pleuratus. Livy fails to mention the Aetolians
for some reason, but they were certainly included; so also
Amynander king of the Athamanians, who was present. The treaty
was duly ratified at Rome, which thereby brought all of Greece
and parts of Asia Minor within its sphere of influence, although
this was probably not realized by any Greek. Any conflict which
subsequently broke out in this area would be Rome's concern. In
token of his loyalty, Attalus secured from the Gauls and sent to
Rome the Black Stone of the Magna Mater from Pessinus, which
they had requested.

ANTIOCHUS III AND PTOLEMY IV

In the meantime, in the eastern part of the Hellenistic world,
Seleucid power was increasing and that of the Ptolemies diminish-
ing. The balance of power which had tended to maintain the peace
between the two monarchies was upset, an event of consequence

for Rome's further involvement in the region. At the beginning, it is true, the fortunes of the Seleucids seemed highly precarious. When Seleucus III was killed by two of his officers in 223, his brother Antiochus was only seventeen years old, and had been left in Syria as regent and heir to the throne. This was an old Persian custom which had already proved its value to the dynasty. The army in Asia Minor declared for the king's cousin Achaeus the son of Andromachus, whose father was the brother of Laodice, the queen of Antiochus II.

Achaeus was mature and able, and loyally continued as field commander while preserving the throne for Antiochus III. He was soon able to press the campaign against Attalus, and in two or three years, while Antiochus was occupied with subduing a revolt of Molon, the general of the Upper Satrapies, had succeeded in winning back most of the Pergamene conquests. He became an ally of Byzantium, which was attacked by Rhodes and Prusias for having increased the Hellespontine tolls, in an attempt to raise the tribute demanded by the Gauls of Tylis. While that issue was soon settled by negotiation and a new Pergamene offensive won back most of northwest Anatolia, by 217 Achaeus, established in the fortress of Sardes, was in a secure position. That was the year when Antiochus, having declared war on Egypt, advanced with his army to the town of Raphia in southern Palestine and was decisively defeated by Ptolemy IV, and on the news of this setback Achaeus took the royal title and seceded. The situation of Seleucus II and Hierax was repeating itself.

But Antiochus III was more able and more fortunate than Seleucus II. In alliance with Attalus, who thought Achaeus to be the more dangerous, he invaded Asia Minor, shut Achaeus up in Sardes, and finally captured him by treachery as he was trying to escape to Egypt (215). He put him to death in oriental fashion and came to a settlement with Attalus, conceding to him Mysia and the Aeolis while he retained Lydia and Phrygia. And in 212 Antiochus set off to the East on a seven-year campaign which was to restore Seleucid sovereignty as far as India and earn for the king the epithet "The Great," for he was felt to have equalled the conquests of Alexander. Actually, Arsaces III of Parthia and Euthydemus of Bactria retained their independence and were recognized as kings, subordinate only to the Great King, and

Euthydemus I of Bactria (tetradrachm)

Sophagasenus in India became a free ally, at the price of furnishing war elephants. Whether or not the kingdom had increased in power, its prestige was very high when Antiochus returned to Syria in 205, about the time Ptolemy IV died leaving the throne of Egypt to a child of about five years.

In the Hellenistic states, any change in ruler was hazardous. The accession of a young and inexperienced king was particularly dangerous, and that of an infant was an invitation to disaster, unless, as in Macedonia in 360 and 229, there was an able male relative to assume responsibility and to command respect. But Ptolemy IV had no brothers or other close male relatives, and the young son was left in charge of two friends, Agathocles and Sosibius, who had little popular support, or at least are so represented in history. In addition to this ominous circumstance, Egypt itself had been seriously weakened during the past sixteen years, or perhaps only during the past ten. Ptolemy IV Philopator is represented in our sources as a weak king, a voluptuary and dilettante, and this is probably untrue, although he was a devotee of the not entirely respectable god Dionysus and his portraits show him inclining to corpulence, a family tendency already observed in his grandfather Philadelphus. He was somewhat offensive to Greek opinion from having married his full sister Arsinoe, from which marriage had come after ten years the only son who was his successor. Perhaps Arsinoe was much younger than her brother-husband, and she is described as a sad queen, without any real influence. Philopator is credited with various dynastic and other murders at the beginning of his reign, including that of his mother Berenice, and in the circumstances of a Hellenistic court this may or may not be true.

But what is known positively about him is not unfavorable. Faced with a serious military threat from Antiochus III in 218, he organized an effective fighting force including seventy-three African elephants and twenty thousand Egyptians organized and equipped in the Macedonian manner. It may be that they received also the right to use the legal status and designation of Macedonian. Never before had African elephants been trained for combat use, and never before since Gaza in 312 had a Ptolemy possessed or used an Egyptian phalanx. Both innovations may have been measures of desperation, as they are presented in our uniformly unfriendly historical tradition, but they testify also to resourcefulness and confidence; and in the event they proved highly successful. Philopator's army, made up otherwise of a Greco-Macedonian corps and Libyan, Gallic, and Thracian mercenaries, won a decisive victory, and the king recovered Palestine and Syria.

Otherwise little is known about Philopator's reign, and the historians probably found it dull, for they liked better martial activities which were by no means necessarily better for the kingdom. He was a builder, in Alexandria and elsewhere, constructing the great Serapeium and the Sema with the royal tombs, and working on numerous Egyptian temples throughout Egypt, notably at Edfu. He reorganized the royal cult, bringing into it Ptolemy I and Berenice, the Savior Gods, who had been omitted previously.

But his reign was marked by two adverse phenomena for which he was not entirely responsible. Literary sources speak of

The Raphia Decree

revolts in Upper Egypt, blaming them on his policy of arming the natives, but earlier Ptolemies had already experienced revolts, about which we can hardly judge, lacking much real information. They may have been little more than riots provoked by rigorous tax-collection, or isolated outbreaks of banditry, producing a temporary breakdown of communications (*ameixia*). On the other hand, the papyri testify to a sudden price inflation due to the disappearance of the silver currency. Thrown back on the non-exchangeable bronze coins of little intrinsic value, people would no longer sell at the old prices, and the situation may well have been made worse by reluctance of the government to accept payments in the token money. This must have had an unsettling effect on Egypt, and it must have made difficult the hiring of outsiders, especially Greeks, who made up at least the mercenary portion of the armed forces. For this, however, Philopator was in no way responsible, since it was caused by the hostilities in Spain, Italy, and Sicily during the Second Punic War (218-201).

This, then, was the situation in 205. Antiochus III, triumphant after his eastern campaign, was ready to advance his dynasty's claims to southern Asia Minor and the Levant, while in Macedonia Philip V, at peace after a not-unsuccessful war against the Aetolians, was eager for profitable adventures in a direction not covered by his treaty with Rome. Their dynasties were traditional allies and traditionally hostile to the Ptolemies, so we have no reason to doubt Polybius' story of some understanding between them when, on the news of Philopator's death, they began moving against the Ptolemaic empire.

PHILIP V AND ANTIOCHUS III

The war which followed is poorly known, and we can see only that it was highly successful for Antiochus, only partly so for Philip. By 201 Antiochus had captured the border fortress of Gaza and in the following year won a decisive victory at Panium (Banias) in northern Palestine, and Ptolemy's guardians sued for peace. Antiochus received Syria and Palestine, Sidon surrendering to him in 199, and it was agreed that Ptolemy V would marry Antiochus' daughter Cleopatra when he came of age. When the marriage was celebrated in 196, Egypt became something of a Seleucid protectorate.

Philip fared more unevenly. Moving east along the Thracian coast, after a campaign to the north had won the friendship of the Odrysians, he had by 202 come into possession of most of the cities north of the Aegean and Sea of Marmora, but some of these were allied to the Aetolians, and thus Philip succeeded in arousing his former opponents who complained vainly to Rome. Swinging south the following year he acquired the Ptolemaic naval base at Samos, but came into conflict both with the Rhodians, who were already actively fighting his allies among the Cretan pirates, and with Attalus. He won an indecisive victory over their combined fleets near Chios and Miletus admitted him, but he was poorly supported by Zeuxis, Antiochus' governor at Sardes, who was doubtless alarmed by Philip's raids on the mainland as far as Pergamum and Thyateira. Philip overran Caria from Cnidus to Iasus, but then found that he had lost command of the sea and was unable to return to Macedonia for the winter. When, in the spring, he was able to get across the Aegean, he had not much strengthened his position. While he retained some Anatolian and Hellespontine possessions, they required troops to protect them, and were not of great immediate value. And now Rome, rid of the war with Carthage, was in a position to consider her eastern commitments.

THE SECOND MACEDONIAN WAR

The result was ten years of war, as decisive as any in the world's history. Fighting successively against Philip, Nabis, and the coalition of the Aetolians and Antiochus, the Romans met their opponents one by one, while they were supported throughout by their other allies; by the Aetolians against Philip; by Attalus and then Eumenes II (197-160) of Pergamum, Amynander of Athamania, the Achaeans, and Rhodes against Antiochus. To a considerable extent, their victories were won by Greek arms, notably at the battle of Magnesia (190) when the legions were hardly engaged, while their enemies were unable to unite. Both of the Greek leagues were friendly to Rome at the beginning, and the Achaeans, Philip's former ally, remained so, accepting Rome as a counter-weight to Sparta instead of Macedon, but the Aetolians shifted to hostility as soon as their immediate enemy, Philip, had been defeated.

All of this contributed to making the Roman victory easier than it might have been, but once war had been accepted, a Roman victory was certain because of the superior manpower and the inflexible determination of the Republic, the discipline and skill of her armed forces, and the higher quality of her weapons. Due to their many wars, the Romans had become, in Polybius' words, complete masters (*athletai*) of war. The consuls, exercising the *jus gladii*, punished any dereliction of duty immediately and mercilessly, so that "men often faced death, refusing to leave their ranks even when vastly outnumbered, owing to dread of the punishment they would meet with." And the Spanish sword which was the principal infantry weapon was of the finest steel and equally effective for thrusting or for chopping. Livy describes the effect upon Philip's army of viewing the first casualties of the war: "When they had seen bodies chopped to pieces, arms torn away, shoulders and all, or heads separated from bodies, with the necks completely severed, or vitals laid open, and the other fearful wounds, they realised in a general panic with what weapons and what men they had to fight. Fear seized the king as well,"[24] and this feeling may explain the great respect with which, in Polybius' narrative, Philip addresses Roman commanders and envoys.

Since war was so profitable a pursuit, both materially and in terms of prestige, to the Roman ruling aristocracy, it is natural to ask whether some Machiavelian purposes underlay the Second Macedonian War. Did the *nobiles* contrive technically just wars, *bella justa*, so that they might conquer the East for their own benefit? If this was so, the evidence for such a plot was well concealed. Philip's action against the Aetolian allies in the Hellespont and then against Attalus was a clear breach of the Treaty of Phoenice, and these were followed by another. After returning to Macedonia in 200, he sent troops to support the Acarnanians in a raid against Athens, in retaliation for the execution of two of their people after a profanation of the Eleusinian Mysteries. Later in the year he marched east, took over more Ptolemaic cities and laid siege to Abydus, probably a Ptolemaic or Pergamene ally. There he was overtaken by a Roman envoy Marcus Aemilius Lepidus, "the handsomest man of his time," who made the formal demand for restitution (*rerum repetitio*) under several heads: 1) not to make war on the Greeks; 2) not to seize Ptolemaic possessions; 3) to stand trial (presumably before a Senatorial commission, but possibly before a group of Greek neutrals) for his injuries to Attalus and the Rhodians.[25]

Giving satisfaction on these points, he might have peace. This would have been a return to the situation of 205 and a surrender of Philip's inconsiderable but hardly won gains since then, and the king attempted to argue that he was not the aggressor. It would be interesting to know how he justified this, for the truth seems to be entirely on the other side. In any case, Lepidus cut in to ask: "And what about the Athenians? What about the Cianians, and what about the Abydenes now? Did any of those attack you first? " In reply, Philip showed how differently a Greek would regard the Treaty of Phoenice than a Roman. He asked that the Romans not violate the treaty by attacking him, as if it were merely a bilateral non-aggression pact. To the Romans it was a permanent area settlement.

The war which followed was desultory in character for two years, due principally to Philip's caution and skill in defense, but became more active with the arrival as commander of Titus Quinctius Flamininus, a Hellenized Roman who understood the Greeks and was also an able commander. A conference was arranged at which Philip tried to negotiate a peace on the basis of a compromise: he would keep half of his conquests and return the rest. But the Romans had no reason to bargain, although the personal relations between Philip and Flamininus are pictured as cordial, and indeed a Roman consul might feel more congenial with a Macedonian king than with a vociferous crowd of Greek politicians. In fact, the demand was now raised: Philip must not only forego war but also pull out of Greece entirely, surrendering the three Fetters, Corinth, Chalcis, and Demetrias. This would be to return to conditions before the reign of Philip II.

The king could not accept, but still tried to avoid the battle which he was doubtful of winning. In the late spring of 197 Flamininus entered Thessaly from the south with an army of twenty-eight thousand men, of which a third was supplied by the Aetolians and Amynander, and Philip went to meet him with a slightly smaller force, almost purely Macedonian in composition, and consisting in great part of new recruits. As the two armies were marching parallel separated by the ridge known as Dogs'

Heads (Cynocephalae) on a hazy morning, their patrols became engaged and a piecemeal combat developed on ground chosen by neither commander, and particularly unfavorable to the Macedonian phalanx. For Philip, as we know from some inscriptions, had studied Roman institutions and particularly those of a military nature, and had modified the Macedonian battle order to meet his opponent. He could not match the Romans in training and armament and so gave up the open, flexible battalion formation employed by Philip II and Alexander in favor of a deep, solid phalanx modeled on that of Epaminondas, designed not to hold the enemy for the decisive cavalry charge but to charge itself and smash the enemy line in a hedgehog formation bristling with spearpoints, wherein even raw soldiers might be effective. Part of this phalanx did get into position and shattered the opposing legion, but the rest was struck on the flank before it was ready, and as the Aetolian cavalry had driven off the Macedonian, the mobile and well-trained Roman maniples could get behind the Macedonian infantry and cut it to pieces. Philip had nothing to do but to sue for peace. The war was over.

THE ROMAN SETTLEMENT IN GREECE

Peace was arranged substantially on the terms which Philip had rejected the year previous. He must give up his Greek possessions and his foreign conquests, dismantle his fleet and pay an indemnity of a thousand talents, but he kept his army and his kingdom, and as a friend and ally of Rome was entitled to her support if he required it. Once the fighting was over, Rome showed herself firm against giving the Aetolians their full claims. Of their former holdings in Thessaly, for example, they received only Phthiotic Thebes. The Achaeans received Corinth, Athens was given Delos and some other islands, Rhodes recovered her Peraea. Before a wildly jubilant Greek crowd at the Isthmian Games in 196, Flamininus announced that the Romans would keep for themselves nothing which had been surrendered to them, and indeed the last Roman garrisons were withdrawn when he returned to Italy two years later. His plan called for the recreation of smaller leagues, such as those of the Boeotians and the Thessalians, probably to make certain that there would be none powerful enough to be a danger. This would keep Greece divided and weak, but with Rome to guarantee the peace, it might be an acceptable arrangement. It is legitimate to regard Flamininus as philhellene, and he may have deserved the honors which the Greeks heaped on him.

It is interesting that he had adopted the old Greek slogan of freedom. The Greeks were to be free, not only in Europe but also in Asia. But the Roman notion of "freedom" as a grant of the Roman people was different from the Greek, and then and later, the Romans saw no contradiction in assigning such freed cities to other Greek powers, if it suited them. His extension of the doctrine to Anatolia, however, while a logical deduction from the Roman connections with Pergamum and Bithynia, could only lead to trouble with Antiochus, who was not yet in the Roman sphere of influence.

With the defeat of Macedon, the humiliation of the Aetolians, and the generally cautious attitude of the Achaeans, there was only one potentially dangerous power left in Greece, and that was Sparta. After Cleomenes' defeat and exile in 222, the revolutionary and nationalistic movement which he had led had by no means ceased, and the socialistic policies of King Nabis (207-192) led many to regard him as a tyrant. He had become possessed of Argos, where he had established a similarly leftist government, inevitably at odds and in conflict with the conservative and propertied classes which were in control of the Achaean League, and which, in general, Rome preferred to support. Nabis had been a loyal supporter of Flamininus during the war with Philip, only repulsing a somewhat unexplained attempt of the Achaeans to capture Argos, but cynically or not, Flamininus felt that Greece would be safer if Nabis were checked. The League of Corinth had been re-created, and Flamininus as president posed in 195 the question, "What should be done about Argos? "

All except the Aetolians, who hoped to have Spartan support in the future as in the past, voted that it should be freed, and an army was assembled and marched both against Argos and against Sparta. Neither place was captured, but a sea campaign against Nabis' Cretan allies and his coastal cities was successful, and Nabis found it necessary to negotiate a peace, surrendering Argos (which was given to the Achaeans), giving up his fleet, and paying the usual indemnity. This was the settlement when Flamininus left Greece, but two years later, taking advantage of the confusion of the Antiochic War, Philopoemen, the Achaean general, secured the assassination of Nabis and the adhesion of Sparta to the Achaean League.

Flamininus returned to Rome to enjoy a triumph, displaying Macedonian trophies and twelve hundred Romans who had been taken prisoner by Hannibal and been sold into slavery in Greece. Characteristically of the Senatorial attitude toward soldiers who let themselves be captured, Flamininus had refused to liberate them, but they had been ransomed by the Achaeans. In addition, there was the booty in gold and silver, nearly two tons of the one and twenty-two of the other, plus nearly fifteen thousand gold staters. Rome, as ever, expected war to be profitable. Greece was much weakened, but some saw in the continued progress of Antiochus III an opportunity to redress the balance. The Romans themselves were conscious of the danger, or perhaps of the opportunity. If warfare in small and poor Greece were lucrative, what would be war in Asia?

THE SYRIAN WAR

A Roman embassy had visited Antiochus first toward the close of his war with Egypt, under the legitimate pretext of urging him to respect the possessions of their friend Ptolemy V. Possibly for this action, one of the envoys, Aemilius Lepidus, was to be remembered in his family annals as a *tutor regis Ptolemaei*. Antiochus cannot have taken this intercession very seriously. At all events, while the Romans were occupied with Philip, he marched north into Asia Minor and liberated or established control over the coastal areas as far as the Hellespont, regardless of whether these belonged then or previously to Ptolemy, to Philip, or to Eumenes. He conciliated Rhodes by returning to her the Carian Peraea, and treated the cities generously, confirming Iasus, for example, in her autonomy and democracy. Only Smyrna and Lampsacus remained loyal to Pergamum. Otherwise his advance was welcomed, and he was able without opposition to cross the Hellespont and begin the rebuilding of Lysimacheia. Unfortunately, however, the Second Macedonian War was now over, Eumenes was a Roman ally entitled to assistance, and Lampsacus, a Phocaean colony and a member of the League of Ilium, sent an embassy to Massilia and then to Rome, asking support in each case on the ground of kinship.[26] In consequence, the Roman attitude toward Antiochus stiffened.

It is hard to accept Polybius's opinion that the Romans feared him, or that he had any idea of interfering in the affairs of Greece. His claim was to recover his ancestral possessions in Asia Minor and in the Thracian Chersonese; it was near Lysimacheia that Seleucus Nicator had been assassinated. For some reason he sent an embassy to Flamininus which was received just after the Isthmian Games of 196 when Flamininus had made his promise to withdraw the Roman garrisons, when, as Polybius writes, "by a single proclamation all the Greeks inhabiting Asia and Europe became free, ungarrisoned, subject to no tribute and governed by their own laws." Flamininus informed Antiochus, who may have intended only to congratulate the Romans on their victory, that "as regards the Asiatic cities, he must leave alone those which were autonomous and make war on none of them, withdraw from those previously held by Ptolemy and Philip and not to cross into Europe with an army." There was logic in this, from the Roman point of view. Ptolemy V was a friend, Philip was a defeated opponent whose possessions were forfeit, Europe was a Roman protectorate, and Rome was a champion of all the Greeks. It is equally true, as later envoys of Antiochus were to point out, that all of these positions were also inconsistent with each other, but the issue was not to be settled by argument.

It was the Aetolians who were responsible for the war. To the extent that Rome wanted it, she was content to wait for a suitable occasion, and Antiochus had no reason for war whatsoever. A 'cold war' state might have continued indefinitely, but the Aetolians were busily trying to build up an alliance which would make it possible to overthrow Flamininus' settlement. Philip and Nabis were approached, and at least the latter was encouraging. In the winter of 193/2, Antiochus was persuaded to become an ally and to send troops to Greece; perhaps he was tired of the endless negotiations with Rome, and hoped by a show of force to prevail on her to leave him unmolested. War was declared in 192, and when the Aetolians had seized Demetrias, Antiochus came to Greece with a small force, and during the autumn and winter, by diplomacy and force, succeeded in winning some support in central Greece. But Philip was cool, and Nabis was extinguished by the Achaeans. In the spring Philip joined Rome, and when Antiochus, who still had only a small army and was feebly supported by the Aetolians, was unable to hold the pass at Thermopylae, he could only retire ignominiously to Asia Minor.

The final decision came in the winter of 190/89, and required very little Roman effort. The Aetolians accepted a truce, Philip was actively helpful, and the Rhodians, forgetful of past favors from Antiochus, joined the Roman side with their fleet. Antiochus lost control of the seas, and was finally defeated in a decisive battle near Magnesia in the Hermus valley. Antiochus had the advantage in numbers and employed the weapons of Asia: elephants, scythed chariots, and mail-clad cavalry. The first, properly used, should have won him an easy victory, but it proved, as often, impossible to control. It overwhelmed the Roman and Pergamene left wing but could not be stopped or turned in a field sodden with rain, and the Pergamene cavalry on the other end of the line uncovered Antiochus' phalanx, which was then destroyed by missiles. Antiochus could have retired to the east and continued the war indefinitely, but chose to accept Roman peace terms.

The Romans may well have been astonished, as have been ancient and modern historians. It is still difficult to understand why Antiochus, an experienced diplomat and soldier who had been a king for over thirty years, should have entered so lightly into a war which he did not want, and have then fought it so badly. In the end he was defeated by Eumenes, for Publius Scipio Africanus, who was in the Roman camp as legate for his brother Lucius, the consul, contributed as little to winning the decision as his old opponent Hannibal, who was with Antiochus, did to prevent it.

The Romans were ready with terms, characteristically harsh. Antiochus must give up Asia Minor as far as the Taurus, surrender his fleet and his elephants, and pay an enormous indemnity. The Romans were to receive twelve thousand talents of silver and nearly a hundred and fifty thousand bushels of wheat, spread out over twelve years. While not a large amount of silver compared with the treasures which Alexander had found in Persia, these four hundred and eighty tons were over forty times what had been exacted from Philip, and twice the sum which Rome realized from Spain, according to Livy, in the forty years between 200 and 160.

In addition, Antiochus was to pay to Eumenes about five hundred talents. He was, also, not to make war on any state in the west, and to give hostages for his good behavior. It is a tribute to the terror inspired by Roman arms that Antiochus accepted the terms without question, and they were faithfully carried out by him and his successor.

This was the Treaty of Apamea, and in view of the professions made by the Romans to Antiochus about the possessions of Ptolemy V, the sanctity of Europe, and the freedom of the Greek cities, it is interesting to see the rest of the settlement effected at the same time. A few towns were declared autonomous and free from tribute: that is, tribute to Rome or to any other overlord. On the other hand, Rhodes was given almost all of Lycia and Caria, regardless of the previous states of these cities (some had belonged to Ptolemy and some to Philip), and Eumenes received all other Seleucid territories and cities including the Thracian Chersonese with Lysimacheia, the occupation of which by Antiochus had been a principal *casus belli*. Never did Rome so clearly betray the one-sided quality of her political and legal standards. Especially clear was the rapaciousness of the Roman commanders. The final campaigns of 189, that of the consuls M. Fulvius Nobilior against the Aetolians and Cnaeus Manlius Volso against the Galatians involved bloody fighting. The two peoples were brought to their knees, but otherwise the expeditions were distinguished by the great quantities of loot captured or exacted. The city of Ambracia may have been the first to experience the Roman fondness for Greek art, but it was not to be the last. It was systematically stripped of its treasures.[27]

The Struggle for Survival

THE THIRD MACEDONIAN WAR — MACEDON PARTITIONED

It was about 187 when the last Roman soldier was withdrawn from Greece, leaving the states of the peninsula autonomous and free both legally and (in some cases) practically, except for the Aetolians, who were under the obligation to protect the imperium and the majesty of the Roman people, and so required to support Rome in any demand. Nevertheless all were, from the Roman

point of view, obligated to live under terms of the latest settlement. These extended not only to Greeks, Macedonians and
Illyrians, but even to the northern tribes, Dardanii, Bastarnae,
Thracians, and Gauls. One of the complaints against Perseus, who
succeeded his father Philip as king of Macedon in 178, was that he
had expelled a Thracian prince named Abrupolis from his territory
in retaliation for a previous attack. Proud and suspicious, the
Senate regarded any change in the political or economic situation
in the East as a matter of concern, and changes were inevitable. No
one wished to provoke Rome. All feared her. All hoped, however,
to improve their own situation under the treaty without rousing
her anger. All wished to be loyal allies, but it was not easy to
know what was permitted. Embassies came and went. Frequently
Rome sent out commissions to hold hearings but these could not
always give answers. Matters must be referred to the Senate, and
this was slow and unsatisfactory for the hearings took much time
and did not always lead to clear answers.

The Senate, for its part, did not readily understand the issues
and was confused by the eloquence of rival Greek orators, thus
preferring to be guided by individuals whom it trusted, such as
Eumenes of Pergamum and the Macedonian prince Demetrius,
Philip's younger son. It also proved to be true that the Senate's
acquiescence in an action did not mean approval. When Rome
decided on war with Perseus in 171, the Romans issued a
statement of charges, one copy of which has partly survived on a
Delphian inscription, and this covered offenses of Perseus and his
father committed over fifteen years.[28]

The declaration of war was as puzzling as it was horrifying to
the Greeks. It must have been decided upon during Eumenes' visit
to Rome the preceding year, and knowledge of this must have
been responsible for his near-death in a stone-slide at Delphi on his
way back to Pergamum, if indeed the slide was not purely
accidental. Polybius, who writes as a Roman apologist, has no
doubt that the attempt was due to Perseus, and this was the
official Roman version, as the Delphian copy of their white paper
shows. Even Polybius, however, perhaps in conscious imitation of
Thucydides, feels it necessary to distinguish between the immediate events which occasioned the war and the ultimate cause, which
was the continued growth of Macedonian power or, as he puts it,

the progressive determination of Philip and then Perseus to attack Rome.

Eumenes, as the proximate cause, may well have felt himself threatened by Perseus' dynastic marriages. He had married his daughter to Prusias II of Bithynia and had himself married Laodice, the daughter of Seleucus IV. She had been escorted by the Rhodian fleet, since neither Macedon nor the Seleucid kingdom was allowed to possess one, and this was a sign that Rhodes, too, was no longer friendly to Pergamum. This general strengthening and independence of Macedon, together with her increased preoccupation with Greek affairs, may well have decided the Senate to weaken or destroy the Antigonid dynasty; even the unfriendly Polybius pictures Perseus as trying to avoid trouble. When some smaller Boeotian communities appealed to him for help, he "replied that it was quite impossible for him to send armed help to anyone owing to his truce with Rome, but he gave them the general advice to defend themselves against the Thebans as well as they could; but rather than fight with the Romans, to remain quiet." The record is clear. Against Perseus the Romans could advance only minor incidents and vague suspicions, and yet they had determined upon war even while negotiations were still in progress, before the final ultimatum, the *rerum repetitio* required by law to ensure that the conflict would be a *bellum justum* and so approved by the gods. In fact, Quintus Marcius Philippus, a traditional guest-friend of the Antigonids, boasted that as envoy he had won six months by inducing Perseus to continue negotiating while Rome mobilized. Both the conduct of the war and the settlement at the end show that the Romans, or at least the Roman generals, were primarily interested in booty, and actually only one consul with a small army was present each year in Greece, as if the ruling aristocracy was anxious to make the war last as long as possible.

Four commanders were in the field in four successive years. Perseus fought cautiously and won an occasional small victory, but kept asking through envoys for terms of peace which were always denied, other than surrender at discretion. In 169 Marcius established an army in southern Macedonia, and on 22 June of 168 Perseus, desperate, drove his phalanx into and almost through the

legions of Lucius Aemilius Paullus in the plains near Pydna, only
to have it cut to pieces and his army destroyed. He can have
expected no less and knew, also, what was in store for him. After
Cynocephalae, a generation earlier, King Philip could treat for
peace on equal terms, but now his son, who had not sought war
but on the contrary had done everything he could to avoid it, was
treated as a public enemy. After a brief attempt at flight, he
surrendered and was taken to Italy with his sons to grace Aemilius'
triumph and die soon after in captivity, while his kingdom was
partitioned into four weak republics. Macedonia no longer existed,
and the spoil belonged only to Rome and the Romans, for they
allowed their loyal Pergamene allies to have no share.

The Roman settlement was universally harsh. Only Athens,
which had met in 171 an enormous requisition of grain for the
war, was rewarded, receiving her old possessions, the islands of
Lemnos, Imbros, and Scyros, as well as the territory of Haliartus
in Boeotia, and the administration of Delos which had been free,
but which was now given to Athens on condition that (in the
words of Strabo) she take good care of the importers and of the
religious rites. These "importers" were Italian merchants, and
when a Rhodian envoy in Polybius complained to the Senate that
by making Delos tax-free (ateles) the Romans had reduced the
value of the Rhodian harbor dues by seven-eighths, he must mean
that the Senate prevented either Athens or Delos from collecting
the usual port fees. Athens' control over Delos must, therefore,
have been custodial rather than possessive. Rhodes had incurred
the wrath of the Senate by proposing a mediated peace with
Perseus in 168, and was punished by the loss of the territory in
Caria and Lycia granted in 188, and also by the restriction of her
right or power to patrol the seas.

The result was an enormous increase in Cretan and Cilician
piracy, directed principally toward satisfying, through the market
on Delos, the insatiable demand of wealthy Romans and Italians
for Greek and oriental slaves. This was, perhaps, the principal part
of the vast booty which Aemilius took back with him, for while he
had secured about ninety tons of silver and nearly a ton of gold in
little and poor Macedonia (better than one-sixth of the precious
metals which Antiochus undertook to pay in 188), a day's raid on
ninety Epirote towns in 167 netted one hundred and fifty

thousand captives to be enslaved, in addition to certainly numerous prisoners taken elsewhere in the course of the war. The impoverishment and terror of Greece was general. Rome's favorite Eumenes was suspected or accused of treating with Perseus, and his influence passed to his younger brother Attalus, while the entirely dutiful Achaeans were charged with disloyalty and required to send a thousand of their leading men as hostages to Rome, the few survivors of whom were not allowed to return until 151. In the meantime, the League was directed by one Callicrates, who was willing to be Rome's tool.

THE ACHAEAN WAR – SACK OF CORINTH

Again Rome withdrew her troops, leaving this time Greece practically defenseless, for in addition to Macedonia, Illyria also had been converted from a monarchy into a group of republics. Polybius refers to the following years as a period of peace and prosperity, and this may have been true in part, but they were equally years of insecurity and unrest. The poor, the former democrats, felt themselves to be and probably were oppressed and exploited by the wealthy class which Rome favored. Border squabbles between neighbors continued, and Greek embassies were constantly on the road to Rome or waiting there for an audience with the Senate, while Roman commissioners as regularly visited Greece. A controversy between Athens and her dependency Oropus was arbitrated by Sicyon greatly to Athens' disfavor and the otherwise unimportant affair provided an occasion for sending to Rome (in 155) her most distinguished citizens and the heads of her great schools, the Academic Carneades, the Peripatetic Critolaus, and the Stoic Diogenes. But, while the intellectual impression created by these philosophers, partly favorable and partly not, was great, the political results of their embassy were small. The Greeks could neither guide their own affairs nor depend on Rome to do so, and the consequent confusion led to the last two desperate and hopeless struggles for survival before Rome accepted the logical result of her policy and converted the peninsula into the *provincia* of a resident magistrate.

The first of these struggles occurred in Macedonia, where the flag of revolt was raised by one Andriscus, who claimed to be a son of Perseus. He stood for nationalism and the rights of the poor, and aroused great enthusiasm. Possessed of some military ability, he defeated one Roman army, but was soon beaten and captured in 148 by the praetor Quintus Caecilius Metellus, and thereafter the Romans regularly sent out a governor to administer the affairs of the four Macedonian districts as well as of Illyria and Epirus, constructing the Via Egnatia connecting the two areas to facilitate military and civil control.

In the following year, under quite different circumstances, the Achaeans found themselves at war also, for in this case Rome was operating not against revolutionaries but against too successful conservatives. The League was still too powerful, even if its policies and interests ran parallel to Rome's own, and the Senate invited those members who wished to do so to withdraw from its membership. The Achaeans made a fight of it, supported by a parallel movement in Boeotia where Thebes was trying to hold her league together also, but a short campaign by Lucius Mummius ended resistance in both areas. Thebes was not illogically sacked for her hostility, but the treatment of Corinth was such as to shock Roman sensibilities in later times. After the defeat of the League forces, Corinth surrendered, but was sacked and destroyed as an example, it was said, but really (as was naturally believed) to satisfy Roman greed. Thereafter no state in Greece was free except in the special way in which Rome understood the term as applied to dependencies.

THE ACCESSION OF ANTIOCHUS IV

In Asia, after the Peace of Apamea, Antiochus III had the status of Friend of the Roman People, with the responsibility of behaving as such in general and of satisfying the obligations of the treaty in particular. This theoretically extended the Roman sphere of influence as far as the most remote Seleucid possessions, and might conceivably have entitled Antiochus to ask for Roman assistance against his Parthian and Bactrian vassals. The Romans, however, confined themselves as always to what was practicable, and concerned themselves little with the king so long as he stayed beyond the range of the Taurus, refrained from rebuilding his fleet, and paid annually the thousand talents of indemnity. Antiochus still had a very large state. In spite of their concern for their friend Ptolemy, the Romans had not required Antiochus to return to him Palestine and southern Syria, while Babylonia remained probably his richest territory. Armenia had become independent but had never been very useful, while in Media, Elam, and Persis, Antiochus possessed the most important Iranian lands, even if the last of these was not entirely dependable. Persis had been independent under a native dynasty in the third century and was to be independent again before the Parthian expansion in the second, but Antiochus had converted it into a satrapy during his eastern campaign (212-205).

Further east, nothing north of the Elburz and the Hindu Kush was under direct administration, but Antiochus had had the mailed cavalry of Turkistan with him at Magnesia, so Euthydemus at least furnished him military support, and the southern districts of Carmania, Drangiana, Gedrosia, and Arachosia were probably all satrapies (our information is very poor on this region). Furthermore, while Asia Minor had been lost, the many Greek or Hellenistic cities founded throughout the realm by the first and second Antiochus, and by Antiochus III himself, were now providing centers of recruitment of soldiers and officials of Greco-Macedonian culture. Thus twenty years later, in his triumph at Daphne, Antiochus IV could parade twenty-five thousand Greco-Macedonian troops, more than any of his predecessors, even if many of these were doubtless of mixed blood.

So the Seleucid kingdom was still powerful although handicapped by vast distances, mountains and desert. With a heterogeneous and often fiercely independent population, the great distances made centralized control difficult, and the kingdom lacked metals, notably silver and iron. Carmania produced silver and copper as well as gold, and some of this may have found its way into the temples of southern Iran, but otherwise much of the Seleucid currency was minted in Asia Minor and then imported. This need for metals was one reason for the friendship between Seleucids and Attalids after 188, when the frontier between them had been drawn and guaranteed by the Romans, but it made more difficult the problem of meeting the Roman indemnity. Antiochus III himself was killed in July of 187 while attempting to collect an assessment from a temple in Elam.

The dynasty was fortunate during the next thirty-seven years in having a succession of mature and able kings, although all of

them died premature deaths. Antiochus III was succeeded by his
son Seleucus IV (187-175) about whom little is known, but he
held the kingdom together and paid off the Roman indemnity. His
brother-in-law Ptolemy V had died in 180, but his sister Cleopatra
acted as regent for the children till 176, and no problem in foreign
policy occurred. An inscription shows Seleucus arranging for the
retirement of one of his father's veterans as citizen of Seleucia in
Pieria.[29] This man may have been a Macedonian, and the citizenship gave him a secure and pleasant residence, for in this way also
the new cities were valuable to the kings. On Seleucus' death he
was succeeded by his young son Antiochus, but his brother, who
had been for more than ten years a hostage in Rome and was then
living at Athens, returned with the approval of Rome and the
assistance of Attalus II. He took over the regency, and later
became king as Antiochus IV. Seleucus' son was put to death for
unknown reasons in the summer of 170, when war with Egypt was
threatening. He may well have been involved in a plot to seize the
throne.

THE EGYPTIAN CAMPAIGN OF ANTIOCHUS IV

In Egypt, with the death of Cleopatra, control of the young
king Ptolemy VI passed into hands unfriendly to the Seleucids. It
is significant that the two regents Eulaeus and Lenaeus, who have
been denigrated like almost all the ministers of the Ptolemies in
history, were said to have been of eastern origin. Their names are
Macedonian, but Eulaeus is called a eunuch and Lenaeus a
Syrian.[30] The Ptolemaic administration of the Levant had been
popular and the Seleucid control was still relatively new. The two
were probably refugees from the Seleucids, and not unnaturally
began to plan the recovery of their country from the new masters.
Unfortunately the resources and the leadership of Egypt in its
reduced state were inadequate to the task, although Egypt was
now unified, with the last recorded rebellion having been sup-
pressed in the year 184/3. But the loss of the Asia Minor cities had
shut off access to those sources of manpower, while other
possibilities, the Aetolians for example, may well have been
discouraged from helping by the Egyptian shortage of silver
currency and the gradual rise of native elements to power.

A few months after Cleopatra's death the regents celebrated

the marriage of Ptolemy VI and his sister Cleopatra (spring, 175), although the royal couple were still very young. Five years later they declared the king an adult and associated the younger brother on the throne with both, and then set in motion an expedition into Palestine. Both they and Antiochus sent embassies to Rome to present their claims but Rome was occupied with Perseus, and Antiochus defeated the Egyptian army and followed it into Pelusium and then Memphis. It was the first successful invasion of Egypt since that of Dareius III one hundred and seventy-three years earlier, for Alexander had not invaded but merely occupied.

It is hard to suppose that Antiochus meant anything but conquest. Then or a little later he sent to Cyprus an expedition which defeated the Ptolemaic field army and began the systematic reduction of the fortified cities. If Rome were to be endlessly tied up in Greece or if Rome had lost interest in the East, he might be able to annex the territories of his nephews and niece, or at least to establish a control over them. It is true that Antiochus was not crowned as pharaoh, and that when Greek embassies came to Alexandria to congratulate Ptolemy VI on his majority (anakleteria) and offered mediation, Antiochus merely advanced his claim to the Levant, but he issued edicts in his own name dealing with local administration and his soldiers occupied the country, doing some damage. In some way he got possession of the young king, but then returned to Syria at the beginning of the Nile inundation in 169, leaving his ward under guard in Mamphis.

But Ptolemy escaped, became re-united with his brother and sister, and Antiochus must come again with his army. At the beginning of summer (168) he was camped in front of Alexandria. But the Senate had sent out Caius Popillius Laenas as a special envoy. As soon as the news of the Roman victory over Perseus at Pydna came, Laenas hurried to Antiochus and, dramatically drawing a circle around him in the sand, demanded an immediate reply, whether for obedience or war. Antiochus knew that the Romans did not jest, and withdrew his forces both from Egypt and from Cyprus, but he kept Syria and Palestine, and can hardly be thought to have lost by the episode. As a matter of fact, there may have been Egyptian booty in the great triumph which he conducted at Daphne near Antioch soon after, in imitation of the Roman practice.

The character of Antiochus has been a puzzle in antiquity and in modern times. He was marked by his long stay in Rome, and is said to have tried to introduce Roman constitutional institutions in Antioch and perhaps elsewhere. Sometimes he behaved as a Roman noble, sometimes as an Athenian democrat, and many stories were told of his pranks and escapades. He was charged with being not Epiphanes (God Manifest), his official epithet, but Epimanes, Mad. It is hard to know how much truth there is in this, but he must have been an able general to have conquered Egypt, and probably possessed a touch of genius which his contemporaries did not always understand or like. At all events, he now fell into the difficulties which have given him his chief fame. Without in any way intending or being conscious of it, he became responsible for the setting up of the first independent Jewish state in over four hundred years, an event with major consequences in world history. It was the unique intellectual climate which followed in Judaea which gave rise to the Christian religion, and it was the inspiration of the Maccabees which supported modern Zionism and the creation of the state of Israel.

THE MACCABAEAN WAR

The Jews had flourished under the Persian Empire and throughout the third century under Ptolemaic domination. They constituted a peaceful temple state, autonomous under the high-priestly family of the Oniads, and without a history, for nothing eventful happened in Judaea. Elsewhere, however, and notably in Egypt, the Jews were becoming important. Their swelling population emigrated in the service of the kings, principally as mercenary soldiers, and this diaspora was at once in contact with foreign influences and in touch with the community which centered on the Temple in Jerusalem. Members of the Tobiad family, whose home was in the Ammonitis, rose high in Ptolemaic service, and constituted the nucleus of a wealthy Hellenizing group which, like the emigres, was somewhat out of sympathy with the conservative peasants and artisans, whose guidance was the Torah and the oral interpretation of the Scribes (the predecessors of the Pharisees).

To this growing tension was added that of conflicting foreign allegiance. Jerusalem was probably occupied by Antiochus III and returned to Ptolemaic control before the Battle of Panium brought

Judaea definitively under Seleucid control, and there were rival groups of Seleucid and Ptolemaic supporters. Thereafter, under the High Priests Simon the Just and Onias III the Jews were autonomous, living under their own laws, but rivalries continued, concerned at first only with the administration of the wealth accumulating in the Temple. Seleucus IV was desperately in need of money to pay his Roman indemnity, and it was easy to win his favor by presents. But after his death in 175, Antiochus IV was persuaded to replace Onias with his brother Jason and to authorize the refoundation of Jerusalem as an Antioch. The refoundation preserved its religion, but superimposed the institutions of an Hellenistic city, council and magistrates, gymnasium and ephebate, based on a restricted citizen group of the well-to-do. Jason continued as High Priest in peace until 172, when he was expelled in partisan fighting, and replaced by one Menelaus, not of a priestly family.

This was the situation at the time Antiochus IV campaigned in Egypt. On his return in the summer or autumn of 169, he visited Jerusalem and collected taxes, but on his departure civil strife broke out again, led this time by an orthodox religious group. On his final return from Egypt in 168, Antiochus was forced to take Jerusalem by storm and it was roughly handled, many of the population being taken and sold as slaves. The activist faction fled into the hills, and a military settlement of hellenized Syrians was established in Jerusalem. These Syrians introduced into the Temple the worship of their Zeus Olympius or Baal Shamin (worshipped in the form of a sacred stone of *betyl*, which became known in Jewish tradition as the "Abomination of Desolation"). Now for the first time the struggle assumed the religious character which it bears in history. Antiochus, who doubtless regarded the whole matter as rather unimportant and had marched or was soon to march east with his army on more urgent matters, left word that the rebels should be hunted down, and that the practice of their religion should be forbidden. For this seemed to him the mainspring of their resistance.

At this juncture, the activists found an able champion in one Judah, surnamed Maccabaeus ("the Hammerer"), who organized an army and suspended such religious practices as Sabbath observance when they conflicted with military duties. Judah won several victories over Seleucid generals, and was not appeased even by a partial amnesty issued in the spring of 164, in which, it is said, a Roman delegation concurred. By December of that year, about the time of the death of Antiochus IV, he got possession of Jerusalem and purged the Temple, in honor of which event the Hanukah festival is still celebrated. Two years later Judah made peace with the young king Antiochus V, and thereafter Judah and his brothers, first Jonathan and then Simon, played an active role in Seleucid politics until, in 142, the garrison withdrew from the citadel at Jerusalem, leaving the Maccabees unquestioned masters in their own territory.

THE DECLINE OF THE SELEUCIDS

Whatever may have been the emergency which drew Antiochus IV east, our sources tell only of operations in Armenia, Babylonia, and Elam, which need have occupied only one campaign season. His death is placed by a Babylonian king-list in November-December 164. Apparently he died of disease, although the pious saw in this a punishment for his having unsuccessfully tried to plunder or to tax a sanctuary of Nannaea, and there is no specific indication that he was concerned with conditions beyond the Zagros Mountains. And yet here momentous events were occurring about which we are poorly informed and which we cannot date.

In Central Asia the great tribal hordes of the Huns and the Tocharians (Yuëh-Chi) were pressing toward the west. In northwestern Iran the Parthian state had gained strength, and under King Mithridates I (191-137) began an expansion to the east and south, penetrating Areia and Media. At the same time the Bactrians, under Euthydemus' successor Demetrius, crossed the Hindu Kush into India, taking advantage of the extinction of the great Mauryan Dynasty. Demetrius himself soon met his death in battle against a rival Eucratides, who may have been a protégé or relative of the Seleucid dynast who got possession of Bactria in Demetrius' absence, but this is all very speculative. It is certain only that a successor of Demetrius named Menander (Milinda) ruled as far as the middle Ganges valley and became a convert to Buddhism, so that an account of his real or legendary career is preserved in the Indian Milinda Panha, and that numerous kings and kinglets with Greek names subsequently flourished in India and struck a voluminous coinage, often distinguished by remarkable portraiture. But the lack of a reliable chronology makes it impossible to bring all of this into clear connection with events in the west.

The next twenty years saw a great decline in the Seleucid state, for the centralized character of the Hellenistic monarchy required a strong and mature king. Dead at the age of perhaps forty-five, Antiochus IV was survived by a son who became king as Antiochus V Eupator. Since he was young, he must have been born of the marriage of Antiochus with his sister Laodice, contracted after 176; he was the first king of this dynasty born from a brother-and-sister marriage. Power rested in the hands of the prime minister Lysias and of the Milesian Timarchus, governor of the Upper Satrapies, but the situation lasted less than two years. In 162 Demetrius, the son of Seleucus IV and Laodice and so the half-brother of Antiochus V Eupator, who had been held in Rome as an hostage, escaped and returned to Syria. He had supporters and became king, Lysias and Antiochus being put to death; and when Timarchus marched west to protect his sovereign, his army deserted to Demetrius, and the only accomplishment was to open Iran to Parthian expansion.

Demetrius I remained king until 150, but his foreign policy antagonized his neighbors, the kings of Pergamum, Cappadocia, and Egypt, and these combined to promote the cause of a certain Alexander who passed as a younger son of Antiochus IV, but who bore also the Syrian name Balas ("Favorite of Ba'al"). He established himself in Ptolemais on the Palestinian coast and a desultory civil war followed, with each side showing its weakness by appealing to the Maccabee Jonathan for help. Finally Demetrius was killed in battle, and Alexander became undisputed king, marrying the daughter of Ptolemy VI, Cleopatra surnamed Thea, the Goddess, who was subsequently in our sources to play a sensational and not entirely helpful role in dynastic politics.

But soon Alexander was challenged by the elder son of Demetrius, who entered Syria from the north with Cretan mercenaries and assumed the diadem as Demetrius II. This time it was the king in Egypt who intervened in force, marching up along the coast and installing garrisons in the cities. He avoided engaging

Jonathan Maccabaeus, who had been operating bloodily against the same cities in the name of Alexander but actually in his own interest. Then Ptolemy, breaking with Alexander, took up the cause of Demetrius and transferred to him the hand of his daughter Cleopatra. Ptolemy VI was in a good position to become ruler if not king in Syria, but he was fatally injured in battle, and with the death of Alexander shortly afterward, the real power rested in the hands of the Cretan mercenary leaders who controlled the young royal couple. Thus the dynasty was fatally weakened at the moment when events in the east most required it to be strong.

EGYPT UNDER PTOLEMY VIII

With the death of Ptolemy VI Philometor at the height of his powers, however (he was little more than forty-five years old), the Egyptian dynasty also suffered a serious loss, for he had been an able and generous if not always very popular king. His reign, from 170 to 145, was pre-occupied or clouded by disputes with his younger brother, Ptolemy VIII (Ptolemy VII was a son of Philometor, and reigned briefly in 145), who was known as Euergetes II or, less flatteringly, as Physcon (the Fat). This danger from Euergetes, however, never became a serious source of weakness, thanks to Roman protection and perhaps also to the skill and tact of the elder brother. The two Ptolemies were associated on the throne with their sister Cleopatra II, the wife of Philometor, at the Egyptian New Year in the autumn of 170, when the regents planned war on Antiochus IV, and this arrangement held, even while Philometor was in Antiochus' hands in 169, until the autumn of 164. Than a palace or Alexandrian plot forced Philometor to flee. Coming to Italy, he made his way on foot to Rome attended by only four attendants, and appealed humbly to the Senate, but as he was back in Alexandria by the spring of 163, the whole episode may not have lasted as long as court storytellers would suggest. Polybius, as a matter of fact, our source for much of the history of this period, is notoriously fond of dramatic or romantic anecdotes of a moral coloring, and must not always be taken literally.

At all events, Philometor brought back a solution of the problem which certainly appealed to the Romans. The realm was divided and Ptolemy. VIII Euergetes went off to the Cyrenaica, where he reigned until his brother's death in 146. There was still trouble between them. Euergetes wished to take Cyprus and even invaded the island, being taken prisoner by his brother and then released. This may have been at the time when Demetrius of Syria was plotting in the island; he may have been working with Euergetes against Philometor. In the next year (154) Euergetes went to Rome to complain, but before going he executed and published a will which has survived on an inscription found in Cyrene. Beginning with the prayer that he might live to get the better of his enemies, he disposed that, in the event of dying childless, he left the Romans as the heirs of his kingdom, and asked them in the meantime to support him by force if he were attacked.[31] A copy of this was taken to Rome, and notice was thus served on Philometor that, if he did procure Euergetes' death, it would do him no good. While this will never came into effect because Euergetes later had children, it served as a model for later bequests to Rome on the part of eastern rulers, and illustrates the intellectual atmosphere of pique or anger in which such ideas arose. Of the internal history of Egypt during this period we are unevenly informed. We hear of a native revolt under a Hellenized Egyptian named Dionysius-Petosiris, a disaffected general and courtier, and the papyri give irregular information of unrest or domestic strife. In particular, Philometor felt compelled to issue in the summer of 163 the first known general amnesty, a type of document (known as *philanthropa*) which appears later in Ptolemaic history, issued by a new king or after a period of trouble as a sign of a new and better era. On the other hand, the policy of ethnic fusion which was to produce a stronger and more uniform Egypt went steadily forward. The archives of a Macedonian private citizen named Ptolemy, a recluse in the Serapeium at Memphis, which cover the years 164-152, show not only friction between himself and Egyptians, official and other, but also his affectionate care for two little Egyptian girls, twin daughters of a woman who had forsaken her husband to follow a Greek soldier.

It is a period when the designations of nationality become simplified and conventionalized with the cessation of immigration and the growth of families of mixed parentage, when a uniform court and archival system is established for both linguistic groups, and when the population loses many of its fixed categories, although the distinction between those in the Land (*chora*) and the citizens of Ptolemais and Alexandria is maintained as strictly as ever. It is a question how far these developments are to be traced either to the weakness, or conversely, to the strength and wisdom of the king. The result was, by and large, good, like the use of the Egyptian phalanx at Raphia and the Egyptianizing of Ptolemy V in the decree of the priestly synod preserved on the Rosetta Stone (196).[32] It was this process of amalgamation, Hellenization and Egyptianization, which helped to preserve the kingdom of the Ptolemies in Egypt longer than any other of the Hellenistic states.

ROME INHERITS PERGAMUM

Significantly, it was the Pergamene state of the Attalids which was the first Asiatic state to succumb. This passed by testamentary succession to Rome in 133 on the death of Attalus III. And yet fifty-five years earlier, at the time of the Peace of Apamea, it had seemed very strong and later escaped the prevailing dangers of dynastic quarrels and regencies for infants. Attalus II was sixty-one when he became king in 159 and had for years been closely associated with his brother Eumenes II, who preceded him, in every area of government. It was neither inexperience nor lack of caution which brought the dynasty to an end. In a letter of Attalus II written at the beginning of his reign and preserved on an inscription from Pessinus, writing to the priest Attis concerning some contemplated military venture, the new king points out that he must undertake nothing without Roman permission, for if he succeeded he would encounter only jealousy, and if he failed he would receive no help, but rather his failure would be welcomed.[33]

Brought up in this atmosphere, the young Attalus III can have been in no doubt as to the means of survival, and he did survive as king until his death after only five years of reign. He was at least twenty-four at his accession and a scientist of sorts, a specialist in poisons and in the culture of herbs, an experimenter in the chemistry of medicine, the author of a treatise on agriculture, and actively interested in sculpture and bronze-casting. It is hard to suppose that he was not older than the tradition states. He died after a brief illness, and he had no son. These were the immediate reasons for designating the Romans as his heirs. But there were other circumstances which made it impossible for the dynasty to continue, even if Attalus had turned to less direct branches of the family for a successor.

The dynasty had rarely been popular with the Greeks, either in Metropolitan Greece or in Asia Minor. The native states of Bithynia, Pontus, and Cappadocia, together with the Seleucid empire, afforded the Greeks the same useful contact with the interior which the Persians had made possible in Achaemenid times, while Ptolemaic control of the coast was for them more often beneficial than oppressive. But the Attalids served no useful purpose except one. They gave protection against the Gauls, and this service, which brought Attalus I the title of king about 230, redounded to the credit of Eumenes and of Attalus in 168-166. The Attalids were generous and their capital was magnificent, and they never failed to emphasize their philhellenic mission. The foundation of national games in honor of Athena Nicephorus, the Bringer-of-Victory, and the construction of the Great Altar of Zeus, one of the wonders of the world, were consequent upon successful wars against Prusias I of Bithynia (186-184; it was in his service that Hannibal died) and Pharnaces of Pontus (183-179).

But all the world knew that Pergamum's greatness was based on Roman support, and the Attalids' possessions were actually granted them by Rome, not independently spear-won. Greece had heaped honors on Eumenes, but when the opportunity came, in 172, all of his monuments were destroyed. This was when Eumenes returned from a mission to Rome, and it was known that he had urged Rome to make war on Perseus. Eumenes' use of Gallic mercenaries in the war which followed must have done nothing to reverse the situation. Significantly, popularity came only briefly to Eumenes toward the end of his Gallic war. He made a personal embassy to the Senate in the winter of 167/6, but when he landed at Brundisium he was ordered not to proceed to Rome but to leave Italy immediately. Humiliated, he returned east, but was met at Delos by a delegation from the Ionian League heaping him with honors, and simultaneously in Greece many of his monuments were rebuilt.[34] All this, however, did the dynasty no real good, for the unpopularity was merely transferred to Eumenes' brother Attalus, Rome's favorite, who succeeded him in 159.

Mithridates VI Eupator

For Rome did not want a strong Pergamum, and the favors shown to Attalus, even the proposal to make him king of a severed half of the kingdom, were designed to weaken the dynasty. The Gauls were declared autonomous after Eumenes had defeated them in 166, and two years later, listening to complaints of Prusias II, the Senate sent out the consular Caius Sulpicius Galus to investigate conditions, and he sat for some days at Sardes, encouraging all who complained about Eumenes. Rome was suspicious of Pergamene eastern policy, as, in 160, her championing of Ariarathes against Orophernes in Cappadocia. Orophernes was the older son of Ariarathes IV, and was supported by Demetrius I of Syria, but his brother had been a student at Athens with Attalus and they were friends.

When Attalus, as king, installed Ariarathes (V) by force, Prusias with Rome's blessing overran Pergamene territory, burning the Nicephorium just outside the city, and it was not until 154 that Rome compelled Prusias to retire to his own territories and make peace. Later, Attalus scored victories in foreign policy in establishing Alexander Balas and Nicomedes (149-128) as kings respectively in Syria and in Bithynia. But both actions may have been welcome at Rome as weakening further the states concerned, and Attalus showed his docility by supporting Rome in Greece, both against Andriscus and at Corinth. The kingdom of Pergamum could have no real strength under such conditions. In 145 the Thracian king Diegylis overran the Chersonese and burned the city of Lysimacheia, and Attalus could do little to hinder him.

This, then, is the background of the decision of Attalus III to extinguish the dynasty and hand his possessions over to Rome. No achievements of domestic or foreign policy are credited to him, and his preoccupation with scientific studies may well have been escapism. One may wonder whether he did not even accomplish his own death, intentionally or not, in the course of some experiment. Rome's pressure on the Greek world was ever increasing, and a buffer king must have been under an almost unbearable strain.

However this may have been, the bequest and its acceptance by Rome proved a great disaster to Asia Minor. A pretender to the throne appeared, one Aristonicus, who claimed to be a member of the Attalid family and called himself Eumenes III. He was accepted at Pergamum, although not generally throughout the Attalid territory. He instituted social reforms similar to those of Cleomenes III of Sparta, notably the freeing and enfranchisement of slaves, perhaps more due to his desperate situation than to political theory, although he called his supporters Heliopolitae, Sun-Citizens. He controlled most of the open country down to Caria and received support from Thracian troops, whether as allies or mercenaries, and held off Roman armies for three years (132-129). Enormous damage was done, and the rich land suffered equally from Aristonicus and from Roman requisitions. Rome was supported by her ally, Mithridates V Euergetes (about 150-120), the son of Pharnaces I and the Seleucid princess Nysa. Curiously enough, he proved to be the major winner in the contest. His father had greatly expanded his kingdom, capturing and making his capital at the great city of Sinope, and Mithridates seized this opportunity to get possession of central Anatolia as far west as Phrygia.

The End of Hellenism

Once more Rome was to illustrate the principle that expansionist powers do not escape their border problems by expanding. With the elimination of the kingdom of Pergamum and the establishment of the Province of Asia (followed later by a Province of Cilicia, concerned primarily with the control of the Cilician pirates) Rome found herself facing a new set of states which furnished new responsibilities. Mithridates V Euergetes was forced to withdraw from his extreme claims, but Pontus remained the strongest of the Anatolian states, followed by Bithynia under Nicomedes II. Between them, on the north coast, lay Paphlagonia, and across the Black Sea, in the Crimea, lay the Bosporan Kingdom under its last king Paerisades, and beyond that, a Scythian state ruled by one Palacus. All, together with the Greek cities of the coast, were under pressure from the Sarmatian tribes of the steppe. In central Asia Minor, the Gauls were weak, but Cappadocia, under Ariarathes VI, was important. And beyond to the southeast lay another splinter state from the Seleucid Empire, Commagene, independent since about 160. Further to the east were Colchis and the other states of the Caucasus, Lesser and Greater Armenia, and in Media and Mesopotamia, the Parthians. Some of these still were outside the Roman sphere of influence, but the reign of Mithridates VI Eupator (121/0-63), Rome's greatest and only voluntary eastern opponent, was to bring them all within it.

Sulla's Defeat of Mithridates

Mithridates' mother Laodice was a half-sister (probably) of his grandmother Nysa; both sprung from full brother-and-sister marriages among the children of Antiochus the Great. Intermarriage between the Mithridatid and the Seleucid dynasties had occurred freely ever since Antiochus II, and Iranian and Macedonian blood was well mixed in both. Antiochus IV was about one-third Iranian, as it may be calculated, and Mithridates Eupator was rather more than half Macedonian (73/128ths, actually). He had more Macedonian blood than Antiochus I. It is perhaps due to this happy mixture of inheritance that Mithridates Eupator owed his brilliant cultural and military abilities, reminiscent of Alexander the Great, and his distinction of being the only Hellenistic monarch to seek a war with Rome. In a conflict which lasted almost thirty years he suffered many reverses as well as winning many victories, but he was never captured or reduced to submission. Against any other opponent he would have found a place in history as a conqueror, and even as it was, his career constitutes the last creditable episode of political Hellenism.

Like Alexander, he became king young, as a boy of eleven years in fact. For a time he was under the tutelage of his mother, but before he was sixteen he succeeded in freeing himself from her and from a younger brother. Like Alexander also, his first concern was to strengthen his kingdom on the north and east, in order to acquire resources of men and materials for the coming struggle. During the first ten years of his unencumbered reign (about 115-105) he extended his territory to the east to include Lesser Armenia and Colchis and perhaps further into the Caucasus, while his able general Diophantus, known only from a long inscription found at Chersonesus, defeated Palacus and the Scythians and annexed the old Bosporan Kingdom as far as Olbia.[35] This was a prize rich in terms of revenues and resources, and it also opened up the recruiting areas of Scythia, Sarmatia, and Thrace. If later on Mithridates could assemble the largest and best armies of the time, this was the reason.

Thereafter Mithridates turned to his major objective. Allied with Nicomedes, Mithridates overran Paphlagonia and Galatia, and these areas were partitioned amicably, but then began a series of rival assaults on Cappadocia, each resulting in a short-lived puppet king. Nicomedes, getting the worst of it, appealed to Rome, and the Senate ordered all captured territory given up, while the nobles of Cappadocia elected their own ruler. But Mithridates tried again, allied now with Tigranes of Armenia who married his daughter Cleopatra. This time Sulla, Roman *propraetor* in Cilicia, intervened with military force (92), and Mithridates saw that operations must be attempted on a larger scale. Four years later, taking advantage of Rome's preoccupation with the Social War and on the basis of extensive preparations, Mithridates struck, and carried all before him.

The moment was favorable. The throne of Cappadocia was still disputed between weak claimants and the young Nicomedes III, who had with Roman help succeeded his father shortly before, was of little consequence. The occasion was just, for the Roman commander in Bithynia had invaded Pontic territory and plundered it. The Romans had furnished a *casus belli,* but they were quite unprepared for the blow which came. In rapid successive victories Mithridates destroyed the Roman military power in the peninsula, and in a well organized campaign, Pontic armies were sent far and wide to receive or compel the adhesion of the cities. Most of these came over voluntarily, a few stood sieges, and in six months all of Asia Minor was in the king's hands, except for the southern coast and such independent cities as Cyzicus. By a concerted plan, all of the Roman or Italian money-lenders and tax-collectors in the former Province were butchered in one day, eighty thousand, it is said. On occasion, they were tortured in ways symbolic of their rapacity by having molten gold or silver poured down their throats. This is testimony to the hatred produced by the Gracchan *lex provinciae* which had opened the Attalid kingdom to Roman greed, but it was planned by Mithridates as a declaration of policy. Previously he had been submissive to Rome, but now he was her open enemy. He was attacking "the common enemy of all mankind" (as he wrote in a letter)[36] and there would be no turning back.

This was the concept behind the invasion of Greece which came in the beginning of 87, after part of the autumn and winter had been spent in a futile siege of Rhodes. However much Greece suffered under the Roman administration, there was no organized resistance to invite Mithridates in the way in which Antiochus III had been invited by the Aetolians.

There is little evidence for conditions in Greece during the preceding sixty years, and what there is is somewhat contradictory. Small towns had tended to disappear, being replaced by the manor houses of large proprietors who felt secure in the general peace. The population in rural areas may have declined, but there was considerable prosperity, and the cities were relatively flourishing. Probably the poor were kept firmly in check while the rich enjoyed Rome's favor. Greece, at any rate, lay under no such *lex provinciae* as afflicted Asia, although Athens, it is true, experienced a revolution, power falling into the hands of one Aristion who led a movement against the propertied classes. Since Rome would not have allowed this situation to continue, Aristion was committed to supporting Mithridates, and the Piraeus became the king's base of operations.

Mithridates did not himself cross the Aegean. Throughout his reign he showed a rare skill at selecting and trusting men of ability, and in the Cappadocian Archelaus he possessed the greatest general of the generation. His strategic plan was a sound one. While the Roman governor in Macedonia was contained by attacks from allied Thracian tribes, an amphibious force under Archelaus was to establish itself in central Greece while the main land army proceeded more deliberately by the coastal route through Thrace. The Pontic fleet was unchallenged at sea, and the army possessed not only a strong cavalry force and numbers of scythed chariots but also highly trained light and heavy infantry, including units made up of freed slaves and Italian refugees from the Social War, who would fight with a fanaticism born of desperation, for they knew that capture meant crucifixion. Mithridates knew that the campaign in Greece was risky and he remembered not only Antiochus the Great but also Dareius and Xerxes. But he realized that only the expulsion of the Romans from the Greek peninsula could bring him any security. His one chance of success lay in boldness and aggressiveness. He very nearly succeeded.

He was defeated by lack of coordination, in part, and in part by the ruthlessness and military genius of the Roman commander

Sulla. The land army did not reach Greece until after Sulla had captured Athens and compelled Archelaus to retire from the Piraeus after a siege lasting all the winter of 87/86. When the land army did arrive, Sulla succeeded in winning two hard-fought battles in Boeotia, in both of which Archelaus displayed great skill and in both of which the decision hung upon a hair. Greece suffered terribly. The treasures of the national shrines, notably Delphi and Olympia, were expropriated, grain requisitioned, food and shade trees cut down, men and animals impressed for combat and support operations. Knowing that his survival at Rome depended on his victory, Sulla let no mercy or no scruple stand in his way. It was Greece's misfortune to support a conflict of giants.

The issue of the war was settled. This was realized by Sulla, by Archelaus, and by Mithridates himself. Although Sulla had no way of getting to Asia without a fleet, and was also awaiting the arrival of an army sent out from Rome by the Marians to displace him, Mithridates began at once to treat with him for peace. Archelaus was as able a diplomat as he was a general, and all proceeded amicably, but he could secure no better terms than the *status quo ante*. Mithridates must surrender all of his conquests, including Paphlagonia, and hand over his fleet. He offered to assist Sulla against his political foes, an offer which may have been neither meant nor taken as insulting. Archelaus declined to enter Roman service, but did accept the gift of some estates in Greece. Characteristically, Roman vengeance was wreaked upon the Greeks, who had been for the most part innocent victims of the whole affair.

The new Roman army played a role which would have been farcical if it had not been so tragic for its victims. The commander, the consul Lucius Valerius Flaccus, had only a small army and prudently avoided Sulla, marching through Thrace so as to invade Asia Minor. On the way he fell to quarreling with his legate, Caius Flavius Fimbria, who maintained no discipline and allowed his troops to plunder as they wished. At Byzantium, which Fimbria's soldiers treated almost as a captured city, the breach became irreparable. Flaccus tried to replace Fimbria, but was himself forced to flee across the straits and was run down and killed at Nicomedeia. Fimbria then brought the whole army into Asia Minor, surprised and defeated a Pontic army, and proceeded to overrun the land, plundering and requisitioning.

Conditions were desperate for the Greeks, already heavily taxed and persecuted by Mithridates, when Sulla's arrival brought peace. Fimbria killed himself, Sulla took his army and turned his attention to the Province of Asia, which was required to pay five years arrears of tribute and the costs of the war. The propertied classes suffered particularly, being subjected to billeting during the winter of 85/84. Each legionary received from his host sixteen drachmae a day and each centurian fifty, in addition to maintenance in luxury and some pilfering. So were the Greeks punished, while Mithridates retired to his kingdom relatively undamaged. Nicomedes and Ariarathes, the ousted kings of Bithynia and Cappadocia, returned to their kingdoms, but with the departure of Sulla's army in 84 there was no real force in existence to keep order. The little fleet of Rhodes could not restrain the pirates, whose depredations added to the economic confusion which made it impossible for the cities to find money to pay the assessment. Delos had been sacked and destroyed by Mithridates, and Italian business moved into the Anatolian cities but did them little good, for these merchants and bankers were not taxable. Instead, the cities were forced to borrow from them at fantastic interest rates to meet their obligations, and the richest part of the Greek world was well started on the road to bankruptcy.

THE END OF THE SELEUCIDS

In the meantime, the once proud state of the Seleucids was going steadily down hill. Demetrius II, king in 145, was young and inexperienced, and his Cretan ministers were unpopular. It was not long before a certain Tryphon, a royal official of unknown origin, raised the banner of revolt in favor of a real or supposed son of Alexander Balas, and was so successful that he killed the young man and took the royal title himself. At the same time the Parthian king Mithridates overran Babylonia, and Demetrius was forced to march to meet him, but ended by being taken captive (139), marrying a daughter of the king, and raising a beard, with which he is portrayed, the first of the dynasty so shown, on his coinage ten years later. He was replaced by his brother, Antiochus VII Sidetes, the last able king of the Seleucid line. Antiochus VII married his brother's wife, Cleopatra Thea, and in a ten year reign

Demetrius II (tetradrachm)

he curbed the independence of the Jews, rebuilt a military power, and launched a great campaign against the Parthians, but the army was surprised in winter quarters (129) and Antiochus was killed. In the meantime, however, Demetrius had been released and returned to Syria, where he reigned until his death in 126. He was succeeded by Cleopatra, who coined in her own name, but after poisoning one son she was herself poisoned by another, who became king as Antiochus VIII Grypus.

For the next generation, the history of the Seleucid house is inextricably entwined with that of the Ptolemies of Egypt. There, on the death of Philometor in Syria in 145, the throne was occupied by his younger brother, Ptolemy VIII Euergetes II, who dated his reign from his coronation in 170. Euergetes killed Philometor's infant son and married his widow and sister, Cleopatra II, later divorcing her and marrying her daughter Cleopatra III, so that the official style was "King Ptolemy and Queen Cleopatra the Sister and Queen Cleopatra the Wife." Ptolemy Euergetes had not been popular in Egypt previously, and he had the misfortune to be very fat. In addition to his nickname Physcon ("pot-belly"), we have the testimony of the philosopher and historian Posidonius of Rhodes, who heard from his teacher Panaetius of a visit to Alexandria with Scipio Aemilianus.[37] The historical tradition about him is almost uniformly unfavorable. He is charged, among other things, with having attacked and expelled the intelligentsia of Alexandria, although he was himself a writer, the author of memoirs.

It is impossible to know what truth there may be in all this. We do know that he did much to promote Ptolemaic trade with the Far East by the Red Sea and the Indian Ocean, and with the West by way of Delos, and was by no means devoid of energy and ability. It is clear that he quarreled with Cleopatra II in about 131, and had to go off to Cyprus, where he remained for two years. After that, for perhaps ten years, Egypt was often or constantly divided between them. Papyri refer to a condition of *ameixia* (lack of communication). But by 118 the brother and sister had made peace, and the event was celebrated by a long amnesty decree, of which a copy was found on a papyrus at the village of Tebtunis.[38] Euergetes died in 116 after the longest reign and one of the longest lives of the Hellenistic monarchs, and left at least a unified country to his eldest son, Ptolemy IX Soter II, but another son and two more daughters were to make trouble in the days to come.

For in Syria there were rival claimants to the throne, Grypus, the son of Demetrius II, and Antiochus IX Cyzicanus, the son of Antiochus VII. Both married daughters of Euergetes II and then each in turn his third daughter, Cleopatra Selene (the Moon). She had previously been the wife of her older brother, Ptolemy IX Soter II, and mother or aunt of Berenice, the wife of her second brother Ptolemy X Alexander I. No one of these was able to command more than local loyalty, and the varying fortunes convert the history of the two dynasties almost into a game of musical chairs among their cities. The Seleucid kingdom was reduced to Syria, since the Parthian power had advanced to the Euphrates and the Jewish state of John Hyrcanus and Alexander Jannaeus occupied practically all of Palestine. Even in Syria the cities were more and more independent, while the Nabataean Arab kingdom under Aretas II occupied the eastern steppe. Egypt was in somewhat better shape, but Cyrene was separated off as a princedom for a third (illegitimate) son of Euergetes, Ptolemy Apion, and on his death in 96 was left as an inheritance to Rome, although Rome waited twenty years to organize it as a province. Cyprus was regularly the residence of the king in exile and so was separated from Egypt in effect, while troubles in Egypt itself culminated in a great revolt in the Thebaid (88-85), finally put down by Soter II with equal ferocity and destructiveness.

Egypt was able to surmount the troubles and confusion of this period with some success, thanks to the ten-year second rule of Soter (89-80), who was skillful enough to avoid involvement in the Mithridatic War. When Sulla's quaestor Lucius Licinius Lucullus came in search of a fleet in the winter of 87/86, he was treated hospitably and forwarded to Cyprus, but nothing was done to compromise the king's position with the Marian government in Italy. Upon Soter's death, Cyprus became practically independent under his younger son, and went its independent way until it was annexed by the Romans in 58, while his elder son, known to history by his nickname Auletes ("the Piper"), held Egypt with varying fortunes for a generation (80-61).

In Syria, however, the remaining Seleucids were too numerous and too weak and too quarrelsome to accomplish anything except the progressive disintegration of the dynasty. Between 83 and 69 the throne was occupied by Tigranes of Armenia, while Seleucid kinglets held isolated cities or languished in exile. When Pompey entered Syria in 64, he refused to recognize Antiochus XIII as king. Wisely so, for he pointed out that this would be only to leave it as prey for Parthians and Arabs and Jews. Although he elsewhere used vassal kings extensively in his settlement of the eastern frontier, he saw that Syria could play a useful role only under the administration of a Roman governor.

POMPEY AGAINST MITHRIDATES

It had waited for Pompey to effect a settlement in the east, for Sulla's victory in Greece and his brief occupation of Asia Minor had not settled anything. When Sulla returned to Italy in 83 he had no leisure to consider the eastern frontier, and at his death in 78 the Peace of Dardanus, which provided at least a *modus operandi*, had never been ratified by Rome. The result was an entirely unjustified invasion of Pontus by the governor of Asia,

Lucius Licinius Murena, and his humiliating defeat (83-82) by Mithridates, who had re-established his authority in Colchis and the Bosporus. Mithridates thus demonstrated again that he was superior to anything except a major Roman effort. The result weakened Roman prestige in the East, and in 78 Tigranes of Armenia, in possession of Cilicia and Syria, overran Cappadocia without Roman interference, to collect inhabitants and treasure for his new capital of Tigranocerta.

Thereafter, their traders and allies suffering from the depredations of the pirates of Cilicia, the Romans put on a flurry of activity. Publius Servilius Vatia conducted a successful campaign in the mountains of Lycia and Isauria (78-76), but the good effect of this was weakened by a disastrous war under Lucius Antonius against the Cretans (74-71). In the meantime, however, the death (74) of Nicomedes III of Bithynia and the Roman decision to convert his kingdom into a province had once more involved Mithridates in hostilities.

It is not clear that Mithridates wished this, although it cannot have been welcome to him to have the Romans permanently established on both sides of the Dardanelles. He intervened in the interest of actual or supposed heirs of Nicomedes, but the rapidity of movement on both sides made them soon forgotten. Mithridates occupied Bithynia without opposition, passing through Paphlagonia and covering his flank by columns in Cappadocia and in Phrygia (against the Gauls). He defeated the provincial governor, Marcus Aurelius Cotta, shut him up in Chalcedon and captured his fleet, but then attempted to capture the free and powerful city of Cyzicus. With its almost invulnerable location, Cyzicus would have given him a naval base of great value.

This proved to be a strategic mistake, however, for the consul Lucullus, who had been given supreme command, moved north from the Province of Asia and besieged Mithridates in his camp. Unable to take Cyzicus by storm and short of supplies, the king had to raise the siege early in 73 with the loss of much of his force, and when he was defeated at sea, he had no choice but to evacuate Bithynia and retire to the east. Cotta and Lucullus followed him, delayed by the resistance of the coastal cities. Heracleia and Sinope held out until 70, in spite of the fact that the issue of the war had really been settled by Roman victories in 72 near Cabeira.

There, Mithridates had won some successes with his cavalry and brought Lucullus into considerable danger, but a partial Roman victory brought panic in the Pontic camp, and Mithridates was compelled to take refuge with Tigranes in Armenia. Lucullus overran Little Armenia, and at the same time his brother Marcus, the governor of Macedonia, defeated and destroyed Mithridates' Thracian and Sarmatian allies as far as the Black Sea, capturing also Callatis, Istrus, and the other Greek cities of the region, which then felt for the first time the force of Roman arms and the rapacity of Roman commanders (72-71).

In the following year Lucullus devoted his attention to the desperate plight of the Greek cities of Asia. He found drastic ways in which they might pay their obligations, it is true, but at the same time he sharply curtailed the demands of the bankers, restricting them to twelve per cent interest and ordering that the total interest in any case should not exceed the value of the original debt. It was a settlement which was perhaps fair, probably workable, and the best which either side could hope for, but it was inevitably unpopular with both. Cicero wrote the same of a similar settlement which he instituted in Cilicia in 50.[39] It gave the cities, at least, the hope of survival, but it made the business class at Rome, the equites or Knights, irrevocably hostile to Lucullus, and they had their revenge three years later.

For Lucullus had, unlike Sulla, attempted to restrict the depredations of his troops, while at the same time he exacted stern discipline and the highest standard of efficiency from them. Part of his army, moreover, was made up of Fimbrian veterans little inclined to be sympathetic with a Sullan commander. He saw that the war was unfinished so long as Mithridates remained free, and in 69 marched into Armenia to compel Tigranes to surrender him. Tigranes was overconfident and under-experienced, and a threat to his capital Tigranocerta brought him with his army to its relief. He was defeated, and Tigranocerta captured. But then troubles began to afflict Lucullus. He tried to march on to the old Armenian capital of Artaxata, but the early arrival of winter and the reluctance of his soldiers compelled him to break off and swing south to Nisibis in Mesopotamia where he wintered (68/67), contemplating a punitive campaign against the Parthians who were Tigranes' allies and weak enough at the moment to make an inviting target. But he had counted Mithridates out too soon. With some support from Tigranes, and taking advantage of Lucullus' preoccupation in another quarter, Mithridates advanced down the valley of the Lycus into his kingdom and was received with acclaim. He defeated the local Roman commander and held Lucullus to a standstill when he came up, for the Roman troops were mutinous and many deserted. This situation prevailed until the beginning of 66, when a new commander arrived.

POMPEY'S SETTLEMENT OF THE EAST

For behind Lucullus' back, so to speak, the Mediterranean world had gotten into a parlous state. For reasons which are not entirely clear, piracy had become general and coordinated from the Levant coast to the Pillars of Hercules at the entrance to the Atlantic, and the alliance which Mithridates had sought from Sertorius in Spain had, even without being formed, become a kind of reality. Rome's business and food supply were alike damaged, if, indeed, the picture painted by the tribune Gabinius in 67 is not to be regarded as wildly exaggerated. It did, at any rate, provide the occasion for giving to Pompey, the champion of the business class, such sweeping powers of command as had never before been granted to any Roman commander. Raising a large army and fleet and apportioning the Mediterranean among his legates, Pompey cleared the sea of the pirates from west to east in a suspiciously easy and rapid campaign ending with the capture of Caracesium in Cilicia, and the war was over. Simultaneously one of the *optimates*, Quintus Caecilius Metellus (later known as Creticus), was fighting a much tougher war to redress the disgrace of Antonius in Crete, a war made none the easier by the interference of Pompey's legate Octavius, and in which Pompey himself later was to dictate the settlement. For the moment, the surrendered pirates were treated sensibly and mildly, being settled in the many cities which suffered from under-population, an evident sign of the times. And for the next year Pompey's *imperium* was extended to the whole of the East.

Lucullus resisted his own replacement, although his legal grounds are not clear, and then departed for Italy. Pompey had fresh troops, enormous prestige, and the backing of the *populares*, and he was also, unlike Lucullus, a diplomat. By promises which, whatever his original intentions, he did not ultimately keep, he persuaded the Parthian king Phraates to break with Tigranes and become a Roman ally. And while Phraates marched on Artaxata and kept Tigranes immobilized, Pompey proceeded against Mithridates. Mithridates used his cavalry and the terrain well, falling back up the Lycus valley to the east, but Pompey was too strong and the Pontic army was caught and defeated. Mithridates was forced to flee to Colchis, for Tigranes was ready to make peace and would not receive him. After taking the surrender of Armenia, Pompey advanced to the Caucasus and wintered in the valley of the Cyrus, skirmishing with the neighboring Albanians. He was preparing triumphs over peoples of whom Rome had never heard.

In 65 Pompey ignored Mithridates, who succeeded in re-establishing himself in the Bosporus, which his son Machares had held since 70 as a Roman vassal. Pompey engaged in desultory operations in the Caucasus, enriching himself and his soldiers and making sure that Phraates did not get into western Mesopotamia, the country of Nisibis and Edessa. In 64 he came down into Syria, putting an end to the Seleucid dynasty and capturing Jerusalem in a three-month seige. He had contemplated a campaign against the Nabataean Arabs, but wisely thought better of it, and then received the welcome news that Mithridates was dead (63). The old king had been killed in an insurrection led by one of his sons, while planning a campaign across the Balkans into Italy. He was magnificent to the end, but his family and his supporters were tired.

This cleared the way for Pompey to make the general settlement of the East which he was authorized to do under the terms of the Manilian · Law. Here he showed himself a great statesman, for the plan lasted in general pattern throughout the Empire. It was a combination of provinces and of buffer vassal states, reaching out to the highlands of Media and the steppe country of Mesopotamia and of South Russia, which provided a kind of natural frontier. Crete and Syria became provinces, and the boundaries of Bithynia and of Cilicia were extended, so that most of Asia Minor west of the Halys was directly administered. Beyond lay the cordon of dependent kingdoms or principalities, beginning in the north with the Crimea under Mithridates' revolted son Pharnaces, and continuing with Colchis, Iberia, Albania, eastern Pontus (under the Gallic chieftain Deiotarus), Armenia, Galatia, Cappadocia, Commagene, and Osrhoene. Syria was rimmed on the east with little princedoms, and Aretas III of the Nabataeans received Damascus as a reward for his submission. Hyrcanus, the elder son of Alexander Jannaeus, received Judaea with the title of High Priest but not king, but Pompey freed the coastal cities which Alexander Jannaeus had come to control. In general, Pompey anticipated the Roman Empire in his policy of favoring the Greek or Hellenized cities, recognizing many of them as *liberae* (free) if only very few as *immunes* (not liable to tax). Taxation continued to be a serious burden, especially as collected by the *publicani*, but the Greeks could have lived under the system if they had been left in peace. In many ways, Pompey's settlement continued or recreated many of the features of the Seleucid system, which itself owed much to that of the Achaemenian Persians.

THE ROMAN CIVIL WARS

Unfortunately for the east, however, it was not yet to be left in peace. There were at most brief periods of respite, as between 63 and 58, a period of peace interrupted by a disastrous Thracian war undertaken by the governor of Macedonia, Lucius Calpurnius Piso. This was preceded, especially in Greece, by recruiting and requisitions accompanied by billeting and pillaging, and followed by a barbarian invasion. The free ally Byzantium suffered especially, and the lasting consequence was the establishment of a unified Thracian kingdom under King Byrebista, with whom the Romans, somewhat unwillingly, found it possible to remain at peace. Later there were Parthian raids into western Mesopotamia and Syria such as preoccupied Cicero during his proconsulship in Cilicia in 51, and more seriously in 41-38 under Pacorus and the Roman renegade Quintus Labienus, when the Parthians penetrated deep into Asia Minor. These were damaging, but hardly more so than Antony's counterattack of 36-33 and his Armenian campaign of the following year, with the inevitable special taxes, requisitions, and impressments.

Even more damaging, of course, were the Roman civil wars. When Caesar fought the Pompeians (49-47), when Caesar's heirs fought his assassins (43-42), and when Octavian fought Antony (33-31), the fighting took place largely in Greece, but all other parts of the Hellenistic world, notably Asia Minor and Syria, were squeezed dry of resources, either as emergency contributions or as punishment for having, of necessity, supported the other side. The vassal princes suffered equally with the Greek and Hellenistic cities, and usually tried to ride out the storm with as little commitment as possible. It was exceptional when Pharnaces, Mithridates' son, tried to recover his father's Pontic possessions in 47, only to be defeated and driven out by Caesar in the brief campaign of which Caesar reported in only three words: *veni, vidi, vici* ("I came, saw, conquered.").

Otherwise the East experienced the normal or abnormal greed of the provincial governors, the burden of Roman taxation, and the exactions of the bankers. Cicero reported in letters from his province how an agent of Brutus had used Roman cavalry to collect a debt owed by the people of Salamis in Cyprus, shutting up the members of the council in the council chamber until some of them died of starvation. He referred to his predecessor, Appius Claudius, as having "starved the province, let blood, tried reducing treatment, and handed it on" to him "drained of life." He explained to his brother Quintus, governor of Asia, that "to conduct yourself so as to satisfy the *publicani*, expecially when they took over the collection of taxes at a loss, and at the same time not to permit the ruin of the allies, seems to demand a sort of divine excellence."[40]

Cicero himself was exceptional if he forewent, as he claimed, gifts of statues and of money from the cities, paid the billeting expenses of his troops out of income, and took measures to reduce interest rates and even capital on outstanding debts. Yet even he admitted to shifting the financial burden, in part, on to wealthy Greeks who were "persuaded" to admit malfeasance in office. Peace was no easy period, and it was only worse, not different, when Brutus and Cassius required Asia to pay ten years' taxes in one, while Antony regarded himself as moderate in only asking for nine years' taxes in two.

THE LAST OF THE PTOLEMIES

During much of the period, Egypt lay outside of the area of

Roman administration, and seemed to be the happiest of the Hellenistic monarchies as well as the longest lasting. This was due, however, rather to Roman hesitation to allow any individual the credit and the profit of moving against her than to scruple or to lack of interest. With the death of Sulla's protégé Ptolemy Alexander II in 80 after a reign of only nineteen days, Rome regarded the throne as vacant, but permitted the Alexandrines to make Ptolemy XII Auletes king on sufferance, while a younger brother was king in Cyprus. In 59, Auletes persuaded Caesar as consul to secure him recognition as king, but this did not prevent the Romans from annexing Cyprus the following year, and the achievement of recognition cost Auletes so much money that he had to go into exile.

He spent 58 and 57 in Rome subsisting on loans from the banker Rabirius Postumus, while a Pontic princeling named Archelaus ruled in Egypt as the consort of Auletes' daughter Berenice. Auletes was restored in 55 by Pompey's friend Aulus Gabinius, governor of Syria. Gabinius was tried and condemned for this the next year in Rome, but Rabirius the banker came to Egypt and became finance minister (*dioiketes*), in which capacity he probably enriched himself rather than the crown. Little is known of internal affairs in Egypt at this time, but they can hardly have been flourishing. There was much temple building, however, and there is little indication of unrest. The Thebaid seems to have been constituted a separate major division of the kingdom, under a governor Callimachus who acted with considerable independence; but it is hard to say whether this is a sign of strength or of weakness.

The last independent reign of the Ptolemaic dynasty is the one which is most famous for its romantic aspects, but one of the hardest to understand. Cleopatra VII was queen in her own right, although first one and then the other of her younger brothers was associated with her on the throne. Her father Auletes was known as a bastard; that is, his mother was not the sister-wife of Soter II but (presumably) a Greek courtesan. If Cleopatra's mother was Auletes' sister, as is likely, Cleopatra may be conjectured to have been one-half Greek, three-eighths Macedonian, and one-eighth Iranian, inheriting a vast ambition and political ability from the one line, charm and versatility from the other. She is credited with

Cleopatra VII

an insatiable curiosity into all technical and scientific matters and with the ability to learn languages, and she was the first Ptolemy to speak Egyptian. She could entertain, counsel, and doubtless advise two of the foremost Romans of her time. Twice she came near to becoming queen of the inhabited world, failing once by the assassination of Caesar and once by the ultimate incompetence of Antony. She bore them both sons, and made Caesarion joint ruler with her in Egypt, she as queen of kings and he as king of kings, while her sons by Antony became respectively king of Armenia and king of Syria. But all of this finally came to nothing, and it was her daughter by Antony, also called Cleopatra, who as the wife of King Juba of Mauretania continued the royal title in the family for two more generations.

Under her reign (61-30) Egypt was able to maintain something of a balance in the first civil war, helping Pompey but not much. Her brother was responsible for the murder of Pompey after Pharsalus, for in the summer of 48 Cleopatra was a refugee, trying to return to Alexandria with an army of Arab mercenaries. When Caesar arrived she was smuggled in to him and received his support, sharing with him the perils of the Alexandrian War when their small force was besieged in the royal palace until the arrival of Mithridates of Pergamum with reinforcements. She followed Caesar to Rome and was a well-known if not popular member of Roman society until his assassination in 44, when she returned to Egypt hastily with Caesarion. She did nothing to help Caesar's heirs until after Philippi, but met Antony at Tarsus in 41 and brought him back to Egypt with her. He was away from 40 to 36, but then returned to stay, and she was his adviser, assistant, and companion during his eastern campaigns and on to Actium.

How much she helped him or hindered him, what were her ambitions for him or for herself, how far she or he were moved by sentiment or passion and how far by deliberation and plan, all these are questions unanswered in antiquity and unanswerable now. For the record, while full, is both romantic and hostile. There is no doubt that the roles of Dionysus and of Isis, which may have seemed genuine or desirable to Antony and Cleopatra and to many of their associates and subjects, would have been repulsive to many Romans and Greeks too. Equally uncertain is the role of Cleopatra at Actium, where she commanded the Egyptian squadron in person and is at least reported to have led the flight. Certainly the fleet of Antony did not put up much of a fight, while his army was hardly engaged. Was this due to ineptitude or to treachery? All that is certain is that the battle was lost and Antony and Cleopatra returned to Alexandria, to be followed in the summer of 30 by Octavian who penetrated Egypt without difficulty and shut up his opponents in their palace. Antony committed suicide, and so did Cleopatra a little later, destroying herself, it was said, by the bite of the royal asp whose poison made one immortal. Octavian waited methodically for the beginning of the Egyptian year (1 Thoth = 29 August) to declare the monarchy at an end.

So only then at length did the Hellenistic World have the peace which it needed to recover, and under Augustus, the policies which Caesar had inaugurated between 46 and 44 were put into effect. The imperial administration became equitable and endurable. Trade, commerce, and agriculture could prosper, depopulated and destroyed cities could be rebuilt, and with the spread of citizenship and the reduction of privilege the gap between

Greek and Roman was bridged. While Rome became now the unquestioned capital, the great cities of the East entered upon a new era of cultural and material prosperity. It is idle to speculate what the Hellenistic World would have become without Rome. Its struggle with Rome for two hundred years affected deeply not only its political and economic history but also its mental, religious, and artistic development. And in the end it found it possible to fulfill its destiny as a part of the Roman Empire. The inexorable ferment of Hellenism continued. The end of political Hellenism was only the beginning of a new phase of cultural Hellenism.

Chapter Three

Social and Economic Aspects
of the Hellenistic Period

1. The Social Aspects

The Hellenistic World was created by the conquests of Alexander the Great, and became the scene of a vast interplay of populations and cultures. The end-product was not to be achieved before the Roman Empire and not even then completely, but the direction in which the process tended was that of the creation of a homogeneous population, speaking or at least understanding the Greek language and enjoying a common culture. This culture would contain not only features and institutions inherited from Greece or from the Orient, but also new elements developed within its frame, answering to the needs of the region and of its people. In the three centuries of Hellenism a counter-tendency making against uniformity, namely particularism or nationalism, occurred only in Judaea in the time of the Maccabees and less markedly in the Iranian world, where Elamites, Persians, and most successfully Parthians accomplished a political independence including and partly based upon the consciousness of a national culture. And yet neither the Jews nor the Iranians escaped the influence of Hellenism, just as they did not fail to influence it.

This process of social and cultural contact took place in a number of ways. Most obvious and best known of these was the migration of Hellenized Macedonians and Greeks from metro-

politan Greece and the coastal cities of Thrace and Asia Minor into
the new kingdoms of Asia and Egypt, and at a later period, in a
somewhat similar way, into Italy. They migrated in a variety of
capacities, as soldiers, officials, technicians, writers or artists, or
business men. Some attached themselves to the courts of kings or
satraps, protégés of the great or themselves great. Some became
permanent members of the new standing armies, either in the field
or lodged in military settlements, or secured irregular service as
mercenaries. Many settled in the newly founded cities of the
Seleucids or in the villages in Egypt. Many became rich; some
continued in a humble station as laborers or servants. All,
however, were in some degree bearers of the Greek language and
Greek culture, and all learned from their environment.

The New Cities

The most interesting and the most important of these events is
the establishment of new cities or of Hellenic colonies in the
Oriental countryside. The total movement of Macedonians was not
large. There were probably no more than twenty-five thousand
Macedonian soldiers in Asia at Alexander's death, and some of
these returned later with Craterus and Antipater. And after 321
there can have been very little further migration. There cannot
have been more than a handful of Macedonian women with the
troops, for the soldiers typically married Asiatic wives, and the
later "Macedonians" who appear in Hellenistic armies over the
next three centuries are either descendants of these mixed marriages or merely soldiers organized and armed in Macedonian
fashion. The great men in the service of the kings, like Aristodicides of Assus with Antiochus I, Apollonius and Zenon of
Caunus with Ptolemy II,[41] and Aristolochus with Seleucus IV,
were few and wealthy and of little demographic importance.
Mercenaries, the *milites gloriosi* of the contemporary stage, would
commonly return to their original homes when their service was
up, with money in their pockets from pay or booty and with
stories to tell, and if they stayed in Asia or Egypt it was because
they joined the stable Greek communities which already existed.

These communities were of a number of types. Some were
quite new, like Alexandria in Egypt, Antioch, Seleucia, Apamea,
and Laodicea in northern Syria, and Seleucia in Babylonia, and of

Tyche of Antioch

their settlement we can form an opinion from the description in Arrian of Alexander's eastern settlements.[42] Walls and a few essential buildings were erected and a Greco-Macedonian citizen population assembled from any available source, partly at least from military veterans or invalids. Then a free native population was introduced to take care of the economic life of the town, and a complement of slaves and agricultural serfs provided. The city's residents consisted, then, of three separate and supporting elements, as at Athens earlier and as provided on theoretical grounds by Plato in the Laws.

But only in exceptional circumstances did the original citizens have Greek wives. Although Greek women were certainly brought out later, the term half-barbarian (*mixobarbaros*) applied later to Antioch must have been applicable in some degree to all such cities. On occasion, as an inscription informs us, this original Hellenic population might be augmented by colonists from an older city. The people of Antioch in Persis, probably near Busire on the Persian Gulf, thank Magnesia on the Maeander for having sent them, on the invitation of Antiochus I, "numerous and excellent men" who certainly brought their families with them, thus increasing the Hellenic element in the blood of future citizens.[43]

More information on the Seleucid city foundations in Iran is becoming available. A Laodiceia has been identified at Nehavend, on the route across the Zagros Mountains from Ecbatana to the Tigris valley and Seleucia on the Tigris, at a point where a route to the south branched off leading to Persepolis. This was a position of strategic importance, guarding these routes and the open country to the west around the modern Kermanshah. A royal edict of Antiochus III concerning the establishment of a satrapal cult of his queen Laodice was communicated to the city by the satrap Menedemus, who from his seat at Ecbatana had a general oversight over the eastern, or "Upper," satrapies. He wrote to a certain Apollodotus and the magistrates and the city of the Laodiceians, who had accordingly not only a civic organization but also a royal resident who presumably exercised some oversight over the city administration as well as commanding garrison troops.[44] This is precisely the situation which we find later in the west, at Seleucia in Pieria and elsewhere, testifying to a uniformity of administrative practice in the kingdom.[45]

Of equal interest is the information which inscriptions furnish from a city of unknown name located at the site known as Aï Khanum, on the left bank of the Oxus River where it breaks out of the mountains. This was a strategic site also, protecting the eastern flank of the satrapy of Bactria. Remains of a palace and a gymnasium have been found dating to the early third century, as well as the tomb (heroon) of the city's founder Cineas, whose name indicates that he was of Thessalian origin. An epigram records the visit to the city of a certain Clearchus, presumably the scholar and traveler Clearchus of Soloi, who inscribed beside it a Delphian maxim, giving the qualities appropriate to various ages. These were, in youth propriety, in young manhood self-control, in manhood justice, and in age wise council. Whether Cineas founded the city in the service of Alexander or the first Seleucus is unknown, but the visit of Clearchus shows that even these remote towns kept in close touch with the culture of the homeland.[46]

A different situation prevailed when a smaller number of Greeks were introduced into a pre-existing native city. This was true of such places as Pergamum, Sardes, Magnesia by Mount Sipylus, and Tarsus. Three of these were great administrative centers, with a garrison and a bureaucracy, but Tarsus received a dynastic name (Antioch) and so must have had some kind of civic organization and citizen body, while Magnesia had only units of the Seleucid regular field army brigaded in it. In the time of Seleucus II, Smyrna gave praise and the right of citizenship to the "military settlers (katoikoi) in Magnesia, cavalry and infantry, to those who are camped outside the city, and to the other inhabitants," as an inscription informs us.[47] While these katoikoi were regular troops, not soldiers responsible for and benefiting from the cultivation of plots of land, like the clerouchoi in Athens and in Egypt, they exercised some political functions, since they were rewarded in this instance for having supported Seleucus' cause. They seem to have been expected to remain permanently or indefinitely in the city and certainly had with them wives and families, whether or not of Greek blood. In all of these cases, the cities developed in the course of the Hellenistic period into normal-appearing Greek cities, complete with magistrates, a council, an assembly, courts, and the other typical institutions of the polis.

The situation in Egypt was different in form because Egypt was not a land of cities, and the Greeks, soldiers or otherwise, lived in villages in the country. But the demographic process was the same. Although most married Egyptian women, a few of them had Greek wives, and they formed social and religious communities based not on the village but on ethnic groups. They had no common political activity, but otherwise lived much as did the Greeks in the new cities, with their schools, festivals, clubs, and social life. Like the cities, they spread Greek language and culture, but they also absorbed native attitudes, especially in religion. They might maintain the cult of imported Greek divinities, but as pagans they worshipped also the local gods of the land. And as everywhere in the Hellenistic World, they supported the cult of the dynastic families, either organized and prescribed for them or on an informal, voluntary basis. And with generations of inter-marriage, the Hellenic blood became more and more diluted.

There were other situations also. Not all of the new cities were Hellenic. Dura-Europos on the mid-Euphrates, a fortress-city known almost solely from the excavations of the French Academy and Yale University between 1922 and 1937, was settled by Macedonians, and not by Greeks. The citizen group remained distinct for five hundred years, even though intermarrying with native Aramaic women, but the institutions were not those of a Greek city. The community was headed by a hereditary or elected general and there were none of the usual Greek civic magistrates, no council, no gymnasium or theater. But Greek education was carried on, and Greek or Hellenistic civil law was maintained with archivists and judges.[48]

Hellenization of the Natives

Side by side with this settlement of Greeks in the new world of Alexander's conquests, with the resultant influence both on them and on their new environment, went a Hellenization of the natives of the new lands, Iranian, Semitic, and Egyptian. From the beginning, following Alexander's example, both Seleucids and Ptolemies employed natives in positions of high responsibility, not merely in the lower administrative posts where their knowledge of the languages and of the traditional methods of the area made it

Plan of Hellenistic Dura-Europus

inescapable that most if not all of the previous officials would have been continued in their employment. In general, the top military and financial positions were reserved for Macedonians or Greeks, and as these had no inclination to learn new languages, it was necessary for the native bureaucrats to Hellenize. This meant something more than merely learning to speak Greek. The author of a well-written letter in the archives of Zenon of Caunus complains of mistreatment and discrimination against him "be-cause I do not know how to Hellenize";[49] and he was clearly one of Zenon's trusted agents in Syria. His name, which has not been certainly read, was probably Aramaic. He lacked the background and probably the manners of the Greeks, and they did not accept him as one of themselves.

The same process of Hellenization occurred in the lesser states also, Pergamum and particularly Bithynia, Pontus, and Cappa-docia, where the ruling families and their nobles (the so-called Friends and Relatives) became bilingual and doubtless in later generations exclusively Greek-speaking, so that Attalus II and Archelaus V were fellow-students together in Athens under the Academic philosopher Carneades. In the later Ptolemaic period many high posts were held by persons with Egyptian names. These would probably have been persons with no Greek blood, and it is impossible to suppose that Paos, for example, who commanded the Thebaid under Euergetes II and had high Greek military and administrative officials under him was not accepted as fully Hellenized in all senses of the word.[50]

But this process spread further. There is no doubt that much of the native population of such cities as Tarsus became gradually assimilated into the citizen body, and were in the end indis-tinguishable from the rest.[51] Many intellectuals and wealthy persons acquired a Greek schooling, and writers such as Manetho in Egypt and Berossus in Babylon were not unique. Liberalism, rationalism, Greek gaiety and excitement had an attraction all the greater because this was the culture of the ruling class, and the new ideas did even more than permeate native mentality. Native cities wished to become *poleis,* at least in superficial form and perhaps in spirit. When under Antiochus IV Babylon and Jeru-salem became Antiochs, they were only following the trend of the times. And even though in Judaea a religio-nationalistic movement swept away much of the Greek surface, the resultant monarchy was quite typically Hellenistic in form and spirit, and Alexander Jannaeus, in particular, continued to wage with the Pharisees the same struggle as the Seleucids had waged with their predecessors, the "activists."

Migrating Individuals

Nor was it only the Greeks and Macedonians who migrated. Large numbers of persons from the periphery of the Aegean World now moved into it in one capacity or another. The Hellenistic armies were filled with foreigners. From Europe came Thracians, Tralians, Paeonians, Agrianians, Epirotes, Illyrians, Scythians, and Sarmatians. From Asia Minor came Bithynians, Mysians, Lydians, Carians, Lycians, Pamphylians, Pisidians, Cilicians, Phrygians, and persons from Paphlagonia, Pontus, and Cappadocia. Their military service and travel, and in many cases their eventual return home, were a large factor in the Hellenization of their Anatolian lands. Gauls came both from Thrace (the kingdom of Tylis) and from Galatia in Asia Minor. Phoenicians served in fleets and Syrians in armies as a matter of course, since they belonged to the Hellenistic World. So also did the Jews, but less closely, and the Idumaeans and Arabs lay rather outside it. In addition to Medes, Persians, and Babylonians, who were integral parts of the Seleucid Empire, Indians served widely, especially as the trainers and mahouts of Indian and African war elephants. From the south came Libyans, Ethiopians, Blemmyes, Nubians, and others, and from the west came, in addition to the Greeks of Magna Graecia, Iapygians, Campanians, Lucanians, Etruscans, and even in the last period an occasional Roman.

In addition, in smaller numbers but even more importantly, came traders. Here, the liveliest picture is furnished by the inscriptions of Delos in its time as an Athenian colony and Roman free port (168-88).[52] In addition to the large numbers of Roman and Italian merchants who resided and traded there, there were Greeks from all over the Hellenistic World. There were many Alexandrians, but also Syrians and Phoenicians, Nabataeans, Minaeans, and Gerrhaeans who brought with them their interests in the trade with the Far East, especially the handling of spices and incense required for the table and for cult purposes. Some of these spices originated in India (notably pepper) and reached the Hellenistic World overland or by sea to the Persian Gulf or southern Arabia, whence they joined Arabian frankincense and myrrh in the movement north by caravan to outlets in Palestine or the Ammonitis.

In the course of the second century, as Italy and particularly the city of Rome enriched themselves with the spoil of East and West, these areas became major purchasers of the wares of the Hellenistic and more distant East, so that merchants and bankers began to establish themselves there. This was a counter-trend to the flow of Roman and Italian bankers to the East, and was certainly much smaller in volume, but it was another contribution to the spread of Hellenism. The earlier influence of the East and specifically of Greece on Rome and Italy was clearly very great, exercised partly directly, partly through the Greek cities of Sicily and southern Italy, partly through the Etruscans. Now came the influence of what we may call Hellenistic Hellenism. The constant stream of embassies from cities and kings ever flowing into Rome was certainly influential, following upon the demonstrable influence of Greek ideas and models upon Roman literature, Roman religion, and Roman law. We have only to recall the momentous visit of the heads of the Attic philosophical Schools, Carneades, Critolaus, and Diogenes, to Rome in 155. There must have been a considerable movement of Greek scholars, artists, and wealthy persons to Rome as visitors, teachers, or technicians.

But, since Rome itself was not always hospitable to non-citizen residents, it is likely that this flow of persons from East to West was not large until the center of this trade shifted to Italian ports. This shift came with the break-up of the commercial colony at Delos in 88, and trade moved notably to Puteoli in Campania where there was a certain concentration of Phoenician and Arabian merchants, who maintained close relations with their homes. By the end of the Hellenistic Period there was a substantial Jewish colony in Italy and even in Rome, a circumstance which accounts for the rapid establishment of Christianity in that city.

Slavery

But most of the Greeks, Orientals, and other Hellenized persons who came to Rome and Italy came as slaves, just as great

numbers of Scythians, Thracians, Gauls, Anatolians, and Semites
had come first into the Aegean area and then into the wider
Hellenistic World as slaves. Both in the East and in the West, these
persons and their descendants, if any, remained permanently as
slaves or as freedmen. The difference between East and West was
that, in general, freed Greek slaves assumed the status of metics,
while the freed Roman slaves became Roman citizens and could
rise progressively from *liberti* to *liberi* until with several generations their servile ancestry might be forgotten altogether. We have
few reliable statistics concerning slavery at any period in antiquity,
but there is no doubt that slavery was accepted as a normal and
unquestioned aspect of life in the Greek and Hellenistic world and
that slaves were numerous.[53]

It is instructive to read Plautus' play, *The Captives,* wherein
the son of an Aetolian, Hegio, had been kidnapped by a runaway
slave, taken to Elis across the Corinthian Gulf, and sold into
slavery. Thereafter this son, ignorant of his parentage, accompanied his young Elian master in a war against the Aetolians. (This
may have been about 241, when the Aetolians took Phigaleia away
from Elis, and before the Elians entered into the Aetolian
alliance.) Both young men were taken prisoner and bought by
Hegio as a possible way of recovering his lost son, but he had no
way of knowing which of the two was previously free and which
was slave, and they actually reversed their roles to deceive him.
The plot ends, of course, with all being recognized and regaining
their freedom, but it is amusing and instructive to see how the
overseer (*lorarius,* himself a slave or perhaps freedman) of Hegio
addresses the young men philosophically:

> *Si di immortales id voluerunt, vos hanc aerumnam exsequi,*
> *decet id pati animo aequo: si id facietis, levior labos erit.*
> > *domi fuistis, credo, liberi:*
> *nunc servitus si evenit, ei vos morigerari mos bonust*
> *et erili imperio eamque ingeniis vostris lenem reddere.*

"Since it is the will of the gods that you have fallen into this
misfortune, you should bear it with calmness; that will be easier
for you. I suppose that you were free men at home. If, now,
you are slaves, it is good manners to adjust yourself to this and

to your master's orders, and so make your condition bearable by adopting the right mental attitude."

It is in the master's interest to speak so, of course. The slave, whom Aristotle called "a living utensil," was useful to the extent that he was cooperative. Nevertheless in Stoic doctrine slavery was purely an external matter, one of those conditions which were indifferent, not affecting the real self which was the soul. Everyone who was not wise was really a slave, and only the wise were free, regardless of anyone's legal status. This attitude had a doctrinal basis, of course, but as a social point of view it is explained by the commonness and the unpredictability of slavery, which might happen to anyone. Plato and Aristotle believed that they could save the utility and avoid the impropriety of the institution by ruling that no Greek should be a slave: all slaves should be "barbarians." But who was Greek and who was barbarian? Isocrates based the difference on culture, not on ethnic origin, and this concept found its fruition in the Hellenistic period, when Greek culture became, to some degree, universal, and purity of blood could not be counted upon by anyone outside a few old Hellenic centers.

Egypt was an exception. Alexandria certainly had slaves in large numbers derived from everywhere, but slaves did not occur in Egypt itself, except rarely and in small numbers as the body-servants or concubines of Greeks or Macedonians, civilian or military. Egyptians themselves were not enslaved, except possibly in the rarest of instances on account of sale in satisfaction of a debt, and no such instance is actually known. In the same way, Ptolemy II ordered in a decree preserved on a Vienna papyrus that no Palestinian should be enslaved, apart from one category: all so held must be reported and released immediately, except for women who were the consorts of soldiers.[54] Presumably also the other Hellenistic kingdoms tried to keep their peasants and workers out of the hands of slave dealers. They probably succeeded fairly well before the advent of the Romans and their purveyors, the pirates, when Nicomedes of Bithynia complained to Rome that half of his subjects had been kidnapped and sold.

But outside of these states the business of the kidnapper or purchaser (for many children were sold into slavery by their parents, and local chiefs may well have sold likewise troublesome subjects or chance visitors) was active as it had always been, especially in the Black Sea region and (to a lesser extent) in the South and East, for Babylonian or Negro slaves were highly valued. War also might always be a fruitful source of slaves, for slavery was commonly the lot of prisoners, and this feature of warfare, rather latent in the third century, became horribly prominent with the advent of Roman armies in the East. From the First Macedonian War on the Romans showed a merciless commercial attitude not only to captured soldiers but to the populations of captured cities as well. It was quite in keeping with Roman standards when Lucius Aemilius Paullus took as slaves one hundred and fifty thousand Epirotes in 167. These numbers did not satisfy the increasing demands of Roman luxury and Roman commercial agriculture, however, and it was in the days of pirate raids, when no ship and no coastal town was safe from them, that Delos boasted of its capacity to clear ten thousand slaves through its auction blocks in a single day.

It is not, however, with the humanitarian or the economic aspect of slavery that we are now concerned, but with the sociological and demographic. By and large it is evident that the arrival and employment of large numbers of foreign slaves in the Greek world contributed to the process of Hellenization. With the exception of the mines, where intractable slaves worked with criminals under conditions such that they could survive only a few years, the farms, factories, and homes where slaves were employed gave them opportunity and indeed required them to learn "to Hellenize." Probably the most favored slaves were Greeks, but many young, intelligent, and attractive "barbarians" must have been trained and employed by their masters. Ultimately, many were given the opportunity to marry, take a salaried position, buy their freedom, and become something similar to what the Romans called "clients" to their former owners. Plato describes such an institution in the Laws, and his picture must be based upon or similar to existing Greek practices. There is no question about the Hellenism of the native women held as slave-wives by the soldiers of the Hellenistic armies. The most famous of these, the Syrian named Elaphion known from two papyri of 285/4 from upper Egypt, seems to have had a business of her own supplying such girls at high prices to the soldiers.[55] Such a business might be viewed askance by strict moralists, but many a Greco-Egyptian in later times traced his origin back to such unions.

If slavery served a civilizing purpose in the Hellenistic world, how much more was this true in Rome and Italy! The slaves who came to the West in vast numbers were either Greek or Hellenized. It is impossible to determine their numbers, but the flow at its height must have run to several hundred thousand in one year, and over the two hundred years from 229 to 30 it is hard to suppose that fewer than several million came in all, and perhaps several tens of millions. These did not, typically, find their way to the chain-gangs of the *latifundia* in Sicily and Italy but came to the cities and primarily to Rome, and in the course of time, slave or freed, must have come to constitute a major element in the Italian cities.

At Rome and as citizens the freedmen were concentrated in two of the four urban tribes, but they can have made up much of the audience to which appealed the Hellenized plays of Plautus and Terence. Later, they would have been in the assembly which supported the reform measures of the Gracchi, themselves advised by a Greek philosopher from the Italian city of Cumae. These slaves were by no means all women or children or uncultured male adults. Many were highly educated — doctors, scientists, literary men, philosophers — and as such found their way into close association and intimacy with wealthy Romans. The Hellenophile circle of the younger Scipio and Laelius, to which Polybius belonged, must have included many such. It was only luck that Polybius himself came to Rome as a free hostage and not as a slave, although he afterwards stayed as a friend.

These, then, were the means by which Hellenism spread, both in the East and South and in the West. It spread both by migration and cross-breeding and by education, formal and accidental. The result was a long step in the direction of a homogeneous race and culture in the Near East and the development of one generally understood language, the Common (*Koine*) Greek. This was used throughout the area beside Egyptian and Aramaic and Iranian and more limited local languages. In the West, Latin, the language of the conquering tribe, retained its supremacy, but Greek became widely known also, and the culture of the Romans became so permeated with Greek and Hellenistic elements that it is difficult in many areas to know what actually remains of a traditional Roman character. Vergil can refer to Rome's capacity to conquer and to rule, but to little else characteristically Roman.

2. The Economic Aspects

The Trading Area

In its economic aspects the Hellenistic World represents more a continuation of existing procedures on an accel_rated or amplified scale, rather than anything specifically new. Greek trade had already been conducted throughout the Mediterranean area on the basis of bottomry loans and bills of exchange. Ships were of good size, up to perhaps a thousand tons burden, and were propelled by lateen sails and guided by celestial navigation. While their operation was restricted to the summer season when the seas were smooth and the winds favorable, they were capable of sailing night and day on direct courses and at good speeds. At the major ports they connected with the routes leading from the interior, either rivers as in Gaul, South Russia, and Egypt, or caravan routes as in the East. There was, perhaps, little progress toward the formation of large companies of merchants or ship-owners, but shippers and traders had wide commercial relationships. While the variety of commodities was not large, business was active and substantial. Most of the cargoes were primary materials like foodstuffs, metals, lumber, stone, or, on the other hand, precious objects of small bulk like metal work, fine pottery, jewelry, imported incense, ivory, precious and semi-precious stones, and perhaps Chinese silk. This basic pattern of trade was continued in the third and subsequent centuries on a larger scale but with little essential change.

For the empires of Alexander and of the Hellenistic monarchies had widened the area known to and accessible to Greek merchants, but had not brought direct contact with basic new areas of production. The tin of Britain, the amber of the Baltic, the gold of central Asia, the silk of China, the spices of India and of southern Arabia, and the ivory and ebony of Ethiopia were still outside reach, still must be brought into Greek hands by foreigners. Access was easier and more frequent, certainly, and in other fields also the Greeks and their Hellenized associates could travel

further, easier, faster, and less expensively. Wheat now entered the
Aegean markets more plentifully than before, as Asia Minor, Syria,
and especially Egypt entered the market as suppliers, so that grain
shortages occurred only in times of political disturbance. Philip V
(and certainly he not alone) stored grain in warehouses against a
time of need. The bountiful export of Egyptian papyrus led
directly to the wide-spread establishment of civic archives and
private and public libraries. Fine woolen or linen stuffs or
clothing, embroidered or dyed with the sea-purple or less precious
tints, appeared on the market in quantity from the coastal cities of
Egypt, Anatolia and Phoenicia, and were soon joined by products
of a native silk industry in Cos and the Levant. Vessels of precious
metals appear beside those of clay and led to new styles, Megarian
and Samian, with appliqué decoration and brown or greyish color
in imitation of bronze, silver, or gold. Glass beads and bowls and
flasks, often gaily decorated in bright colors, were plentifully
manufactured in Egypt, in Syria and finally in Italy, especially
after the discovery of the technique of glass-blowing in the first
century B.C.

Slaves, on the other hand, were probably less plentiful in the
first half of the Hellenistic period, since the monarchies all tried to
protect their subjects from the slave-traders, but after Pydna the
markets were full of slaves of all sorts on their way to Italy.
Unemployment is no more mentioned than over-production. At
times, as in the Fayum in Egypt about 257, labor was scarce.
Children were regularly used as apprentices. Labor-saving devices
were scarce, but the Archimedian screw was introduced for raising
water. One used the hand lathe, potter's wheel, loom, adze. There
was much drudgery and hours were long, but except in the mines,
where the work was inhuman, no one probably worked very hard.
And there were many religious holidays, dynastic and otherwise.

Technology

For Hellenistic trade was sensitive rather to politics than to
technology. Advances in physics, in mathematics, and to some
extent even in chemistry, led to inventions in the field of military
and naval engineering and to curiosities devised for kings and other
wealthy customers, but did not contribute directly to industry.
Siege engines and artillery, the latter operating with the torsion

capability of women's twisted hair, reached a high state of efficiency and sophistication in the armies of Alexander and the Hellenistic kings. A fifty-pound stone ball could be flung up to five hundred feet. The most notable engine was the great *helepolis* ("City Taker") constructed for Demetrius Poliorcetes at the siege of Rhodes, an armored wooden tower one hundred feet high supported on eight wooden wheels, swivel-mounted so that the crew of three thousand four hundred men could push it in any direction.[56] There were nine stories in all, connected by wide stairways, and each fitted with covered ports for missiles or for rams. At the top, overtowering the walls of the city, was a square platform thirty feet on the side. It was one of the wonders of the day and brought Demetrius close to victory, but its construction was coarse and illustrates well why no machine age was then possible.

Metallurgy was in a rudimentary state, permitting only an inadequate and irregular production of steel plate or alloys for special purposes. Wire produced by extrusion was unknown, and so were bolts and screws, while nails were primitive. There were no precision tools or adequate micrometers, wood-working methods allowed only a limited use of hardwoods, and lamination was unknown. There were no roller- or ball-bearings, no springs, no proper adhesives, rope, or twine, and no real lubricants. The use of soda and oil for cleaning cloth failed to lead to the discovery of soap. Meshed gears and even pulleys were little understood. Under such circumstances machines, even the steam engine invented by Hero of Alexandria (who may have been of Roman rather than of Hellenistic date), remained only toys, although it was possible to build bigger ships than ever before. And Archimedes at the siege of Syracuse (213-211) invented many useful gadgets to employ against the Romans, whether or not he employed compound burning glasses to set their engines on fire.

The Athenian triremes of the classical period had long been obsolete. Their three banks of oars were clumsy and slow, and they required great skill and strength on the part of the rowers. They could carry few marines and were designed primarily for ramming opponents. Dionysius I of Syracuse (406-367) had introduced a basic innovation, larger vessels propelled by long oars manned by four or five rowers each (quadriremes and quinque-remes), which were faster and could carry larger numbers of fighting men. This served as the inspiration of Antigonus I and Demetrius Poliorcetes and their successors in the third century, who built larger and larger fighting ships with more and more rowers and marines until Ptolemy IV reached the limit with a colossal "forty," so large that it was useless. It was four hundred feet long, fifty feet wide, and its prow and stern towered seventy feet above the water, while it carried a complement of four thousand rowers. The same Ptolemy built for himself a vast houseboat for travel on the Nile, capable of holding a complete royal villa of great luxury.

It is possible that Hellenistic palace architecture also showed technical advances over earlier periods, including the use of balconies supported on cantilevers as they are portrayed in later frescoes and mosaics, but there is little evidence on the subject. The Attalid palaces at Pergamum have nothing essentially novel about them, nor have such temporary but magnificent structures as the pyre of Hephaestion or the funerary carriage of Alexander.

Even in the matter of developing new commercial routes the Hellenistic period was not noteworthy. There is no evidence for systematic road construction. The Mediterranean routes and har-bors[57] remained what they had been, with a few modifications due mainly to Alexander, like the mole at Alexandria extending out to the island of Pharos and the lighthouse on the island itself, the "Pharos" tower three hundred feet high constructed by Sostratus of Cnidus. It is possible also that the Colossus of Rhodes, the great statue of Helios which spanned the entrance to the harbor, served as a lighthouse, but even if so it was overthrown in the great earthquake about 228 and never rebuilt. Few even of the kings had wealth or imagination for such construction, and even the great Nile-Red Sea canal built in Persian times was allowed to fill with silt.

It was only when a country's economy was seriously affected that invention occurred. So long as they possessed Palestine, down through the third century, the Ptolemies had control of the southern routes to the Orient and the routes to the South which were maintained by the Nabataeans and the Gerrhaeans. These were the routes by which spices and incense, gold, ivory, and

The harbor of Latakia

slaves came to the Mediterranean. With the Battle of Panium (199) these passed into the hands of the Seleucids, but it was possible for Ptolemy VIII Euergetes II, the fat and despised Physcon or Kakergetes of the Greek historians, to redress the balance by developing a sea route to the East via Coptus and the Red Sea port of Berenice. He appointed an admiral over "the Red and the Indic Seas," and these activities, signalized by two very profitable voyages of Eudoxus of Cyzicus, led at a later time to the discovery and systematic study of the southwest monsoons by one Hippalus, to make direct trade with India easy and safe. Little Ptolemaic currency has been found in southern Arabia and in India, however, and the volume of this trade may have been small. In the same way, late in the Hellenistic period, the occupation of the northern Syrian steppe by the Parthians led to the development of a southern route through and by Palmyra.

From the end of the fourth century and for a hundred years thereafter, the Mediterranean world was divided into two economic spheres determined by two rival systems of currency. The Seleucids continued minting on the standard of Philip, Alexander, and Lysimachus, itself a continuation of the Attic standard, but Ptolemy I went over to a lighter standard which was in use in Phoenicia and the Phoenician west. Thus Greece, the Aegean, and the Black Sea belonged economically to a free trade area of the Greek cities, some of which were controlled politically from time to time by Seleucids, Attalids, Ptolemies, or other Hellenistic dynasties, but which were not subject to economic controls; the southern and western Mediterranean belonged to the Ptolemies, who exercised a strict control over their traders by a system of export and import licenses and currency controls when they did not actually ship and exchange goods on their own account through their own agents. Their methods are known only from a few papyrus letters, but the importance of this western trade to the Ptolemaic economy is shown by the disastrous results of its interruption during the Second Punic War, when inflation and revolt broke out in Egypt.

Actually, favorable conditions never returned after the beginning of the second century, for, except during the years of Rhodes' commercial supremacy (down to 168), the economic life of the Mediterranean fell more and more into the hands of the

Italians. Settled first in Delos and then everywhere in the Greek and island and Anatolian cities, they often became citizens and settled down permanently (like the Cloatii at Gythium in Laconia) to serve as intermediaries with the Roman government and to be honored as benefactors by their fellow citizens. Under these conditions the Ptolemaic currency ceased to be international and appears rarely outside of Egypt.

Internal Economics

One curious feature of Hellenistic economy which is not easy to explain is the general rise of commercialism even in the field of small and inexpensive fungible goods, along with the progressive reduction of domestic production. Food, clothing, and common pottery were purchased, not made at home, and this small trade resulted in a high division of labor and was maintained by a plentiful small local bronze currency. As early as the fourth century the cynic Diogenes had sneered that taverns supplied the Athenian counterpart of the Spartan eating clubs — the Athenians purchased their food rather than preparing and consuming it at home. It may be that good cooks, familiar characters in the New Comedy, were less common in real life than in literature. The highly differentiated economic life which the papyri show in Egypt seems not to have been exceptional but typical. This means that a monetary economy was much more general than in previous centuries, and it is likely that a partial cause, at least, was the steadily growing supply of monetary metals, although much of this metal was diverted to other than monetary uses. Offerings of gold and silver objects in temples had always occurred, and benefactors of cities were commonly tendered golden crowns (often, however, adaerated into cash), but the use of gold and silver plate for domestic dining and drinking increased greatly. Respectable people did not use pottery, and the best ceramics were imitations of metal ware.[58]

It is impossible to prepare statistics on currency for too much evidence is lacking, but there can be no doubt that Alexander's conquests put into circulation vast quantities of silver (and gold too, though gold was never important as a monetary metal in antiquity) accumulated by the Persian kings and now paid out or spent or given to favorites. This should have resulted in a large increase in purchasing power and a considerable stimulus to business, even if most of it may have been spent initially on luxuries, fine clothes, rare foods, elegant Attic courtesans. We have many anecdotes about the exotic tastes of Alexander's nobles, fantastically rich and with little to spend their money on. So long as much of this currency remained in circulation, business should have been good, and the characteristic wealthy citizen of the Hellenistic cities, like Bulagoras of Samos, must have gotten rich directly or indirectly through this means.

Also, as money begets money and the Hellenistic period opened up new as well as maintaining old sources of silver, we should expect something of a boom economy far down into the third century at least, and there is evidence in the Delian accounts, for example, of high prices.[59] On the other hand, in Egypt where silver was rare, prices were quite low before the inflation under Philopator. There may well have been local and temporary or even general and protracted periods of monetary scarcity and deflation, but none has been certainly identified. With the flow of silver to the West after Roman intervention however, the affluent conditions of the third century became progressively less general. With the Mithridatic and the Civil Wars of the first century the Hellenistic East was bankrupt, forced to convert its temple treasures and privately owned silver plate and jewelry into cash, and to borrow at high rates of interest from Italian bankers in order to meet Roman taxation and Roman requisitions.

It is especially difficult to determine the role of free enterprise in the Hellenistic period. In the little treatise on Economics which is preserved among the works of Aristotle but which belongs to the early third century, the economy of the private individual is limited to agriculture, the lending of money at interest, and a third field not clearly defined but which must include trade and industry like the manufacture, transport, and sale of goods. In contrast, the economy of satraps and of cities includes also taxation (that is to say, fees and licenses) and the exploitation of natural resources, mines, quarries, and forests. It seems likely from the analogy of fourth century Athens that the cities handled these two activities as concessions sold to private bidders, tax-farmers and entrepreneurs. But what was the situation in the monarchies? In the tightly knit economy of Egypt, tax-farmers played a routine part, but under such conditions that they can hardly have made much money honestly, and seem actually to have drawn a salary. The able and well-connected Greeks in Egypt in the third century, like Zenon· of Caunus, were probably able to engage in a variety of commercial and administrative activities for or in spite of the government, in such a way as to become rich but certainly not so as to build industrial or commercial empires of their own. In addition to government banks, private banks were permitted and engaged in deposit and lending operations. Even in the field of agriculture, when Zenon was manager of the ten-thousand aroura estate of the *dioecetes* Apollonius, there is no indication that he was concerned to improve it and turn it into a model or experimental farm. Some letters tell of rare or cross-bred animals sent by the Jewish prince Tobias in Amman to the king, but there is no suggestion that these were anything but curiosities. It is particularly notable that the olive was never grown much in Ptolemaic Egypt, although imported oil was very highly valued by the Greek population. In contrast, the olive was grown plentifully in Roman Egypt. The same general conservatism or lack of enterprise appears to have prevailed also in the Seleucid kingdom, for which there is, it is true, little evidence. Iran was a land of fruits unknown at that time to the Mediterranean, notably the peach, but this does not seem to have been transplanted into new areas at this time.

Chapter Four

Hellenistic Culture

1. Philosophy

Philosophy dominated the intellectual life of Greece in the fourth century. Plato and his contemporaries had been concerned with man's conduct as the tragedians and historians of the fifth century had been concerned with his religion, that is, his destiny, and the problem posed in each case was the same. How might a society or an individual live securely in an often hostile world? Religion helped if one supposed that the gods were, or could be brought to be, friendly or at least just, so that the good need have no fear. Socrates, however, if we may believe the testimony of Plato in the *Apology,* and later on Plato himself, went further and argued that the good were capable of finding their own security. What happened to one externally at the hands of men or gods, properly viewed, was unimportant. Importance in the matter of true happiness lay only in what happened to a man internally, in his soul, and here no one could harm him but himself. Here he was master of his destiny; so that Socrates could say, "No evil can happen to a good man living or dead." This thesis and its practical application continue on with no interruption and little change into and through the Hellenistic period. In this area it is hard to see any influence on men's thinking exercised by the conquests of Alexander.

In addition, Hellenistic philosophers continued the other preoccupations of their predecessors of the fifth and fourth centuries in the fields of theology, physics, medicine, mathematics, logic, politics, and rhetoric, but these tended to become localized specialties. After Isocrates, rhetoric went its separate way, commonly associated with grammar, prosody, and other educational matters, until it was brought back to philosophy by the polymath Cicero. The exact and experimental sciences went to the Museum in Alexandria, which also, with the Library, became the home of literature and philology. The study of mathematics was widespread in both pure and applied forms, with Archimedes of Syracuse, who had no school, as the outstanding personality. Theoretical physics became, in different forms, the doctrinal basis of Epicureans and Stoics, while logic or dialectic was employed by all for the purposes of controversy. The arguments, retorts, and witticisms of the various schools against each other must have made Athens an amusing place to live in. Dialectic as a study for its own sake belonged to such individuals as Pyrrho of Elis (360-270) and to the so-called Middle and New Academy of Arcesilaus (318-242) and of Carneades (213-129), who used its contradictions to deny the possibility of knowledge. They spoke of seeming, not of being, hesitated to make any positive statement, and were ready to argue equally on either side of any question. And this *eristic,* as it was called, tended to make them distrusted and disliked, as happened notably in the case of Carneades during his embassy in Rome in 155, when public opinion was so outraged by his display of virtuosity that he was ordered to leave the city forthwith.

Character portraiture and the delineation of individual character were among the interests and accomplishments of the fourth century, and this interest found expression in a number of histories of the philosophers. The first and most notable of these histories was that of Antigonus of Carystus (ca. 290-235), a writer and sculptor, who lived first at Athens and then at Pergamum. He was a pupil of the eminent Menedemus of Eretria, philosopher and statesman, a friend of Antigonus Gonatas, and wrote a book on portrait sculpture. After him came others, Hermippus of Smyrna, Sotion of Alexandria, and Heraclides Lembos, all of whose histories form the basis of the *Lives of the Philosophers* of Diogenes Laertius (second century A.D.). They are concerned with the succession from teacher to pupil, and present a picture of philosophical schools deriving by this means from Socrates.

And in fact, while there were individuals like Stilpo of Megara, the teacher of Zeno and of Crates, and later on Aristo of Chios, a renegade Stoic who rejected the school's logic and physics, most of the prominent philosophers are grouped in formal schools, with one head succeeding another both as the bearer of the school's doctrine and as the owner and occupier of the school's property at Athens. The same attitude is shown even toward the Cynics, although they owned no property and, lacking formal doctrine, constituted no formal school. Thus, of Socrates' pupils, Plato was the founder of the Academy, from which later the Peripatos split off under Plato's pupil Aristotle. Antisthenes of Athens became the teacher of Diogenes, the first proper Cynic (there are chronological difficulties here). From *his* pupil, the Theban Crates, Zeno of Citium separated and founded Stoicism, while the hedonist Aristippus of Cyrene was the inspiration, or the forerunner at least, of Epicurus. At the time of Plato's death in 349 it was still difficult for a foreigner to own property in Athens, but later the schools became completely international and the city took on its formal role of teacher of the Greeks, a role which it had played in fact since Pericles' time.

The Academy

Precedence in dignity as well as seniority in age belonged to Plato's school, known as the Academy from the place where it had its buildings, sacred to the Attic hero Academus. After Plato's death it was directed by his nephew Speusippus (to 339) and then by Xenocrates of Chalcedon (to 314) who as a revered and elder citizen was sent as envoy to Antipater after the Lamian War (322). He was succeeded by another Athenian, Polemo (to ca. 276), and in his time Crates of Athens and Crantor of Soloi were prominent in the Academy. The former was credited with being the teacher of Zeno as well as of Arcesilaus and of the Cynic Bion, a testimony to the vitality of the school doctrine at this time. But with Arcesilaus, head of the school until 242, a gracious gentleman from Pitace in the Aeolis who was a friend of kings, Eumenes, Attalus, and Antigonus Gonatas, the trend was more toward *eristic*, heavily overlaid with wit. When asked, for example, why many joined the Epicureans but no one ever left them, he replied:

"Because men may become eunuchs but eunuchs cannot become men." Thereafter the Academy boasted few prominent members, at least until the time of Carneades, who served as envoy to Rome and was the teacher of Attalus II and Ariarathes V.

The Peripatetics

When Aristotle returned to Athens in 335 shortly before Alexander's departure on his Asian campaign, he was assigned by the city as residence the Lycaeum, the sanctuary of Apollo Lycaeus, and here the colonnades (*peripatoi*) gave the school its name (Peripatetic). He had been a pupil of Plato's for twenty years, and after that had been with the tyrant Hermaias at Atarneus, at Mytilene, and at Pella as Alexander's tutor. His immense learning and his research in every field of knowledge, fortified by the materials and reports sent him by Alexander, established the Peripatos as a vast research institute. After his death his pupil Theophrastus of Eresus (to 286) continued working on an almost equally encyclopaedic scale, although most of his writings have not been preserved. We have his great *History of Plants,* a collection of *Character Sketches,* and fragments of a treatise on contracts to testify to his ability. During his tenure his pupil Demetrius of Phalerum, ruler of Athens 317-307, went to Egypt after Cassander's death (297), taking to Ptolemy an enthusiasm for and interest in research. He helped to establish the Museum and the Library, and assisted the king in the preparation of a law code. Thereafter the Peripatos was less distinguished, although Strato of Lampsacus (to 268) instructed Ptolemy II in physics, Lyco of Troas was a friend of Eumenes and Attalus and refused an invitation of Antiochus (III) to join his court, and Critolaus of Phaselis was a member of the famous Athenian embassy to Rome in 155.

The Cynics

More colorful and more generally influential than these traditional seats of learning were the schools primarily concerned with human conduct, especially that of the Stoics. This was an intellectualized offshoot of the Cynic tradition which was traced back to Antisthenes, although he was probably dead when Diogenes of Sinope came to Athens in the mid-fourth century.

Diogenes wished to "overstrike the coin," to make a basic change in human habits. His motto was "Live according to nature," and by this he meant to live as simply as possible, to have as few needs and possessions and as few and as unabashed pleasures as the dog (*kyon*), to which people were quick to compare him and his followers, and which gave them their designation. The Cynic badge was the wallet, the staff, and the worn cloak, together with a bluntness of speech and a biting humor. What affected the soul was either good or bad, as it had been to Socrates, and everything else was indifferent, but the Cynics were not unintellectual. Diogenes wrote a *Republic*, carrying further and simplifying Plato's ideas, but his motto was self-sufficiency. His pupil was Crates of Thebes, who was himself a teacher of Zeno. With time the Cynic doctrine became more generous and less harsh, and this trend was continued in the third century when there were many Cynics of differing sorts.

Bion the Borysthenite, from Olbia on the Black Sea, was a wandering preacher, the first world-citizen (*kosmopolites*), who through diatribes, the models for the Christian sermon, taught people how to endure exile, poverty, and suffering. Extensive remains of his teaching exist in the writings of a certain Teles, a Cynic preacher of a later generation. Other notable Cynics, all of the third century, were Menippus of Gadera, the inventor of the Menippean satire, a serio-comic mixture of prose and verse which later influenced Varro, Horace and Lucian. Another Cynic, also of Gadera, was Meleager, who compiled the first collection of epigrams under the title of *Stephanus* or *Garland*; and the Megalopolitan statesman and lawgiver Cercidas, the friend of Aratus, was a Stoic, responsible for curious *meliamboi*, extensive fragments of which have been discovered in the papyri. A fondness for curious verse forms appears also in Timo of Phlius, whose *Silloi* or *Lampoons* are a product of third century Cynicism also. This activity was of short duration, however, and there are no more important Cynics until the Roman Empire.

The Stoics

The Stoic school, which had its own property but took its name from the founder's fondness for the Painted Porch (*Stoa Poikile*), was an intellectualized offshoot of Cynicism which attracted a series of very able men who created the most important philosophic doctrine of the Hellenistic period. Zeno of Citium in Cyprus was often called a Phoenician, but such epithets do not necessarily indicate ethnic origin. So the Olbian Bion was called a Borysthenite, Dionysius of Byzantium, the grammarian, was called a Thracian, and the Stoic Diogenes from Seleucia on the Tigris was called a Babylonian.

Opinions differ sharply as to the presence of Semitic, Phoenician, or Jewish elements in Zeno's system. Certain is it only that, coming to Athens in the time of Demetrius of Phalerum, he became a pupil not only of the Cynic Crates but also of the Academics Xenocrates and Polemo and of the Megarian Stilpo, from whom he derived his logic. He was learned, a little shy, much admired at Athens, a friend of Antigonus Gonatas, and he wrote extensively on a great variety of subjects, beginning with a very Cynic-like *Republic*. He accepted the Cynic dogma of living according to nature, but defined nature differently than they. Nature, as defined in Stoic physics, was an expression of the wisdom or Providence of God, and it was man's duty to live in agreement with it, and so virtuously. Wisdom was the important thing, carrying with itself incidentally the Cynic ideal of insensitiveness (*apatheia*). While externals were still generally indifferent, they showed various degrees of desirability, so that the Stoic did not separate himself from the world as a Cynic did but was interested in everything. He was not, like the Cynic, an anti-intellectual, nor was he anti-religious, but rather a strong defender of conventional religion and a firm believer in immortality. This led him to accept suicide as normal and reasonable if one had reason for doubting the value of further life.

While not scientists, the Stoics accepted and used the Greek heritage of science, even when this led to odd concepts like that of the periodic conflagration of the world (*ekpyrosis*) which they took over from Heracleitus. The reasonableness, breadth of vision, and wide humanity of the Stoic doctrine attracted many of the most thoughtful and noblest Greeks and Romans throughout antiquity. So even Cicero, a professed adherent of the Academy, showed himself very sympathetic to the doctrine of the Stoa, especially in the fields of religion, politics, and ethics.

Zeno lived until 264 and was given a state funeral and a public burial in the Cerameicus. His place at the head of the Stoa was taken by his pupil Cleanthes of Assus, who wrote on many subjects but particularly on physics, and was the author of a remarkable hymn to Zeus, strongly monotheistic in its tone, which was quoted before the Council of the Areopagus by the apostle Paul. His pupil Chrysippus of Soloi, another Cypriot, was the greatest scholar and writer of the early Stoa, developing ethics further than Zeno and giving to logic the final Stoic form. He was the founder of orthodox Stoicism, and later writers found it difficult to separate his contributions to dogma from those of his two predecessors, for he used, transformed, and advanced everything. With him ended the so-called Early Stoa, and the two most notable Stoics of the Middle Stoa, Diogenes of Seleucia and Panaetius of Rhodes, did not affect doctrine in any notable way, although they were of great importance as teachers.

Both were men of outstanding personality. The former was a member of the Athenian embassy to Rome in 155, and made a much better impression on the Senators than his two relativist colleagues, Carneades and Critolaus. Panaetius also came to Rome and was a prominent member of the circle around the younger Scipio. The Stoic Blossius of Cumae, the friend of Tiberius Gracchus and of Aristonicus, was a fellow student with him at the feet of Antipater of Tarsus, Diogenes' pupil. It is at least interesting that so many Stoics came from the East. The outstanding personality of the first century was Poseidonius of Apameia who counted as Panaetius' pupil, and lived in Rhodes rather than Athens because of the political and economic conditions after the Mithridatic War. He was a man of immense learning and industry, philosopher, geographer, scientist, and even historian, for he was the author of a continuation of Polybius' *Histories* describing events at least down to Sulla's seizure of power in Rome. It was evidently of great value, but unfortunately it has almost completely perished. He was a friend of Pompey, who visited him twice, and of Cicero.

The Epicureans

The traditional rival of the Stoics was Epicurus' school, which boasted few great names because of its devotion to the words of the master, but which had many adherents and some imitators.

Epicurus was an Athenian who had been a cleruch on Samos, but returned to Athens when the Samians recovered their freedom in 322/1. There he founded his school in his walled Garden, remotely influenced by the hedonistic doctrines of Aristippus but based upon the atomic doctrine of Democritus, which he took over, apparently, without modification. This explanation of the universe as based upon atoms and the void, brought into various combination by chance (emphatically not by Fate or the goddess Fortune), while it did not eliminate the gods, made it unreasonable to suppose that the gods interfered with or cared for men. Thus it removed any compulsion to act because of honor, justice, or such a duty as the Stoics posited, leaving self-interest as the only human motivation.

This existentialist doctrine was saved from chaos and despair by two considerations, that the only real pleasure was freedom from emotional disturbance (*ataraxia*) and that the greatest pleasure was friendship. Epicurus' group lived as friends behind the garden walls frugally and temperately, not only because luxury and self-indulgence often lead to subsequent physical discomfort but because dependence on luxury produced desires which were disturbing. Epicurus himself attained an almost saintly composure. We have a letter which he wrote just before his death: "On this blessed day, which is also my last, I write this to you. My continual sufferings from strangury and dysentery are so great that nothing could increase them, but against all this stands my joy at the memory of the conversations which we have shared."[60] In times of trouble such as that caused by the siege of Athens by Demetrius, the members of the group shared their last scraps of anything edible with great cheerfulness.

Critics of the doctrine found much to attack, notably the easily distorted doctrine of hedonism practiced by a society which avoided the public eye. Epicurus' contemporary Theodorus of Cyrene, called an atheist as were the Epicureans themselves, made a shrewder point in arguing that pleasure was too precarious and uncontrollable a goal and substituted for this the concept of joy, contrasted with grief, which could be attained by a right mental attitude (*phronesis*). But the school of Epicurus maintained itself at Athens and made converts elsewhere, and did not entirely avoid intellectual activity in a variety of areas. We are fortunate to have

in charred papyri found at Herculaneum the remnants of the
library of a certain Epicurean Philodemus, who had himself
composed a long list of volumes on the topics beloved by all the
schools, on anger, on death, on freedom of speech, on piety, even
on music and the aesthetics of poetry, as well as on kingship and
on the errors and shortcomings of Stoicism. This is not profound
thinking, but it is interesting as giving us a glimpse of the topics
and the treatment of them which have otherwise so largely
perished. It may be that Campania was an Epicurean center. At all
events, it is certain that Lucretii Cari lived at Pompeii, and since
Epicureanism was rarely respectable at Rome, it is a plausible
suggestion that the greatest Epicurean document, the *De Rerum
Natura* of Lucretius, was due to his connection with this family.

2. Science

As with philosophy, the Hellenistic developments in science
were a direct continuation of the researches and speculation of the
fourth century, and occur mainly before the end of the third.
They represent the highest achievements of the Greeks in this
field, and such men as Euclid and Archimedes, Apollonius and
Philo, Aristarchus and Hipparchus, Eratosthenes and Seleucus, and
Herophilus and Erasistratus reached heights of genius comparable
to those of Plato and Aristotle earlier, although in each case in a
more specialized area. With some exceptions the center of their
activity was Alexandria, where the Museum and the Library
founded by the first Ptolemy, and supported and expanded by his
two successors, provided a living, a meeting place, and a collection
of research materials for scholars of widely varied origin. While the
schools at Athens were concerned primarily with teaching and the
establishment of dogma, their counterpart at Alexandria was
interested in advancing the frontiers of knowledge. Since such
modern concepts as mathematics, physics, and so on were not yet
isolated, the work of these scholars may be described briefly under
two heads, one dealing with studies based on mathematics and
mechanics, and the other based on botany and biology.

Mechanics, Astronomy, and Mathematics

It is probably the encouragement furnished in the fourth

century to the invention and improvement of machines for
military purposes by such rulers as Dionysius of Syracuse and
Philip II of Macedon which brought about the great advance in
knowledge of mechanics which was to flower in Alexandria with
Ctesibius, Philo of Byzantium, and Hero (unless he is of a later
date), the first and third of whom are called Alexandrians.
Aristotle shows a familiarity with lever, balance, and pulley, and
certainly the siege engines of the period of the Successors were
based upon knowledge of the cog wheel and the worm gear or
endless spiral. Soon thereafter the propulsive power based on
torque (as in the catapult) was supplemented by water power
(hydrostatics) and compressed gases, steam and air.

It is impossible to determine the history of these developments in detail, but to Ctesibius, Philo, and Hero are credited not
only military machines of many sorts but games and curiosities: a
water pump worked by compressed air for extinguishing fires, a
water clock and a water organ (where air pressure in the tubes may
have been supplied by depressing them in water), an automatic
theater, animated dolls, automatic dispensing machines, and many
others which were certainly subsidized by the wealthy Ptolemies.
Of a more practical character were surveying instruments with
micrometer adjustments, which contributed to notable advances in
both geography and astronomy, and which made possible such
scientific instruments as the planetarium of Archimedes of Syracuse. Archimedes, while more of a theoretician, employed the new
knowledge to invent useful devices. He aided King Hiero by
devising a method of launching his great ship and by inventing
military engines for use during the siege of Syracuse (213-211).
And in Egypt he gave his name to the Archimedian Screw, still
used there to raise water.

Together with these practical uses of the new techniques went
their scientific study. Aristotle's pupil Strato of Lampsacus explained the compressibility of gases by the revived concept of
empty space, and Archimedes came on the principle of specific
gravity when faced with the problem of determining the propor-
tion of gold and other metals in Hiero's crown. Hero is credited
with isolating the physical principle of action and equal reaction
and interested himself in thermal transmission, both being involved in his rotary steam engine. Aristoxenus of Tarentum,

another pupil of Aristotle, studied harmonics both aesthetically and physically. The study of catoptics and refraction, notably by Archimedes, led to the discovery of burning and magnifying lenses, although the poor quality of glass available prevented the development of telescopes or microscopes. Greater exactness of measurement became possible with the division of the day into twenty-four hours and of the circle into three hundred and sixty degrees, both units further subdivided into sixty minutes or sixty seconds each (the old Babylonian system).

Astronomy did not progress beyond the Pythagorean notion of a circular motion of the planets which Eudoxus of Cnidus, a pupil of Plato, had explained by a cumbersome system of homocentric spheres. Eudoxus also had prepared the first catalogue of the fixed stars, and had calculated the earth's circumference, although his figure was much too large. This was later improved on by Dicaearchus of Alexandria and Eratosthenes of Cyrene, the latter of whom came close to the actual figure. He also prepared a map of the earth's inhabited surface, controlled by parallels and meridians. The notion of a rotating earth developed by the Pythagoreans, opposed by Aristotle, was revived and became generally accepted, leading Aristarchus of Samos to posit a solar-centric universe. This hypothesis, accepted by Seleucus of Babylonia who explained the tides, was unfortunately rejected by the most exact observer of the period, Hipparchus of Nicaea, who anticipated Ptolemy in locating cities and other terrain features by latitude and longitude and who discovered the precession of the equinoxes. Since he was followed by the great popularizer Poseidonius, the heliocentric doctrine went out of fashion and out of men's minds.

In mathematics, the period saw a substantial advance in many directions. Attention was focused principally on the uses of the method of exhaustion or the method of the infinitesimal, invented or first popularized by Eudoxus. It was employed both for proofs in solid geometry (spheres, cylinders, cones) and for calculation, and led Archimedes to something very close to the modern Calculus. Using the methods of Euclid, whose secular textbook was published in Alexandria and immediately became popular, problems of solid and analytical geometry were widely studied, leading to better and better proofs and demonstrations. The principles of the infinite and of the irrational were accepted and used. A whole doctrine of conic sections was worked out by Apollonius of Perga, especially. Hero developed a trigonometry and improved methods of extracting cubic roots. In short, while this account must be brief and superficial, it may be said that the first two centuries of Hellenism saw a development in all these fields greater than any until modern times.

Biology and Medicine

The situation in the biological and medical field is similar, but the advance was not as far or as general. In botany and zoology there was little or no advance after the tremendous accomplishments of Aristotle and his pupil Theophrastus. Aristotle's numerous writings on all aspects and kinds of animals (parts, movement, generation, etc.) show an extraordinary capacity for analysis and classification which has rarely or never been surpassed. He and his pupils collected information from everywhere and themselves practiced dissection and vivisection, discovering much of the anatomy and physiology of vertebrates. They also interested themselves in invertebrates to include some rather low orders of animals, but speculated on the boundaries between the animal and vegetable kingdoms. Some low orders, like the sea nettles, seemed to partake of both. It is traditional that Aristotle received notes and specimens from Alexander, although these are not specifically mentioned by him, but there is no doubt of the influence of the new discoveries on Theophrastus' great *History of Plants*, the best treatise on botany produced before modern times.

Neither of these lines, however, was pursued by scholars in the next two centuries. These looked to zoology only for information on the human body, and to botany only for *materia medica* and pharmacology and especially toxology, developed to a high technique by (among others) Attalus III and Crateuas, the physician of Mithridates Eupator. But there is little known of progress in this area which could be regarded as an anticipation of organic chemistry.

In medicine, the Hippocratic notion of the normality of health based on a strict regimen of diet and exercise prevailed. Nevertheless, the greatest of the physicians and doubtless most of the thousands of lesser medical practitioners employed drugs too, as well as the popular cupping and bleeding to equalize the traditional four bodily humors. There were, no doubt, improvements in treating diseases and injuries, although in view of the lack of microscopes and chemistry no real advance in pathology was possible.

The really notable advances were in anatomy, based traditionally upon the possibilities of dissection and perhaps vivisection of criminals and prisoners supplied by the Ptolemies. Earlier generations were not entirely ignorant, because of the information derived from the examination and treatment of wounded soldiers. Alcmaeon of Croton, in the fifth century, had identified the brain as the seat of sensation, and it was only later that the heart was credited with the emotional properties ascribed to it in fiction and current speech. But it was the Alexandrian scholars Herophilus of Chalcedon and Erasistratus of Cos, perhaps his pupil, who determined the anatomy and the function of the nervous system, including the distinction of sensory and motor nerves. In a similar way they discovered the function and diagnostic value of the pulse and the function of heart, veins, and arteries. However, lack of knowledge of the capillaries and misunderstanding of the lungs led to some odd concepts, as that which had the arteries convey air. Or was this actually only a fumbling way of defining the function of blood in distributing oxygen to the bodily tissues? Their systems are known only from later attacks upon them, and so are subject to distortion.

An important curiosity of the late Hellenistic period was the herbal written by Crateuas and illustrated by drawings, some idea of which may be formed from later copies and imitations.

3. Religion

The Greek Background

In the field of religion, also, the Hellenistic period saw only a continuation and extension of processes going back to our earliest Greek records. For Greek religion had long been a complex thing. Foreign influences were always present. The Oriental fertility goddess Aphrodite appears with established attributes among the Olympians in Homer, and may probably be recognized in a nude female figure accompanied by doves represented on a plaque from a shaft grave at Mycenae. The Carian Hecate is credited by Hesiod in the *Theogony* with almost universal powers, influential alike in the heavens, on earth, and in the sea. She rewards and protects her worshipper, giving him victory, wealth, and honor, but she is also concerned with justice, and guides aright the judgments of kings. The Anatolian Mother (Meter) gave her name to the Metroum at Athens, where the civic archives were kept in the fourth century, and Bendis from Thrace acquired an official cult at the end of the fifth: Plato's dialogue the *Republic* took place in the Peiraeus because Socrates had come down from Athens to see the first celebration of her nocturnal festival. The Athenian Alcibiades consulted the oracle of Ammon at Siwah in the Libyan desert, and Sabazius, the Phrygian god, was known to Aristophanes. In so far as Hellenistic religion was concerned with non-Greek gods, it was no new phenomenon.

It may be that the earliest stratum of Greek religion consisted of that essentially pagan concept, *do ut des* ("I give that you may give"). The god, located in and identified with a specific object, place, or natural phenomenon, possessed a certain power (*dynamis* or *energeia*) which a worshipper could bring into play for his benefit or avert from causing him harm, by certain procedures. Such a notion is seldom absent from any religion, ancient or modern, at least on the popular level, but in its crudest expression it approaches magic, where the worshipper controls the god, compels him to do his will. So Plato asked sarcastically in the *Euthyphro* if religion were a matter of huckstering with the gods, giving (sacrifice) and asking (prayer); and in the *Laws* he insisted that while there were gods, and while these cared about men, they could not be diverted from their righteous course by gifts. Individual gods, whose identity, names, and proper cult could be learned from Apollo at Delphi, were concerned with all the various aspects of human affairs, but collectively they were concerned with righteousness, the same or approximately the same righteousness as man himself could discover with his own reason. Thus human ethics came to be supported by religion. If the apparently good man did not always experience good fortune, it was because he possessed flaws invisible to man but visible to god, or because god had a different and higher idea of human good than man had, or because earthly adversity built character or wisdom, he recognition of which would occur in the world to come if not in this existence. "In experience lies understanding" was an old Greek proverb, as Aeschylus pointed out in the *Agamemnon*.

And so, already before the Hellenistic period, by an inevitable process of logic, the Greeks had transformed a chaos of blind and impersonal but probably to some extent controllable powers into an ordered universe of responsible and admirable gods. The gods were concerned with man's material and moral well-being, so that the good might look forward, if not necessarily to prosperity in the present world, at any rate to happiness in the world to come. And with the acceptance of man's immortality and the organized decency of the gods with whom he came into contact went the idea of a higher, unified purpose. As the working gods, according to myth and belief, had experienced a coming into being at a given time in the past and were as much a part of the universe as man himself, although immortal and more powerful, this unified purpose must be that of a deity outside the universe, the great cause, model, and maker of all things. This went beyond henotheism or pantheism to something very close, perhaps, to monotheism as it appears in Islam. This achievement was the spiritual inheritance of the Greeks of the Hellenistic period, and they applied its various elements in various ways to the wider horizons opened by Alexander.

Alexander the Great

Religious speculation in the schools has been described above. It may most conveniently be surveyed in Cicero's pamphlet *On the Nature of the Gods,* where the conflicting points of view are presented by an Epicurean, a Stoic, and an Academic. On a more practical level, the religious experience of the Hellenistic Greeks may be seen in the case of Alexander the Great, the first, greatest, and most typical Hellenistic individual. His concern was not with problems of the universe, divine purpose and human freedom of will, nor indeed with the gods as upholders of moral law. He was concerned with the gods as they affected him, as and to the extent that they assisted or might oppose his purpose. These were, in the first instance, the gods of Macedon and of the royal family. Before leaving Pella he conducted with great magnificence the feast of Zeus and the Muses, and at the beginning of his last fatal illness he gulped down the enormous Heracles cup of wine, in honor of that god's festival in Thessaly. At Ilium he sacrificed to Athena, Achilles' patron deity, and Dionysus was honored not only by frequent drinking celebrations of the kind known as comuses but also by dramatic performances.

On the other hand, Alexander was almost equally as mindful of deities whom he encountered in their native habitat. Melkart at Tyre was regarded as a form of Heracles, and Alexander undertook the seven-months' siege of Tyre, at least in part, so that he might sacrifice to him on the island. In Egypt he was crowned Pharaoh, which meant that he became a son of the god Re and an incarnation of Horus, and his image was placed in all the Egyptian temples both as worshipper and as a fellow god. In Babylon he certainly respected and worshipped Bel and Marduk, although he never was in the city at the spring equinox to take Marduk's hand in the traditional New Year's festival. In the Iranian lands he at least maintained the fire temples, although there is no other evidence of his attitude toward Iranian religious concepts, whether Mazdaean or Zoroastrian. But the support which he looked for and found in the Iranian nobles would have been impossible had he not treated their religion with respect. This is what we should expect of a man of Greek education, for there were few Greeks who would challenge any existing religious institutions, even if novel or bizarre.

The Ammon of the oracle at Siwah was almost as much Greek as he was Egyptian. The Greeks called him Zeus, and his oracle was all the more respected for being somewhat inaccessible. It was natural for Alexander to consult it, as he had consulted Delphi before his departure for Asia, and it, like Delphi, pronounced him invincible. But it went further and pronounced him Ammon's son. No witnesses to this are named, but Alexander would not lie in such a matter, and the report spread rapidly throughout the army to be greeted with hostility by the Macedonians, untroubled acceptance by the Greeks.

For to a Greek, as divinity was capable of residing in any material object, statue or talisman, so it could reside also in a human being. This is why later Greeks were so ready to accept Jesus Christ as God and the Son of God. But divinity must prove itself by deeds, and when Alexander's conquests began to surpass those of Heracles and Dionysus, many others and himself too began to take Ammon's words seriously. This is the background of the demand or request issued by Alexander in his last year that the Greek cities establish formal cults for his worship. Little seems to have been done, for the time was too short. But after his death the divinity of Alexander was generally accepted, even by the Macedonians, so that Eumenes could employ the sanctity of Alexander's tent, throne, and scepter to hold together his reluctant and suspicious generals. The dynastic cults which later flourished in all of the kingdoms as symbols and expressions of loyalty were headed by Alexander, the divine ancestor of the kings.

These cults were organized both regionally (on a kingdom-wide basis) and locally, in cities and towns and on an individual basis. In Egypt the Ptolemies as Pharaohs were worshipped in all of the native temples, and were combined with Alexander in a cult carried out at the royal necropolis in Alexandria. Under the Seleucids, the cult was organized officially in each satrapy. What the cities and the rest did was left to their own initiative, although presumably royal approval had to be secured. One form which this cult assumed was that of annual festivals under dynastic names, such as the Antiocheia at Laodiceia on the Lycus River in Phrygia. With one exception, the Ptolemaia established in Alexandria by the second Ptolemy in honor of his father, these were local and lacked the pan-hellenic standing which was claimed for numerous festivals in Anatolian cities in the course of the third century.[61]

Universalism

Alexander's example was followed, *mutatis mutandis,* by his soldiers and by his friends, and by the thousands of Greeks who migrated into the new areas in the next hundred years. They brought with them their own gods. They accepted the gods of the country, sometimes but not necessarily calling them by Greek names. And they accepted the dynastic cults of the kingdom where they were, and which in the form of the worship of individual kings were not restricted to the kingdoms. There were numerous royal cults at Delos, and at Rhodes, even while the cult of the city's ally, Ptolemy, was being maintained, alongside it the cults of Antigonus and Demetrius were meticulously observed even while Demetrius was laying siege to the city.

The temple at Edfu

The same mixture of cults existed in the cities. A great capital such as Alexandria had cults of all the usual Greek gods as well as of Alexander, Hephaestion perhaps, and the Ptolemies, but also of the Egyptian deities Isis, Anubis, Bast, Horus, Apis, Ammon, and many more, of Adonis and the Great Mother, of the Babylonian Astarte, and of the Syrian Atargatis.[62] A little Macedonian town like Dura-Europos on the mid-Euphrates worshipped its founder, Seleucus Nicator, and certainly the other kings of the dynasty, as well as Apollo and Artemis, a variety of gods called Zeus (mostly local Syrian Ba'als), the Syrian Hadad and Atargatis, the Palmy-rene Bel (and other Palmyrene deities), Adonis, and many others. Delos in the second century must have included every deity known to Hellenism.

These were all, in general, typically pagan cults, locally maintained for the material benefit of the worshippers, whether few or many. But the taste for universalism was not dead, and the notable development in Hellenism lay in this direction. The source of this was Greek, not Oriental, although universalism attached itself by preference to Oriental deities the cults and character of which were, in Greek eyes, strange and flexible. Universalism had attached itself earlier to Zeus, but the recognized cults and myths of Zeus served as an obstacle to innovation. The same was not true of the Jewish Jehovah (Jaweh or Jao), but we are far from being able to trace the Hellenistic influence in the maze of Jewish literature and thought of the last three centuries before Christ. Scholars generally admit that the influence was extensive, but agree on little else.[63] On the other hand, we are better informed about Isis and Serapis, the two Egyptian deities who become universal in the Hellenistic period and continue so during the Roman Empire, Isis was an old Egyptian deity, the cult of Serapis something of a Hellenistic creation.

Isis and Serapis

The Hellenization of Isis had taken place earlier and it required only the prestige of the Ptolemaic dynasty to make her widely popular, the bearer of all the age-old wisdom and mystery of the land of the Pharaohs, the cradle of civilization. A number of hymns in her honor have survived, some of which go back to the early Hellenistic period, but none is more remarkable than the

Seleucus relief from Dura-Europus

group of four found inscribed on the vestibule of her temple in Medinet Madi on the southern edge of the Fayum Oasis.[64] These were the composition of one Isidorus, perhaps a Thracian, and may be dated about the year 100. They celebrate the goddess in various aspects, but her universality is most clearly defined in the first of the series. She is not only great-named but many named:

"The Syrians call her Astarte, Artemis, and Anaia; the Lycian peoples call her Lady Leto; the Thracians, the Mother of the Gods; the Greeks, Hera of the mighty throne, and Aphrodite, good Hestia, Rheia, and Demeter; the Egyptians Thiouis, for you alone are all the other goddesses named by the nations."

The competence of Isis was as comprehensive as that which Hesiod ascribed to Hecate. She was the bringer of wealth, the source and the support of justice, the protector of those in danger, the bringer of the fruits of the earth and of fertility among animals and man, and the special guardian of King Ptolemy. In the same manner the goddess herself speaks in an earlier inscription found at Cyme in the Aeolis:

"I am Isis, ruler of the whole earth. I was educated by Hermes and with Hermes discovered letters . . . I gave laws to men . . . I separated earth from heaven. I showed the paths of the stars, and ordered the journey of the sun and the moon. I found the uses of the sea . . . I brought together man and woman. I ordained that women should bring forth a ten-months infant into the light . . . I made the true to be held good . . . I made nothing to be more feared than an oath."[65]

Isis offered something which the Greeks could call mysteries. These, as we see in the *Metamorphoses of Apuleius,* under the Empire offered both a revelation of the secrets of the universe and the offer of blessed immortality, like the Greek mysteries of Eleusis and of Samothrace. They gave to the devotee both salvation and a way of life. So Isis offered to the Hellenistic world much which later was to be offered by Christianity.

Serapis was in many ways her male counterpart, although he was never her consort. The cults were separate, and must have been more or less rivals. His origin is less than certain, although it is clear that he developed out of the Osiris-Apis of Memphis, whose sanctuary was the dwelling of the living bull called Apis and the tomb of each dead and mummified bull Osiris. This was called in Hellenistic times a Serapeium. It was a large and important sanctuary, which in ways not entirely clear to us accepted persons as protracted or permanent recluses. The archives of one of these, a Macedonian named Ptolemy, have been found, but they tell more about his personal affairs than they do about the temple life. It is not even clear that there was a cult of Serapis, properly speaking, there.

The center of Serapis' worship was in Alexandria, where there was a world-famous shrine and precinct and the cult image made by the sculptor Bryaxis early in the third century, representing the god with the traditional attributes of fertility and the underworld, much like the Greek Pluto. He was also an oracular god, whose temple was frequented by those who had made or were to make journeys, or who wished to pray for absent friends. Little is known of his cult, but he also was a universal deity. As one of his oracles states, the heavens were his head, the earth his feet, the waters his belly, while the sun was his all-seeing eye. His cult spread very rapidly both in the Ptolemaic empire and elsewhere, and was believed to have been the invention or the discovery of the first Ptolemy, assisted by the Egyptian Manetho and the Athenian Timotheus. But the *Journal* of Alexander the Great mentioned a Serapeium at Babylon in 323, and the early establishment of the worship at Alexandria (by 320 or soon after) somewhat argues that the god existed a little earlier than the beginning of Ptolemy's satrapy.

A recently published inscription from Hyrcania, southeast of the Caspian Sea, shows the cult of Serapis established there in the early third century, and it seems possible to think of Alexander himself as the propagator of the cult.[66] Perhaps this was one of the gods of whom Ammon had told him at Siwah. In any case, would a satrap of Egypt, even a Ptolemy, have promulgated a new deity in the troubled first years of the wars of the succession, a time when this Ptolemy was playing otherwise an exceedingly cautious and correct role? The question cannot be answered, but in any case, the cult spread widely and rapidly and continued increasingly popular under the Empire under the slogan "One Zeus Serapis," a claim to supremacy and universalism if not actually to monotheism.

Astrology

In these cults, oriental in name, there remained very little of the oriental, although the professional clergy and the foundation of the doctrine in sacred books based on divine revelation were not Greek. Much stronger oriental influence was present in the growth of astrology. It is true that the Pythagoreans and Plato had imagined a mystical relationship between the heavenly bodies and men, but astrology itself grew more out of the combination of the astronomical lore of Babylon made known through the writings of Berossus (time of Antiochus I), the Egyptian concept of divine wisdom incorporated in the god Thoth, and Greek rationalism represented by such exact astronomers as Hipparchus. These concepts produced in Egypt about the middle of the second century the first astrological handbooks, associated thereafter with the Greek counterpart of Thoth, Hermes the Thrice-Great. Often opposed, but more and more accepted in the Greco-Roman world, especially by the Stoics, the notion was that the fortunes of an individual were determined by the position of the planets and constellations at his birth and that future events could be forecast by a study of the heavens. Astrology became rapidly popular, and is attested not only by the surviving technical manuals, but also by numerous individual horoscopes preserved on papyrus or scratched on the walls of buildings.

Scientific or pseudo-scientific, astrology served in part as a substitute for religion rather than as a religion. Not only were the seven planets, at least, themselves gods, the whole system was a product of and directed by divine wisdom, a concept very close to that of the Stoic divine providence. And in general the great scientific achievements of Hellenism did little or nothing to reduce the intense religiosity which characterized both Greeks and Orientals. Even the cult of the living ruler should not be dismissed as lacking a strongly religious element, although it was likewise regarded as an expression of loyalty and gratitude toward a living benefactor. A fragmentary inscription recently found at Paphos in Cyprus preserves part of a petition addressed probably to Ptolemy VI by certain soldiers who have no doubt that he will help them "since you are a god."[67]

4. Literature

Prose

It requires a special combination of circumstances to produce great literature. A mastery of form and expression attainable only when a number of writers are in contact and competition must be combined with a depth of feeling and insight provoked by an anxious contemplation of vital human problems. When this combination of qualities is possessed by writers of wisdom and perhaps serenity, then we may hope for such eternal masterpieces as the epics attached to the name of Homer, the Attic tragedies of the fifth century, and the writings of Plato and of Demosthenes. Nothing comparable to these was produced in the Hellenistic period. Nevertheless, the vast and rapid spread of literacy and the development of a common dialect (the so-called *Koine* based upon a simplified Attic), together with the availability of papyrus in any desired quantity for book manufacture, greatly widened the reading as well as the listening public. Furthermore, the financial support offered writers by kings and cities encouraged all to write who could or wished. And as a matter of fact, the literary output of these three centuries was certainly enormous. Most of it has perished, either because it was absorbed in or superseded by writings of a later date (as happened with technical tracts, philosophical, philological, or scientific) or because it was no longer admired under the Empire. A great deal thus disappeared in one way or another, yet enough remains to show its character, and it is clear that, for whatever reason, form and feeling had become separated.

Serious writing was almost exclusively confined to prose. Philosophers wrote much but with little regard for style, and they so borrowed from and attacked each other that an original idea must have been rare, even in such towering personalities as the Stoics Zeno and Chrysippus. What the scientists wrote concerned man and his destiny or place on earth, but this lacked both feeling and form. There was a vast deal of oratory, not only the epideictic — oratory for oratory's sake, like Isocrates at his worst — but also political and perhaps forensic. Cicero shows that great eloquence may occur before a single judge or a small panel of jurists quite as well as before a great popular jury such as called forth the court speeches of Lysias and Demosthenes. And political oratory must have resounded in kings' courts as well as in the assemblies of the cities, many of which had sufficient political freedom to require almost as much public debate as Athens in the classical period. The literary letter too had become a recognized form of expression in the fourth century, and a number of these are preserved from Hellenistic times, written principally by philosophers, but they are no more notable for style or wisdom than are the examples of diplomatic correspondence preserved on inscriptions.

Historiography in the Hellenistic period never reached the heights of Herodotus or Thucydides or even the vigor, interest, and elegance of Xenophon. Historians varied between the factual and dull and the rhetorical and vacuous, if our impressions of Hieronymus of Cardia and Phylarchus of Athens are correct. We naturally deplore the loss of the information which they would have given us, but can hardly mourn them as monuments of literature. They were known and used under the Empire, but not read through to the end for pleasure, and only the Arcadian Polybius, fired by the dramatic spectacle of Rome's expansion and her conquest of the Greek and Hellenistic states, has survived to us in substantial part. Polybius was an important person in his own right and an interesting personality, full of prejudice, partisan, not above distortion, a captious critic of other historians whom he criticizes unfairly and at great length. But his concept of history does not rise above a Fortune guiding human events to unexpected or to astonishing conclusions, and his style is the *Koine* at its worst, crabbed, verbose, sloppy. Where we have Livy's paraphrase the contrast is striking. Factually Livy is inferior, but Livy's style and philosophy of history make his writing literature. Polybius' history is a valuable document.

Nevertheless, although substance in Hellenistic writing failed to be clothed in form in some areas, the feeling for form was certainly not lacking in the Hellenistic period. Quite the reverse. Form was elevated to the position of primary importance in the two centers which produced important, original, and influential literary monuments at this time, Athens and Alexandria.

Drama

Athens was the home of the drama, first of tragedy and then

of comedy, and in the fifth century the two differed so greatly in form and structure as to constitute two separate literary types. By the end of the century, however, the decline in the choral elements in both had eliminated most of the formal differences, and in the hands of Euripides the treatment of the tragic themes of Greek myth assumed a naturalism which gave his plays a very mundane character. His gods and heroes spoke and acted like ordinary Athenians, as Aristophanes complained. And in Aristophanes' last plays, too, much of the fantasy of his earlier productions disappeared, so that his characters also became everyday people and the distinction between tragedy and comedy became one of theme, whether sad or happy. Plato could wonder whether it were not possible for the same man to write both. Both types were written and produced in quantity throughout the fourth century, although tragedy relied more and more on the revival of the old plays of the great masters, and we have little knowledge of the new tragedies of the period. Comedy, however, forbidden after 403 to engage in political satire, rapidly developed into a comedy of manners concerning the interests and adventures of the Athenian bourgeoisie.

It is customary to distinguish between the Middle Comedy, of which we have numerous quotations but no complete plays, and the New Comedy, represented principally by Philemon, Menander, and Diphilus. The categories overlap, however, with writers identified with the Old Comedy continuing to produce plays as late as 362 and those of the Middle Comedy as late as the first decades of the third century. It is impossible to establish a satisfactory basis for a distinction between Middle and New Comedy, the latter dated from Philemon's first production in 326. In both, it is clear that the plots usually concern Athenian citizens of the upper middle class, fairly opulent but undistinguished politically or otherwise, uninterested in anything except their families and estates. Humor is supplied by slaves, flatterers ("parasites"), prostitutes (*hetaerae*), and especially cooks, who engage in repartee, often of a gnomic character.

The Middle and New Comedy was very quotable, and most of what we possess consists of quotations from later writers. The hero or heroes are young men of good family and the plots concern their amours. Typically, the hero falls in love with an *hetaera* of not yet or not otherwise tainted virtue who proves eventually to be the long-lost daughter of a wealthy neighbor, so that the two may marry and live happily thereafter. Sometimes soldiers appear, the coarse and braggart mercenaries of the time, and all the characters tend to become stereotypes, like the "Characters" described by the contemporary Theophrastus in the series of sketches published under that title. When an actor put on the mask representing an old man or a slave, a young man or a parasite or an hetaera, it was clear in general how he would behave. Nevertheless the playwrights showed great skill in writing and in inventing plots. Our best evidence comes from the Latin adaptations of Plautus and Terence, supplemented by four substantial fragments of Menander preserved on a papyrus discovered in 1905 and now by a complete play, the *Dyscolus*, or *Peevish Man*, published in 1958 from a papyrus from Geneva. Substantial fragments of other plays, but not complete, have been discovered, providing an outlet for the ingenuity of numerous scholars.

The *Dyscolus* was an early play of Menander, produced in 317/6, with which he won his first victory, and it was surprising in that it failed to contain the usual recognition scene. The plot is quite fantastic, consisting of the efforts of a wealthy young man of good family to marry the daughter of the Dyscolus, also relatively well off but living a life of toil and solitude in the country, rejecting all visitors. The dialogue lacks humor, at least to the modern taste, and the resolution of the plot is accidental: the Dyscolus falls into his well for no good reason and is rescued by the suitor, toward whom, accordingly, his hostility begins to soften. Thereafter the suitor's suit is successful, the suitor's sister is betrothed to the Dyscolus' stepson, and the Dyscolus himself is finally induced, complaining still, to join in the nuptial celebration.

It is possible that the play had political overtones not obvious to us, for this was at the beginning of the rule in Athens of Demetrius of Phalerum. Can the Dyscolus stand for the Athenian people (*demos*), compelled reluctantly to accept an unwelcome situation? Otherwise the play is rather dull, unless one can take seriously the banal romance upon which it depends. There were certainly better plays than this in the New Comedy, cleverer and more amusing, but it is the type itself which is of significance. It is the product of a society which was comfortable and complacent to the extent of having no real problems, or none of which it wished to be reminded. Once established, this type became popular and somewhat normative for our theater, in antiquity and in modern times, and so deserves historical recognition.

The Alexandrian School

Equally important historically and more enjoyable to the modern taste was the circle of poets which centered upon Alexandria. Most of them were neither Alexandrians by birth nor residing exclusively there, but they were as closely associated with the Library as the scientists were with the Museum. Some of them were philologists and literary historians as well as poets. It was with reference to this group also that an Alexandrian historian named Andron could claim for his countrymen the honor of being teachers of all the Greeks and barbarians in the time of the first Ptolemies.[68]

In these poets there came together, in addition to learning and a refined taste, two non-Attic traditions of Greek literature, the Dorian mime of Sicily and the eroticism of Aeolis and Ionia. With these went a fondness for wit and tenderness, which led to the popularity of the epigram and a terror of boredom leading to a dislike of long poems and of the obvious and simple. Rare words and recondite allusions, allusiveness and suggestion rather than direct statement were valued. Writers were interested in the morbid and the topical, in the warped and perverted. Elegance was prized more than sympathy, except in the epigram, and the result was a manner and form of court poetry which flourished again at the court of Augustus in Rome and in later courts where wit, learning, and a touch of superciliousness were present. Of all these writers, first place was held by Callimachus of Cyrene, both for literary excellence and for versatility, but his slightly older contemporary, Theocritus of Syracuse, had the greater subsequent influence.

THEOCRITUS

As a Syracusan, Theocritus inherited the mantle of Epicharmus and Sophron who were active about 500 and 400 respectively and so hardly form a school. Their mimes, comic skits written in the Doric dialect and concerning humble or grotesque persons, were very popular. Theocritus himself left Syracuse under Agathocles and came to Cos. There he began to write hymns, epigrams, and his own modified mimes which became known as "little poems," *eidyllia* or idyls, dealing commonly with erotic themes in myth or painting, folk songs, lovers' laments, wedding songs, praises of lovely girls or boys.[69] Sometimes the poet sang in his own character, sometimes the singers were mythological or fictional human characters. Commonly they were neatherds or goatherds singing responsively or in rivalry in a rural Sicilian landscape, with names, temperaments, or problems which suggest that they are only masks for the poet's own friends and acquaintances. Quickly Theocritus attracted the attention of Ptolemy Philadelphus, whose praises he had hymned or was to hymn, and he came to Alexandria where he remained for some years, perhaps returning to Syracuse and King Hiero II only on Ptolemy's death.

The grace and charm of his idyls have made them generally admired in antiquity and modern times. The fancy of choosing a scene in an imaginary, "idyllic," country setting led his successors, Bion and Moschus, to develop a specific bucolic type of poetry, which was later further developed and popularized by Vergil, with the transfer of the scene from Sicily to Arcadia in Greece. The mime proper was continued rather by one Herodes or Herondas of whom little is known, but from whose pen came, in whole or in part, nine mimes found in a papyrus manuscript published in 1891. They concern bawds and brothel-keepers, slaves, school masters, and fashionable women, and are uniformly coarse in tone, intended to amuse a sophisticated society with glimpses of the lower classes and of their own foibles. The Ionic dialect and the choliambic meter mark Herodes as an imitator of the sixth century Ionian poet Hipponax, but it is a natural assumption that he lived in Alexandria.

CALLIMACHUS

Callimachus also has benefited from the papyri, for previously there was known of him only the hymns to Zeus, Apollo, Artemis, Athena, and Demeter, and a collection of epigrams, with some quotations. They showed his quality as a poet but not his variety, and he was known mainly for his quarrel with his friend, pupil, and associate in the Library, Apollonius of Alexandria, called the Rhodian from the city to which he retired late in life. Apollonius was the author of an epic poem in four books and six thousand lines (half as long as the *Odyssey*) describing the adventures of Jason and the Argonauts, and various remarks of Callimachus together with the stories of ancient grammarians make it seem that he disapproved of this. In addition to the summary remark dear to every student and every librarian, "A big book is a big nuisance," Callimachus sneers in his hymn to Apollo at "the great stream of the Assyrian river which carries much filth and refuse," and in an epigram he states: "I hate the cyclic poem."

In view of this he has been credited with the invention himself of the short epic, called in modern times and probably in antiquity an epyllion, of which an example would be his poem about the aged Attic woman Hecale, hostess of Theseus, and perhaps also a poem on the *Lock of Berenice,* vowed by the queen of Ptolemy III for his safety and subsequently become a constellation. Other examples of short epics are known from papyrus fragments, notably of the Chalcidian Euphorion, and the type was passed on to the Roman writer of the late Republic, Catullus and his associates. But papyrus discoveries have greatly enriched our knowledge of Callimachus beyond this. A list of summaries (*diegeseis*) of his poems has been found, showing the number and variety of his output, and extensive remains of his iambs (or rather, choliambs) have shown that he, too, wrote in the tradition of Hipponax, like the later and more moralistic Phoenix of Colophon and Cercidas of Megalopolis, they too known from papyrus finds.

In his scholarly capacity, Callimachus composed not only many books on philology and literary history, as well as a catalogue of the Library (the so-called *Pinakes*), but also four books of *Origins (Aitia),* a pseudo-historical explanation of myths, cults, and geographical names throughout the Greek world, long enough to earn his own condemnation. It is now evidently impossible to subsume Callimachus under any simple formula. If he was the inventor of the epyllion, he was also a contributor to every literary and philological activity of his time. Almost alone of his contemporaries he appears free of eroticism, for although there is little erotic in the *Argonautica* of Apollonius, his central character is the love-struck Medeia, who was to be the model of Vergil's Dido. And his epigrams show a warm human sympathy, already anticipated by the epigrammatist Leonidas of Tarentum and frequently found in the collection of epigrams made in the third century by Meleager, but never surpassed in sincerity and restraint. One may be quoted in entirety:

"Twelve years old his father Philip laid here his son,
Nicoteles, his hope for greatness."

OTHER WRITERS

Later writers in antiquity, as well as the ever generous papyri from Egypt, have given us names and excerpts from many other writers of the Hellenistic period. One should mention Aratus of Soloi in Cilicia, the pupil of Menedemus and of Zenon, who lived at the court of Antigonus Gonatas and there wrote his astronomical poem called *Phaenomena*. Based on a work by Eudoxus, it was important enough to provoke three books of commentary by the eminent astronomer Hipparchus. At about the same time Lycophron of Chalcis in Euboea was writing in Alexandria his *Alexandra,* an exceedingly obscure and learned work which purports to be a prophecy of Priam's daughter Cassandra describing how Troy's fall will be balanced by the rise of a new Troy, Rome, in the West. This is one of the earliest as well as the most remarkable acts of recognition by a Greek of Rome's coming greatness, although the phenomenon had not escaped Callimachus' attention, either. In Alexandria also wrote Sotades, a Cretan poet of professionally obscene character, whose witticism at the marriage of Philadelphus with his sister Arsinoe brought about his death at the hands of his outraged patron. And at the opposite extreme one should mention the noblest piece of religious poetry of Hellenistic times, the hymn to Zeus by the Stoic Cleanthes, pantheistic in tone but expressive of a deep religious feeling.

Thus in volume, in variety, and in importance, the literary output of the Hellenistic period is considerable. Characteristically, like most other flowerings of Greek genius at this time, it occurred mainly in the first half of the third century. To the same period belongs the greatest philological activity of the Alexandrian school, although the grammatical studies continue on later, represented for example by Dionysius the Thracian in the second century. These studies, to which we owe very much of what we know of Greek literature as well as the form in which that literature has come down to us, were occasioned by the new possibilities and requirements of the great Library and the intelligent patronage of the second Ptolemy.

With the accession of tens and hundreds of thousands of rolls of literature, it was necessary to catalogue, to classify, to compare, to organize and explain. The task belonged to the series of librarians, although it is not necessary to suppose that there was a single chief librarian or that all of those listed held that position. Many of the scholars associated with the Library were more or less contemporaries: Zenodotus of Ephesus, Callimachus, Apollonius, Eratosthenes, Aristophanes of Byzantium, and Aristarchus of Samothrace. Eratosthenes was more scientist than philologist, but to the rest we owe our text of Homer, our canon of the Attic dramatists and Attic orators, the lexicographical information necessary to read the authors, and the paraphrases and commentaries which not only explain difficult passages but give historical information helpful in criticism. Worth mentioning, because it also has been partly recovered in a papyrus, is the commentary on Demosthenes by Didymus of Alexandria, the most voluminous philologist of all time, called from his industry the Bronze-Hearted (Chalcenteros). Every student of the Classics owes Alexandria a profound debt.

5. Art

Art is a somewhat subjective term. It is the skill of men applied to or expressed in the doing or the making of things useful or otherwise, a concept which the Greeks expressed by *techne*. Every fashioned object from antiquity, every artifact, is the product of art, but not every artifact is of interest to the historian of art. The art historian, by necessity as well as convention, interests himself only in those objects which convey an esthetic meaning or pleasure to him, to the experienced beholder, to the common taste of mankind or of an age. This is the limited sense in which the concept will be considered here. Not every product of *techne,* the planetarium of Archimedes, for example, if it could be reconstructed, would be considered by us to embody art. Since we have no treatises on art in this sense from any period of antiquity, it is by no means certain that we are not applying to this study criteria which a Greek would not accept. Persons and things, natural and artificial, are called beautiful, but beauty and art are not synonomous, and beauty is also subjective. We know that Praxiteles regarded a statue of Eros as his most beautiful work and this, were it preserved, would certainly be regarded as a work of art, although the ancient practice of tinting marble statues in naturalistic colors might require us to readjust our thinking to regard the Eros in its original state as beautiful.

On the other hand, the numerous descriptions of statues and painting which have come down to us from antiquity (these constituted a recognized form of literary composition known as *ekphrasis*) do not praise their beauty or their artistic qualities either (form, line, space, color, and the rest) but only their subject matter and their naturalism. Such descriptions go back to the Shield of Achilles in the Iliad. Their popularity in Hellenistic times is shown, for example, by the description of the rustic drinking cup in the first *Idyl* of Theocritus, with its scene of courtship, its aged fisherman, and its little lad plaiting a trap for locusts instead of watching the vintage, while two foxes threaten, the one the vintage, and the other the lad's lunch. The description is full of subjective interpretation of the figures and their thoughts and feelings, but the cup itself, if we had it, would probably prove to be a poor specimen of Pergamene ware with relief decoration, and not a work of art at all, its excellence lying entirely in the imagination of the poet. We must admit, therefore, a certain anachronism in describing the art of the Hellenistic period. It is a modern rather than an ancient concept.

Artifacts

Many varieties of artifact have survived to us from the centuries after Alexander, but not all of them are relevant to our purpose. The painted Attic pottery of the sixth and to a lesser extent the fifth and fourth centuries is interesting to art historians, and some of it is very fine, but the same cannot be said for Hellenistic pottery. Attic or imitation Attic pottery is still common, but it was no longer painted with figured scenes but bore a uniform black glaze in imitation of metalwork. More interesting are the types of relief pottery, red in color, and distinguished into types called Megarian, Samian, or Pergamene, although the decoration was separately made in molds and the wares could be produced anywhere. Still less valuable for an art historian is the wide range of commonware, painted and unpainted, and the numerous clay lamps of Hellenistic date, also with appliqué decoration, are not of high artistic quality. Lamps and pottery alike were for poor folk who could not afford vessels in silver and gold, which might have shown a higher quality of art. But few of them have survived even in fragments, and they may be disregarded. The same is true of jewelry, glass, and gems, although all three categories contributed to the elegance of gentle living among the wealthy, and there must have been many objects of these sorts which were then regarded as of great beauty.

Figurines are a special problem. Broken or whole, tens of thousands of these have survived from antiquity, many of uncertain date and most of them crude or ugly. Some, however, must have had charm and even beauty in a miniature way in their original colors. They were made in many places, notably at Tanagra in Boeotia, Myrina in the Aeolia, and Alexandria, and they are of great historic importance as showing costumes, implements, personal types. But they were pressed in molds, not carved, products of a large-scale industry, and need hardly be included in a survey of art. In the same way, the silver coinage of the period may be noted only in passing. Much of it shows the high quality of die-cutting of the classical period, and some of the royal portraits are of extraordinary beauty and liveliness, especially those of the coins of the kings of Bactria, Euthydemus and his successors. They are notable examples of portraiture, which was one of the arts most highly developed in the period.

Essentially our concern is with painting, sculpture, and architecture, and since very little Hellenistic painting survives, it will be possible to take this up only in connection with other objects. Most of it is funerary, grave stelae from Alexandria, from Pagasae, and from Sidon, but the quality is not high, although the subjects and their treatment are valuable for the history of style. Architecture will be treated separately. Like sculpture it benefited from the affluence of the first half of the Hellenistic period, before the worst of the Roman plundering. Architecture can ordinarily be dated fairly well. In dealing with sculpture, it is a major problem to determine what is of Hellenistic date and what is later, especially since so many surviving statues are at best Roman copies which may reproduce inadequately the Hellenistic original. The remarks of such writers as Pliny and Pausanias are often helpful, and make possible the identification at least of distinctive types. Otherwise the only certainly datable material is the relief sculpture on dated buildings, notably the Great Altar at Pergamum.

Portraiture and Sculpture

The first type of art prominent in the Hellenistic period is portraiture. Portraiture, or at least the realistic representation of living persons, begins in Greek art in the fourth century and perhaps in Asia Minor, thus showing from the start Oriental influences. The coin portraits of Pharnabazus and Tissaphernes about the year 400 may be caricatures but they are clearly likenesses, and the same may be said of the slightly later statue types of Socrates and Mausolus. Contemporary portraits were made of fourth century philosophers and statesmen and then the practice became general, but this should not obscure the revolutionary nature of this development, the explanation of which is not easy. Images of gods were made in Greece for cult purposes and appeared on coins of their tutelary cities, and this continued throughout antiquity. Images of individuals, especially victors in the games, were set up in sanctuaries as *exvotos,* symbols of their enduring worship and dedication, and the same explanation may account for the discobolus of Myron and the doryphorus of Polycleitus, but such victors were believed to have taken on a certain divine quality. Images, mainly in relief, were made also for tombstones, but the dead too partook of divine nature and were entitled to cults of their own, however humble.

And so the generalized and idealized Hellenistic grave stelae are only logical successors of the Attic funerary reliefs of the fourth and fifth centuries, themselves looking back to the stela of Aristion of Peisistratid times. But coin representation of mortals was something else. The Persian satrapal coinage with representations of Pharnabazus and Tissaphernes was preceded by the royal coinage with a very schematized rendering of the Great King, in no sense a portrait. Even the dynasty of Mausolus did not put portraits on its coins, nor did any other ruler of the Greek world till Alexander, and then only late in his reign. And as with all the kings after him, this may be connected with the royal cult: the portrait was that of the king as god, not as ruler, even in the case of the rare portraits of Antigonus Gonatas. Realism or beauty were tributes to, not distractions from divinity. But the free portrait statue is more of a problem.

It is logical to suppose that this has the same origin and history. That is to say, that the portrait statue, herm, bust, or relief or representation in painting or mosaic was designed properly for either funerary or cultic purposes and was never, or only late in antiquity, purely honorific or "art for art's sake." Honoring with a statue or other likeness had for long religious overtones. Philip II was represented by a statue, sitting among the Twelve Gods. The twenty-five bronze statues of Alexander's companions killed at the Granicus were funerary. The fourth century portraits of Socrates, Plato, and the rest were either funerary or cultic, like the reported images of Alexander, Jesus, and Apollonius of Tyana in the lararium of the Emperor Alexander Severus. The numerous contemporary portraits of Alexander the Great by Lysippus, Apelles, and other artists were *exvotos* intended for shrines of one sort or another, public or private. It is true that there were other currents of portraiture which flowed into the Hellenistic artistic *Koine,* one native to Egypt which began producing striking likenesses from the Saite Dynasty down, and one native to Etruria which contributed to late Hellenistic Roman portraiture, and it may be that these had different origins. That is another problem, but there too, a religious rather than a secular conception seems likely. At all events, there is no reason to regard the portraiture of the Greek world in at least the early Hellenistic period as non-functional. Later the attitude may have changed, probably did change. It may be, although proof is impossible either way, that the statues of Dioscurides and his wife Cleopatra found in a private house of the late second century in Delos meant no more than statues do today.

The supposed change in attitude may have occurred through mere familiarity. Statues and other likenesses became so common that they ceased to attract attention. On the other hand, such a tendency would seem to be supported by another feature of Hellenistic art. In common with science and literature, art characteristically and conspicuously was interested in "truth." Quintilian uses this word of the fourth century sculptors Lysippus and Praxiteles, adding that they did it "best." The somewhat earlier Demetrius of Alopece, perhaps the first avowed Greek portraitist, on the other hand, to Quintilian's dislike, cared more for likeness than for beauty. And while we have no certain examples of Demetrius' work, the comment on his two greater successors is quite proper; their work is clearly beautiful, while approaching naturalism on the one hand through softness, languor, and graceful curves, and on the other through the representation of active movement and such pathological states as drunkenness or such subtler emotions as the nostalgia (*pothos*) of Alexander.

Both Lysippus and Praxiteles pictured figures, gods or men, in arrested motion or in actual motion; both represented such mythical but grotesque figures as satyrs. Lysippus, at least, represented groups in hostile action. This had been done before, of course, at least in painting and relief, but the manner was now different, adding a third dimension to the earlier notion that a statue should be viewed from the front only. The way was open to the vast array of realistic and scientifically interesting but often ugly or even repulsive figures which appear in later art. Many of the figures exist only in copies of Imperial times and it is not certain that they arose in the Hellenistic period, but there are enough certain attestations to make this likely, at least in the main. We are told by Pliny that it was Boethus of Chalcedon who created in the times of Antiochus IV the eternally popular group of a chubby boy wrestling with a goose, and Myron of Thebes, perhaps about the same time, is credited with another popular figure, that of a hideous and drunken old woman. With these may well go the dwarfs, pygmies, negroes, actors, acrobats, slaves, fishermen, artisans, fashionable young men and women, soldiers, pedagogues, and every other imaginable type of person, male or female, young or old, who appear in great quantity and variety in the Hellenistic figurines and also in marble and in bronze, miniature or life-size.

It is impossible to suppose that these representations, which differ only in degree from proper portraiture, were intended exclusively for religious purposes. Nevertheless, we must not forget that ancient religion concerned itself with what are to us less publicized aspects of human life, notably the mechanics of reproduction, and the not infrequent obscene figures or groups may well have had cultic significance. As with the mimes of Herodes and with the scientific studies of the Peripatos and the Museum, many of these figures from daily life may have served no other purpose than scientific or idle curiosity. In this they do testify to a lively interest on the part of Hellenistic man in the world around him. The popularity of the mime with its exotic characters may have played a role here, too.

Representations of the gods continued to be produced in large numbers for worship or admiration, in the fourth century and later, and all of the sculptors and painters whose names are preserved made them. For some reason, perhaps religious conservatism, the classical treatment prevailed here in contrast with the baroque style which characterizes most of the art of the period. Representations of Zeus, Apollo, Artemis, and the rest continue in the manner of Praxiteles and Scopas. Only in the rendering of the slightly more bizarre Heracles and Dionysus, and the companions of Dionysus, was more liberty of innovation allowed, and this may reflect the great popularity of these two benefactor gods with their strong human sympathies. Perhaps for the same reason Aphrodite with her little son Eros was also very popular. The Aphrodite of Praxiteles, for long the great glory of the city of Cnidus, was commonly regarded as the finest statue of the Greek world. It was only the first in a long series of undraped or partially draped female figures, presumably Aphrodites, to be produced throughout the Hellenistic times, down to the most tender Aphrodite of Cyrene, and the most famous of them all, the Aphrodite of Melos, both the work of unknown sculptors. With these, nakedness was a novelty but the treatment is classical in spirit, and the same is true of the few instances where new divine types were created — or at least the few known to us.

It is possible that in such border areas as the Syrian steppe, new and somewhat un-Greek types emerged, such as we find there in Roman times, but there is no adequate evidence for the Hellenistic period. In the creation of the cult statue of Serapis, entrusted by Ptolemy II to the second Bryaxis (grandson of the Bryaxis of the fourth century), only classical concepts derived from Zeus and Pluto were employed, and the same was surely even more true in the Apollo of Daphne made by the same sculptor for Antiochus I. And in the same way the Tyche of Antioch, the work of Lysippus' son Eutychides, is a conventional goddess type with added attributes, the turreted crown and the River Orontes. The same may be said of the Tyche of Alexandria, known from a second century mosaic signed by an otherwise unknown Sophilus.

Standardized iconographical types were developed not only for the major deities and for Tychae but also for the Muses and for such personifications as appear in the relief known as the Apotheosis of Homer, signed by the sculptor Archelaus of Priene. This was found at Bovillae in Latium, near Rome, but is usually regarded as Alexandrian in origin. Homer is crowned by Chronus and Oecumene (Time and the World), supported by the Iliad and the Odyssey, and acclaimed by Myth, History, Poetry, Tragedy and Comedy, Nature, Virtue, Memory, Faith, and Wisdom, while Apollo and the Muses are in upper registers, with Zeus at the top. The writing belongs to the period around 200 B.C., and some regard the crowning figures as Ptolemy IV and Arsinoe, since this Ptolemy is known to have built a temple of Homer.[70]

Especial importance attaches in the Hellenistic period to the handling of groups, in painting, in relief, and in sculpture. These are all, of course, legacies from earlier periods of Greek art, but they shared in the various currents of Hellenistic style and produced notable and familiar monuments of Hellenistic art. Groups of Alexander and his generals fashioned by Lysippus and Apelles have perished without trace, but the painting of the battle of Issos by Philoxenus may have inspired the great mosaic in the House of the Faun in Pompeii (its use of perspective shows it to be later in date). The so-called Alexander sarcophagus from the royal cemetery at Sidon, the work of an unknown Attic sculptor of the time of the Successors, one of the few ancient marbles which still retains its original color, is a glory of the Istanbul Museum. Both give us an idea of the brilliance of the art of this early period, when there were great artists and money was plentiful.

Our loss of original masterpieces is enormous, but from the times of Eumenes II and Attalus II we have the largest and probably the most important single work of Hellenistic sculpture, the frieze of the Great Altar at Pergamum showing the giganto-machy. Here we have typical features of Hellenistic sculpture: violent action and strong emotional expression in face and figure, heavy figures with strong musculature, elaborate drapery and contorted poses, worked into a close-knit and interlocking pattern of movement in a single plane. In contrast, the smaller and poorly preserved Telephus frieze from the same monument was divided into scenes and may be the earliest preserved specimen of narrative art in the Greek world. It includes some elements of landscape background but does not yet employ linear perspective.

The period saw also great technical advance in the handling of groups in free-standing sculpture, a matter of engineering as well as of art, although the fact that the representation may be viewed from all sides and not merely from the front does present artistic problems also. Perhaps for both reasons there was a tendency to produce a pyramidal effect, and the use of props, tree-stumps, shields, drapery, and the like, was known from early times and handled with great skill, for example, by Praxiteles in the Hermes at Olympia. The first Hellenistic examples, known only from later copies, are the Niobids being shot by the arrows of Apollo, the Gallic monuments at Pergamum and Athens, Artemis with Iphigeneia and a stag, and many more. Simpler architecturally and more symbolic is the representation of the River Nile surrounded by his animals and the little putti, each representing a cubit in the river's rise. Here may be mentioned the figure of Nike descending upon a ships's prow found at Samothrace and now in the Louvre.

But the most astonishing technically of all these groups, a credit rather to the skill than to the taste of the late Hellenistic period, are those of Dirce and the bull and of the Trojan priest Laocoön and his sons, both erected and still preserved in Rome. Both are identified by Pliny with Rhodian sculptors, but it is probably unsafe to think of specific local schools of sculpture in the Hellenistic period. (The Laocoön is, on stylistic grounds, otherwise dated in the second century and associated with the Pergamene altar, while some think the Dirce belongs to the Imperial period.) The great sculptors whose work has been preserved either through fortunate finds or through later copying were well rewarded, and travelled and worked where they would or where they found patrons. While Hellenistic art would certainly not seem entirely uniform if we had more monuments and more information, nevertheless, as in the other areas of culture, there was a common taste and style, complex but recognizable. And even more than the other cultural expressions, art benefited from the wealth and social freedom created by Alexander, but was touched, hardly if at all, by its oriental associations, at least in so far as our evidence goes.

Architecture

The same conclusion and the same caution apply equally to Hellenistic architecture. A number of Hellenistic cities have been carefully excavated, notably Miletus, Delos, and Priene, but these lie so firmly embedded in Hellenic culture that they inevitably yield architectural forms which derive from it, except as the large Italian population of Delos between 168 and 88 introduced western features into the houses, notably paintings of Lares upon their altars. The same is true of such well explored cities as Athens and Cyrene, where also most of the buildings recovered belong either to an earlier or to a later (Roman) phase. At Pergamum, there was much Roman building and rebuilding, while at Dura-Europos on the Euphrates, the little frontier Macedonian city founded by the first Seleucus, very little of Hellenistic date has been found, and that of the simplest.

The Seleucid capitals of Antioch on the Orontes and Seleucia on the Tigris have revealed that they were laid out on the Hippodamian plan and so was Alexandria, with its two great avenues running east and west the length of the city, paralleled by other narrower streets and intersected at right angles by transverse streets to form the grid. Strabo tells us that about a third of the city's area was given over to the royal quarter, with its vast rambling palaces where each king in succession had added something, the Museum, and the Sema. The latter was an enclosure containing the royal graves, a kind of heroön for the dynasty, while the former included colonnades, an exedra or auditorium, and a great dining hall. Otherwise there were in the city sanctuaries and parks, a theater, gymnasium, and law court, together with a market, warehouses, ship sheds along the waterfront, and the gleaming white marble Pharos on the island of the same name. Outside to the west lay the necropolis, and to the·east, in the suburb Nicopolis, the amphitheatre and hippodrome.

This list of Strabo's can be supplemented from other evidence. He mentions only a temple of Poseidon near the market, but there were many temples, notably the great Serapeium, in the south-western part of the city. There was a great agora for public business in the center of the city. There were public buildings including a town hall (*prytaneium*). There were colonnaded streets, shops, factories, and many private houses which certainly varied in size and style with the wealth and the nationality of the occupants; for many nationalities, notably Egyptians and Jews, shared in the life of the city even if full citizenship was restricted to Greeks. (Macedonians presumably could, but would not neces-sarily, become citizens.) Most of the public architecture was certainly the standard Greek style, cut stone with column and lintel in some one or some combination of the three orders — Doric, Ionic, Corinthian — with gabled roofs covered with tiles. The city must have had a generally Hellenic look, for Callixeinus reported as something unusual the use by Ptolemy IV of Egyptian columns in his great river barge. Private houses and the poorer parts of other buildings would have been constructed of sun-dried brick upon rubble foundations, and here certainly the flat roof of the Orient was standard. Beams, timbers, trim, and doors were of wood. Tile and cement were rare, but surfacing with plaster was normal, and this could be painted. There would have been little use of the vault, except in foundations, or the arch, except for monumental gateways in the fortifications and in public precincts, for Greek architecture disliked these as much as it disliked building with tiles and cement mortar, and the dome was not yet invented.

It is probable that a similarly Hellenic manner of construction prevailed throughout the Hellenistic world, for it appears in a naturally poor and simplified fashion in the early buildings of Dura-Europos, such as the market buildings in the agora and the Temple of Zeus Megistos, and continues to dominate the buildings of the city in later periods. Roofs are flat in the Oriental fashion, but building lines are horizontal, and public and private buildings consist of a congeries of courts, peristyled or not, with rooms and

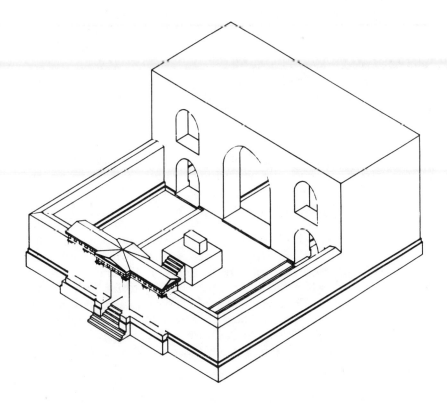

Temple of Zeus Megistus at Dura-Europus

apartments opening from them. This court architecture is common to Greece and the Orient. In the later periods such more specifically oriental features as the arched "liwan" doorways and benched rooms entered from the middle of a long side ("diwans") are common. These might be expected in Hellenistic cities of the East, especially in the smaller ones and in private houses, but we should not expect them in public buildings in the royal capitals.

A general feature of the interior appointments of the great buildings, palaces and temples, of the Hellenistic dynasties was the lavish use of luxurious materials. So Callixeinus describes the houseboat of Ptolemy Philopator:

"As one first came on board at the stern, there was set a vestibule open in front, but having a row of columns on the sides. In the part which faced the bow was built a fore-gate, constructed of ivory and the most expensive wood . . . Connected with these entrances was the largest cabin. It has a single row of columns all round, and could hold twenty couches. The most of it was made of split cedar and Milesian cypress. The surrounding doors, numbering twenty, had panels of fragrant cedar nicely glued together, with ornamentation in ivory. The decorative studs covering their surface, and the handles as well, were made of red copper, which had been gilded in the fire. As for the columns, their shafts were of cyprus wood, while the capitals, of the Corinthian order, were entirely covered with ivory and gold. The whole entablature was in gold. Over it was affixed a frieze with striking figures in ivory . . . Over the dining saloon was a beautiful coffered ceiling of cypress wood. The ornamentations on it were sculptured, with a surface of gilt."[71]

Other features of the barge were columns of Indian marble and a shrine covered with a mosaic of gold and precious stones containing portrait statues of the royal family in Parian marble. Here as well as in a dining pavilion of Ptolemy II also described by Callixeinus, there was a liberal use of curtains and tapestries in purple, scarlet, and other brilliant colors. The effect might be a little barbaric to our taste, but there is no evidence that Greeks found it distasteful.

In the stricter traditions of Greek architecture, especially those concerned with temple construction, classical standards were maintained with slight modification and development, and Hermogenes of Alabanda, the architect of the Temple of Artemis at Magnesia, is quoted with approval by Vitruvius two centuries later. Like the unknown architects of many temples known from the third and second centuries, he weakened the distinctions between the orders. Even Doric columns were made tall and slender with small capitals, and the entablature over them was reduced in size so as to give the effect of a strong upward thrust and lightness to the structure. Ionic becomes somewhat preferred over Doric, but the two are used in the same building, Ionic on the exterior and Doric in the interior, and Corinthian begins presently to be used also on the outside of buildings.

Many of these temples were very beautiful, like the Temple of Athena at Priene dedicated by Alexander and the Temple of Athena Nicephorus at Pergamum of a century and a half later, of which part has been erected in the Berlin Museum. With the increased wealth of the period, large buildings were undertaken, like the Temple of Zeus at Athens, of which construction was advanced by Antiochus IV, and the great Didymaeum near Miletus, where the oracular shrine was a small temple in an open sunken court within the temple proper. The Serapeium in Alexandria must have been a very ambitious building, although only parts of the walls of the peribolus in which it stood have been recovered. The temples of Pergamum, generally large and handsome in themselves, had the advantage of an unrivaled setting on the slopes of the citadel of the Attalids, and they were companioned by one of the wonders of the Hellenistic world, the Great Altar of Zeus. This was a high foundation 112 by 120 feet cut into by a flight of twenty-four steps on the west, and enclosed at the top on the other three sides by a wall and colonnade making an enclosure preceded by a propylaeum, within which was the altar proper. The frieze depicting the battle of the gods and giants, for which the altar is mainly famous, ran around the top of the podium, except where this was interrupted by the steps. The structure stood in a conspicuous place on the western side of the hill and was of such fame that it became known later to the Christians, from its shape, as Satan's Seat.

A number of other types of public buildings of the period are known from preserved examples or reconstructed examples. Stoas and colonnades are common, either lining main streets or agoras or standing free, like the two-story Stoa presented to Athens by Attalus II, recently reconstructed in the Athenian Agora. Other public meeting places took such forms as the Hypostyle Hall at Delos. The earliest preserved library was found at Pergamum, which had the second largest collection of books after Alexandria. Council chambers, roofed and with tiered seats like theaters, have been preserved at Miletus and Priene. Public fountains of an elaborate sort (*nymphaea*) began to be erected, although not as lavishly as under the Roman Empire. Both Priene and Pergamum have well preserved gymnasia, open courts for exercise, wholly or partly surrounded by colonnades, and with rooms for dressing and bathing. Even that typically Roman institution, the public bath with hypocausts for steam bathing, has appeared in Crete and may be dated to the second century. At the end of the period is the clock tower or horologium erected in Athens near the Agora of Julius Caesar and still standing,[72] an octagonal tower with sundials and indicators showing the direction of the wind.

Theaters of the Hellenistic times are not uncommon, and examples occur at Pergamum, Priene, and many other places, but these show no real change during the period. The theaters follow the model of Epidaurus (of the mid-fourth century) and of the theater of Lycurgus at Athens, and have something more than a semicircle of seats surrounding a nearly circular orchestra. However, since with the New Comedy the actors appeared no longer in the orchestra but on the proscenium before the permanent stage building, it was impossible for them to be seen in any position by all of the spectators. This was a defect which it remained for the Romans to remedy.

City walls, with towers, walks, and battlements, offered a rich field for the Hellenistic military architect, and some fine examples of fortifications remain or can be reconstructed, as at Priene and Miletus. With smoothly tailored and fitted stones in regular courses, well proportioned round or square towers, and handsome gates, these fortifications must have been things of great beauty, but they were of course primarily functional, and wall construction and design were intended more to meet the latest techniques of siege warfare in artillery fire, sapping, and ramming, than in looking beautiful. The walls of the later period tend to be squat and solid for strength, rather than tall and graceful. We possess a fine description of all types of walls in the writings of a Hellenistic specialist on military affairs named Philon.

Architecture was less concerned with comfort than was the individual architect, but the building activity of the Hellenistic period, domestic and public, shows commendable concern for the comfort of its customers. Streets began to be paved as well as lined with colonnades for protection against rain and sun. A more plentiful water supply permitted not only public fountains but also public latrines and public baths, while street drains permitted solid and liquid wastes to be flushed away. Water was even led into private houses, at least those of the wealthy, both for drinking and for family hygiene. With their plastered and artistically painted walls (for the incrustation style familiar at Pompeii, the First Style, was a Hellenistic invention), their windows and courts and gardens,[73] their floors paved with cement or with mosaic, and their furniture, hangings, objets d'art, lamps and landscaping, the better houses of the Hellenistic period must have been pleasant places in which to live.

Epilogue

The Hellenistic states lasted long enough to assure the survival of Hellenism. Not so many states have had the longevity of the three hundred years of Ptolemaic Egypt, and few collections of states have had, amidst political conflict and continued warfare, a common heritage and language which made it possible for individual men to feel at home wherever they might go over a wide area, under any number of rulers hostile to each other. Throughout the East the language of government and culture was Greek, and an educated man could settle where he would, and prosper. A Theocritus could emigrate from an old Greek city like Syracuse in Sicily, travel to Cos and then to Alexandria, respected as a poet at the court of Ptolemy. Ordinary people could travel all over the eastern Mediterranean, some to settle in new homes, others to transact business, like manumission of slaves at Delphi. Anyone could find his way into a theatre anywhere, and would find public and private buildings familiar in almost all cities of the East. Letters on official and private matters crisscrossed land and sea routes; by the end of the period, news of Egypt was gossip in Rome a few weeks after the event. And all this went on while royal armies clashed and Roman consuls triumphed over Greek forces.

Although the immediate heirs to Alexander's empire seemed no more able or inclined to live at peace with each other than had been the Greek city-states of earlier centuries, their successors worked out a political *modus vivendi* which was more or less successful. Spheres of influence provided both framework for peace and cause for war: borders generated continual disputes, but a ruler rarely tried to destroy another in his heartland. And political adventurism and hostility had some of the feeling of family squabbles. Rulers were often related to one another, and wars and conflicts were sometimes settled (or postponed) by marriages. Withal, the dynasties were conscious of the stakes in the game they were playing, and each wanted to survive. Since kingship and power were personal, not territorial, associated with the men and money a king could muster, the loss or gain of a patch of land had less significance than the mystique of power which a ruler could muster: kings remained kings regardless of the successes of their ventures. Some, like Antiochus the Great, might have been seen to be more kingly, but even Cleopatra's poor little brother Ptolemies were kings until they were snuffed out as part of the dynastic power play. To the people the kings were kings; the world was a warlike place, and much was to be endured under the best of circumstances. But daily life did not change much in Palestine, for example, whether it was carried on under Seleucid or Ptolemy. The great change came with the removal of the kings. First in Greece, then in Asia Minor, Syria and Mesopotamia, the Romans solved their problems of awkward borders by extending them. Big kingdoms were turned into little ones, into protectorates, then into provinces. Political problems were solved in terms of Roman law, as some kings left their possessions as legacies to the Romans, and others tried to protect what they had by making the Romans their heirs. Finally, caught up in the Romans' own internal strife, the Hellenistic states were drained of men, money, and materials, until with Egypt the last of them fell under the domination of the emerging Empire.

But Hellenism persisted through all this. During the centuries of Roman rule, and under the Byzantine Empire which survived Rome, the language of the East remained Greek, and all the traditions of Hellenism lasted in the schools and academies of the centers of culture. Although the Romans extinguished political Hellenism, Hellenic culture remained the basis of civilization of the East for all the centuries of Roman domination, preserved for the Arabs, who themselves kept and returned much of it to Europe over a thousand years after the death of Alexander the Great.

Bibliography

While systematic histories of the Hellenistic World, or of any single aspect of it, are not numerous, articles and books dealing with special problems and the interpretation of source material are innumerable. The best guides to this material are the bibliographies in the *Cambridge Ancient History*, Vols. VI-X, 1927-1934, and the two handbooks:

H. Bengtson, *Griechische Geschichte*, 1960 (from the earliest times to the late Roman Empire)

E. Will, *Histoire politique du monde héllenistique*,1966-1967 (from 323-30 B.C.)

The political history of the Hellenistic Period is covered in detail by

B. Niese, *Geschichte der hellenistischen Staaten*, 1893-1903, (from 336-120 B.C.)

and more briefly by

M. Cary, *History of the Greek World 323-146 B.C.*, 1932.

The relevant chapters in the *Cambridge Ancient History* are excellent and detailed, but somewhat discontinuous, since they are by several different scholars: Benecke, Bevan, Cary, Ferguson, Frank, Holleaux, Ormerod, Rostovtzeff, Tarn.

All aspects of the period are treated by

P. Jouguet, *Macedonian Imperialism and the Hellenization of the East*, 1928;

and

W. W. Tarn, *Hellenistic Civilization*, 1952.

The fullest treatment of the social and economic aspects is

M. Rostovtzeff, *Social and Economic History of the Hellenistic World*, 1941 (later editions add nothing substantial).
Among the special studies which may be mentioned are the
following:

E. R. Bevan, *The House of Seleucus*, 1902

E. Bevan, *History of Egypt under the Ptolemaic Dynasty*,
1927

W. S. Ferguson, *Hellenistic Athens*, 1911

E. V. Hansen, *The Attalids of Pergamon*, 1947

R. G. McShane, *The Foreign Policy of the Attalids of
Pergamon*, 1964

H. A. Ormerod, *Piracy in the Ancient World*, 1924

W. W. Tarn, *Antigonus Gonatas,* 1913.

For the chronology of the period should be consulted

E. J. Bickerman, *Chronology of the Ancient World,* 1968

B. D. Meritt, *The Athenian Year*, 1961.

The following bibliographies are primarily concerned with indicat-
ing the major literary sources, but some modern books are
mentioned for further reading.

Chapter I

We are fortunate in having five substantial biographies of Alexander. These are, in chronological order:

Diodorus Siculus, Book XVII (a sober account from generally
good sources, written in the Augustan period)

Curtius Rufus, (agreeing closely with Diodorus, but including
much rhetorical material; first century)

Plutarch, Life of Alexander (an interpretation rather than a
biography; cf. also his "Fortune of Alexander" in the
Moralia; written about A.D. 100)

Justin's abridgement of Trogus' Philippic History (Trogus was
an earlier contemporary of Diodorus)

Arrian, *Anabasis* (based on Alexander's contemporaries
Ptolemy and Aristobulus, this is the fullest, most detailed,
and most authorative life, written in the second half of
the second century).

The best modern lives of Alexander are the following:

G. Radet, *Alexandre le Grand*, 1931

U. Wilcken, *Alexander the Great*, 1932

C. A. Robinson, Jr., *Alexander the Great*, 1947

W. W. Tarn, *Alexander the Great*, 1948 (the second volume is devoted to a detailed study of special problems)

F. Schachermeyr, *Alexander der Grosse*, 1949.

Chapter II

For the period down to 302, we have a detailed and sober history in Diodorus, Books XVIII-XX, based on the contemporary Hieronymus of Cardia. The same source lies mainly behind the *Lives* of Eumenes, Demetrius, and Pyrrhus by Plutarch. For the Greece of the later third century B.C. there are the *Lives* of Aratus and of Agis and Cleomenes, with the narrative of Polybius. For the period of Roman intervention, there is Polybius and Livy, and Plutarch's *Lives* of Philopoemen and Flamininus, followed by that of Aemilius Paullus. For the period of Roman domination there are numerous Roman *Lives*: Ti. and C. Gracchus, Marius, Sulla, Lucullus, Pompey, Cato the Younger, Caesar, Brutus, and Anthony. This last period is also richly documented from Roman sources, notably Cicero's speeches and letters, Caesar's *Civil War* and the later historians Appian and Dio Cassius. Much of Ptolemaic and Seleucid history is known only from inscriptions and papyri, for which the reader is referred to the General Bibliography above.

Among modern books touching on special periods or problems are the following:

C. Wehrli, *Antigone et Demetrios*, 1968

J. A. O. Larsen, *Representative Government in Greek and Roman History*, 1955; and *Greek Federal States*, 1967

M. Holleaux, *Rome, la Grèce et les monarchies héllenistiques au IIIe siècle av. J.-C.*, 1920

E. Badian, *Studies in Greek and Roman History*, 1964

P. Lévêque, *Pyrrhos*, 1967.

Chapter III

The best accounts of the social and economic aspects of the period occur in the books of Rostovtzeff and Tarn cited in the General

Bibliography. One may also consult:

G. Glotz, *Ancient Greece at Work*,1925

R. Bogaert, *Banques et banquiers dans les cités grecques*,1968

A. G. Drachman, *The Mechanical Technology of Greek and Roman Antiquity*, 1963

A. Neuburger, *The Technical Arts and Sciences of the Ancients*, 1930

R. J. Forbes, *Studies in Ancient Technology*, 1955; *A History of Science and Technology* (with E. J. Dijksterhuis), 1963; *The Conquest of Nature; Technology and its Consequences*, 1968.

The evidence is almost entirely derived from inscriptions, papyri, and archaeological monuments.

Chapter IV

1. Philosophy

The major texts are assembled in

J. de Vogel, *Greek Philosophy* III, 1959.

Among the histories may be cited:

H.C. Baldry, *Unity of Mankind in Greek Thought*, 1965

E. Bréhier, *The History of Philosophy in the Hellenistic and Roman Age*, 1965

D. R. Dudley, *A History of Cynicism*, 1937

R. D. Hicks, *Stoics and Epicureans*, 1961

L. Edelstein, *The Meaning of Stoicism*, 1966.

2. Science

There is a convenient survey in the *Cambridge Ancient History*, Vol. VII, Chap. IX, by W. H. S. Jones and T. L. Heath. Otherwise one is referred to:

O. Neugebauer, *The Exact Sciences in Antiquity*, 1951

G. Sarton, *A History of Science*, 1952-1959

B. Farrington, *Science and Politics in the Ancient World*, 1947

M. Clagett, *Greek Science in Antiquity*, 1955.

3. Religion

On Hellenistic religion there is no lack of books. I may mention:

E. Bevan, *Hellenism and Christianity*, 1921

S. Angus, *Mystery Religions and Christianity*, 1925

A. D. Nock, *Conversion*, 1933

C. H. Dodd, *The Bible and the Greeks*, 1935.

C. N. Cochrane, *Christianity and Classical Culture*, 1937

E. Hatch, *The Influence of Greek Ideas on Christianity*, 1945

F. C. Grant, *Hellenistic Religions, the Age of Syncretism*, 1953; *Roman Hellenism and the New Testament*, 1962

F. Legge, *Forerunners and Rivals of Christianity*, 1964.

On the history and dispersion of the cult of Serapis, I may mention

P. Fraser, "Two Studies on the Cult of Serapis in the Hellenistic World," *Opuscula Atheniensia* 3, 1960; "Current Problems Concerning the Early History of the Cult of Serapis," *Op. Athen.*, 7, 1967

4. Literature

Among the many books dealing with Greek literature, the following deal particularly with Hellenistic writing:

F. A. Wright, *A History of Late Greek Literature*, 1932

H. J. Rose, *A Handbook of Greek Literature*, 1942

R. Pfeiffer, *Callimachus*, 1949-1953; *History of Greek Scholarship*, 1968

T. B. L. Webster, *Hellenistic Poetry and Art*, 1964.

5. Art

The fullest collection of material on Hellenistic art is in

M. Bieber, *The Sculpture of the Hellenistic Age*, 1961.

One may usefully consult the chapters in the *Cambridge Ancient History* by J. D. Beazley (Vol. VI, Chap. XVII) and B. Ashmole (Vol. VIII, Chap. XXI).

On architecture and town planning may be cited:

T. Fyfe, *Hellenistic Architecture*, 1936

F. Haverfield, *Ancient Town Planning*, 1913

A. von Gerkan, *Griechische Städteanlagen*, 1924

R. E. Wycherley, *How the Greeks Built Cities*, 1949.

In addition, more general books are useful:

A. W. Lawrence, *Late Greek Sculpture*, 1927; *Greek Architecture*, 1957

John Boardman, *Greek Art*, 1964

G. M. A. Richter, *A Handbook of Greek Art*, 1959.

Notes

The following notes are intended only to give the source of quotations or references from authors or other documents in the text. Inscriptions are commonly published without translation; an exception is my *Royal Correspondence in the Hellenistic Period*, 1934, hereinafter cited as *RC*. Other abbreviations are *OGIS* (W. Dittenberger, *Orientis Graeci Inscriptiones Selectae*, 1903-1905) and *SIG* (W. Dittenberger, F. Freiherr Hiller von Gaertringen, and G. Klaffenbach, *Sylloge Inscriptionum Graecarum*, 1915-1924.

1. Arrian, *Anabasis*, 3. 6. 5; Plutarch, *Life of Alexander*, 10. 3. The five named were the Macedonians Harpalus and Ptolemy, the Greeks Nearchus and the brothers Erigyius and Laomedon.
   2. The crucifixion of Pausanias is mentioned in Justin, 9. 7. 11.
   3. *RC* 1.
   4. *RC* 5.
   5. Cf. *RC* 6-7.
   6. *SIG* 398.
   7. *SIG* 434/5.
   8. E. Vanderpool, J. R. McCredie, A. Steinberg, *Hesperia* 31, 1962, pp. 25-6; 33, 1964, pp. 69-75.
   9. The new evidence in the form of an inscription from Maroneia is published by me in the Festschrift G. Klaffenbach, *Klio*, Beiheft 1970.
   10. R. Herzog, G. Klaffenbach, *Asylieurkunden aus Kos*, 1952, pp. 18 f., no. 7 (A. G. Woodhead, *Supplementum Epigraphicum Graecum* XII, 1955, 374).
   11. O. Kern, *Die Inschriften von Magnesia am Maeander*, 1900.
   12. Theocritus, XVII, 86-90; *OGIS* 54.
   13. *Inschr. Magnesia* 91.
   14. L. Robert, *Comptes rendus de l'Académie des Inscriptions et Belles-Lettres*, Paris, 1958, p. 189. A second Greek inscription is published by D. Schlumberger, *ibid.*, 22 May 1964.
   15. *RC* 25.
   16. Scarlat Lambrino, *Revue des Etudes Roumaines*, 5-6, 1960, pp. 180-217.
   17. *OGIS* 266.
   18. J. J. E. Hondius, *Supplementum Epigraphicum Graecum* I, 1923, 366.
   19. *RC* 10-13, 18-20.
   20. L. Robert, *La Carie* II, 1954, pp. 285-302, no. 166.
   21. *Inschr. Magnesia* 61.
   22. Polybius, 30. 5. 5-6; Livy, 45. 25. 9.
   23. G. Klaffenbach, *Der römisch-ätolische Bündnissvertrag von Jahre 212 v. Chr.*, 1954.
   24. Livy, 31. 34 (trans. E. Sage, Loeb Classical Library).
   25. Polybius, 16. 32; Livy, 31. 18. 1-5.
   26. *SEG* 591.
   27. Livy, 38. 9. 13.
   28. *SIG* 643.
   29. *RC* 45.
   30. Diodorus, 30. 15.
   31. J. J. E. Hondius, *Supplementum Epigraphicum Graecum* IX, 1954, 7.
   32. *OGIS* 90.
   33. *RC* 61.
   34. *RC* 52.

35. *SIG* 709.

36. *RC* 73-74.

37. Athenaeus, *Deipnosophists* XII, 549e, with note of C. B. Gulick in the Loeb Classical Library, p. 493.

38. B. P. Grenfell, A. S. Hunt, *The Tebtunis Papyri* I, 1902, 5 (A. S. Hunt, C. C. Edgar, *Select Papyri* II, 1934, 210; Loeb Classical Library).

39. Cicero, *Ad Atticum*, 6. 2.

40. Cicero, *Ad Atticum*, 6. 1 (trans. E. O. Winstedt, Loeb Classical Library); *Ad Quintum Fratrem*, 1. 33 (trans. W. Glynn Williams, Loeb Classical Library).

41. M. Rostovtzeff, *A Large Estate in Egypt in the 3rd Century B.C.*, 1922.

42. So Arrian, *Anabasis*, 4. 4. 1.

43. *Inschr. Magnesia* 61.

44. L. Robert, *Comptes rendus de l'Académie des Inscriptions et Belles-Lettres*, 1967, pp. 281-297.

45. *RC* 45; E. Bikerman, *Institutions des Séleucides*, 1938, pp. 162 f.

46. P. Bernard, *Comptes rendus de l'Académie des Inscriptions et Belles-Lettres*, 1967 pp. 306-324; 1968, pp. 263-279; L. Robert, *ibid.*, 1968, pp. 415-458.

47. *OGIS* 229.

48. M. Rostovtzeff, *Dura-Europus and its Art*, 1938.

49. W. L. Westermann, C. W. Keyes, H. Liebesny, *Zenon Papyri* II, 1940, pp. 16-21, no. 66.

50. *OGIS* 132.

51. C. B. Welles, *Mélanges Université St. Joseph* 38, 2, 1962, pp. 43-75.

52. J. A. O. Larsen in Tenney Frank, *Economic Survey of the Roman Empire* IV, 1938, pp. 334-356.

53. W. L. Westermann, *The Slave Systems of Greek and Roman Antiquity*, 1955; M. I. Finley, *Slavery in Classical Antiquity*, 1960.

54. H. Liebesny, *Aegyptus* 16, 1936, pp. 257-291.

55. O. Rubensohn, *Die Elephantine-Papyri*, 1907, 3-4.

56. Diodorus, 20. 91.

57. But on the harborless north-Syrian coast, the early Seleucids built artificial harbors at Seleucia in Pieria and Laodiceia (Latakia; this harbor is still in use). See H. Seyrig in W. Ward, *The Role of the Phoenicians in the Interreaction of Mediterranean Civilization*, 1968, pp. 53-63.

58. So II Timothy, 2.20: "Now in a great house there are not only vessels of gold and of silver, but also of wood and of earth; and some unto honor and some unto dishonor." Pottery fell into the latter class, however elegant.

59. Larsen, above, note 49.

60. Diogenes Laertius, 10. 2 (trans. R. D. Hicks, Loeb Classical Library).

61. A list is given by L. Robert, *Laodicée du Lycos*, 1969 p. 253. The literature on the ruler cult is enormous. A good outline in English is given by W. S. Ferguson, *Cambridge Ancient History* VII, 1928, pp. 7-22. Cf. further M. P. Nilsson, *Geschichte der griechischen Religion* II, 1950, pp. 125-175; C. Habicht, *Gottmenschentum und die griechischen Städte*, 1956; L. Cerfaux, J. Tondriau, *Le culte des souverains*, 1956.

62. C. E. Visser, *Götter und Kulte im ptolemäischen Alexandrien*, 1938.

63. See however especially E. Bickerman, *From Ezra to the Last of the Maccabees*, 1949; *Four Strange Books of the Bible*, 1967.

64. J. J. E. Hondius, *Supplementum Epigraphicum Graecum* VIII, 1934, 548-551.

65. Published by A. Salac, *Bulletin de Correspondance Héllenique* 61, 1927, pp. 378-383; on the whole collection see R. Harder, *Karpokrates von Chalkis und die memphitische Isispropaganda*, 1944.

66. Cf. C. B. Welles, *Historia* 11, 1962, p. 290.

67. T. B. Mitford, *American Journal of Archaeology* 65, 1961, pp. 100 f., no. 4.

68. Athenaeus, *Deipnosophists* IV, 184 b-c.

69. G. Lawall, *Theocritus' Coan Pastorals*, 1967.

70. Described with earlier bibliography by A. H. Smith, *A Catalogue of Sculpture in the ... British Museum* III, 1904, pp. 244-254, no. 2191. Cf. M. Bieber, *The Sculpture of the Hellenistic Age*, 1961, no. 497.

71. Athenaeus, *Deipnosophists* V, 205.

72. The building and its technical operation are described by D. J. deS. Price, *National Geographic Magazine*, April 1967, pp. 587-596.

73. Cf. the description of a great house and its gardens in Achilles Tatius, I, 15.

Index

THE HELLENISTIC DYNASTIES

EPIRUS

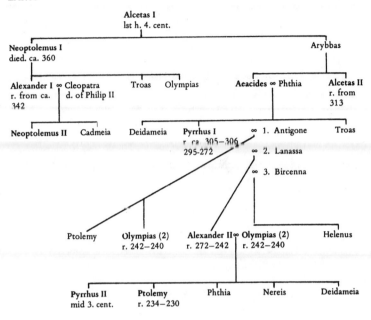

THE ATTALIDS

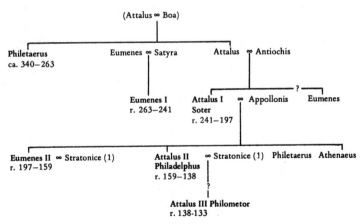

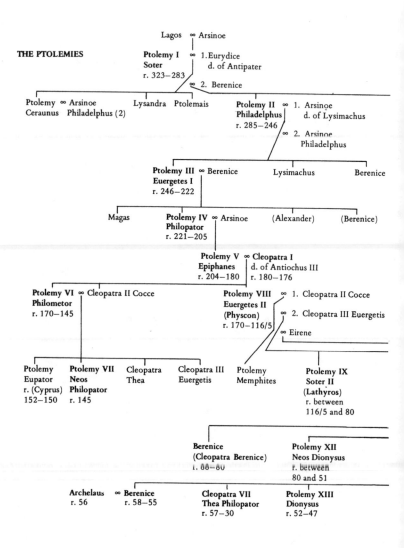

THE PTOLEMIES

Lagos ∞ Arsinoe

Ptolemy I ∞ 1. Eurydice
Soter   d. of Antipater
r. 323–283
∞ 2. Berenice

Ptolemy ∞ Arsinoe   Lysandra Ptolemais   Ptolemy II ∞ 1. Arsinoe
Ceraunus Philadelphus (2)   Philadelphus   d. of Lysimachus
                                                      r. 285–246
                                                      ∞ 2. Arsinoe
                                                          Philadelphus

Ptolemy III ∞ Berenice   Lysimachus   Berenice
Euergetes I
r. 246–222

Magas   Ptolemy IV ∞ Arsinoe   (Alexander)   (Berenice)
         Philopator
         r. 221–205

Ptolemy V ∞ Cleopatra I
Epiphanes   d. of Antiochus III
r. 204–180 r. 180–176

Ptolemy VI ∞ Cleopatra II Cocce   Ptolemy VIII ∞ 1. Cleopatra II Cocce
Philometor   Euergetes II
r. 170–145   (Physcon)   ∞ 2. Cleopatra III Euergetis
                                         r. 170–116/5
                                                      ∞ Eirene

Ptolemy   Ptolemy VII   Cleopatra   Cleopatra III   Ptolemy   Ptolemy IX
Eupator   Neos   Thea   Euergetis   Memphites Soter II
r. (Cyprus) Philopator   (Lathyros)
152–150   r. 145   r. between
                                                               116/5 and 80

Berenice   Ptolemy XII
(Cleopatra Berenice)   Neos Dionysus
r. 88–80   r. between
                            80 and 51

Archelaus ∞ Berenice   Cleopatra VII   Ptolemy XIII
r. 56   r. 58–55   Thea Philopator   Dionysus
                           r. 57–30   r. 52–47

Arsinoe
Philadelphus

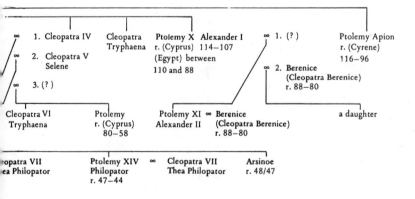

∞ 1. Cleopatra IV   Cleopatra   Ptolemy X Alexander I   ∞ 1. (?)   Ptolemy Apion
                   Tryphaena   r. (Cyprus) 114–107   r. (Cyrene)

∞ 2. Cleopatra V   (Egypt) between   116–96
     Selene   110 and 88   ∞ 2. Berenice

∞ 3. (?)   (Cleopatra Berenice)
                                          r. 88–80

Cleopatra VI   Ptolemy   Ptolemy XI ∞ Berenice   a daughter
Tryphaena   r. (Cyprus)   Alexander II (Cleopatra Berenice)
              80–58   r. 88–80

opatra VII   Ptolemy XIV ∞ Cleopatra VII   Arsinoe
ea Philopator   Philopator   Thea Philopator r. 48/47
             r. 47–44

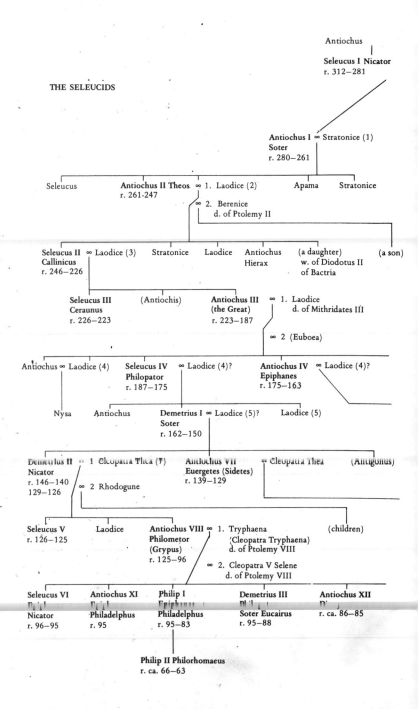

THE SELEUCIDS

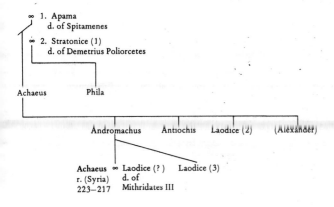

∞ 1. Apama
    d. of Spitamenes

∞ 2. Stratonice (1)
    d. of Demetrius Poliorcetes

Achaeus   Phila

Andromachus   Antiochis   Laodice (2)   (Alexander)

Achaeus   ∞ Laodice (?)   Laodice (3)
r. (Syria)   d. of
223–217   Mithridates III

Cleopatra I   Antiochis

Antiochus V   Laodice
Eupator

Alexander ∞ Cleopatra Thea
Balas   d. of Ptolemy VI
usurper
150-147

          Antiochus VI
          Epiphanes Dionysus
          r. 145–142

Antiochus IX   ∞ 1. (?)
Philopator
(Cyzicenus)   ∞ 2. Cleopatra IV
r. 116–95   d. of Ptolemy VIII

           ∞ 3. Cleopatra V Selene

Antiochus X Eusebes Philopator ∞ Cleopatra V Selene

Laodice Thea   r. 95–83
Philadelphus

         Antiochus XIII (Asiaticus)   (a son)
         r. 69–64

**THE HOUSE
OF LYSIMACHUS**

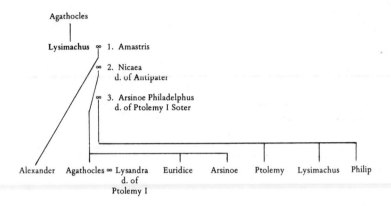

Agathocles
|
Lysimachus ∞ 1. Amastris

∞ 2. Nicaea
    d. of Antipater

∞ 3. Arsinoe Philadelphus
    d. of Ptolemy I Soter

Alexander Agathocles ∞ Lysandra   Euridice   Arsinoe   Ptolemy   Lysimachus   Philip
                  d. of
                Ptolemy I

THE ANTIGONIDS

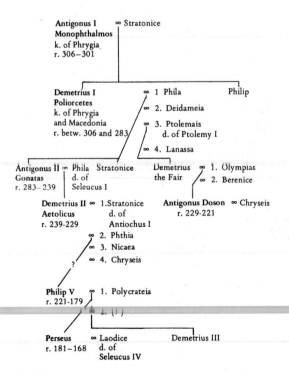

Antigonus I   ∞ Stratonice
Monophthalmos
k. of Phrygia
r. 306–301

Demetrius I   ∞ 1 Phila   Philip
Poliorcetes
k. of Phrygia   ∞ 2. Deidameia
and Macedonia
r. betw. 306 and 283 ∞ 3. Ptolemais
                         d. of Ptolemy I

                     ∞ 4. Lanassa

Antigonus II ∞ Phila Stratonice   Demetrius ∞ 1. Olympias
Gonatas   d. of   the Fair   ∞ 2. Berenice
r. 283–239   Seleucus I

Demetrius II ∞ 1.Stratonice   Antigonus Doson ∞ Chryseis
Aetolicus   d. of   r. 229-221
r. 239-229   Antiochus I

              ∞ 2. Phthia

              ∞ 3. Nicaea

         ?   ∞ 4. Chryseis

Philip V   ∞ 1. Polycrateia
r. 221-179
              2. (?)

Perseus   ∞ Laodice   Demetrius III
r. 181–168   d. of
                Seleucus IV

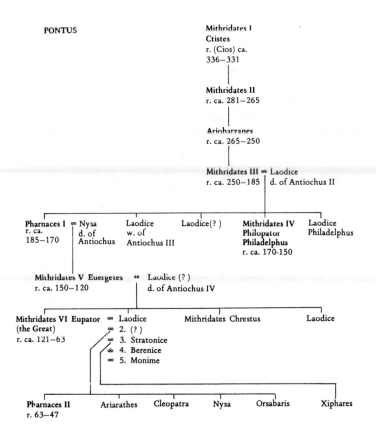

PONTUS

Mithridates I
Ctistes
r. (Cios) ca.
336–331

Mithridates II
r. ca. 281–265

Ariobarzanes
r. ca. 265–250

Mithridates III ∞ Laodice
r. ca. 250–185 | d. of Antiochus II

Pharnaces I ∞ Nysa Laodice Laodice(?) Mithridates IV Laodice
r. ca. d. of w. of Philopator Philadelphus
185–170 Antiochus Antiochus III Philadelphus
r. ca. 170-150

Mithridates V Euergetes ∞ Laodice (?)
r. ca. 150–120 d. of Antiochus IV

Mithridates VI Eupator ∞ Laodice Mithridates Chrestus Laodice
(the Great) ∞ 2. (?)
r. ca. 121–63 ∞ 3. Stratonice
 ∞ 4. Berenice
 ∞ 5. Monime

Pharnaces II Ariarathes Cleopatra Nysa Orsabaris Xiphares
r. 63–47

THE HOUSE OF ANTIPATER

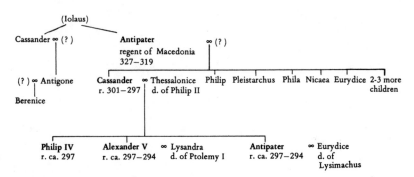

(Iolaus)

Cassander ∞ (?) Antipater ∞ (?)
 regent of Macedonia
 327–319

(?) ∞ Antigone Cassander ∞ Thessalonice Philip Pleistarchus Phila Nicaea Eurydice 2-3 more
 r. 301–297 d. of Philip II children
Berenice

Philip IV Alexander V ∞ Lysandra Antipater ∞ Eurydice
r. ca. 297 r. ca. 297–294 d. of Ptolemy I r. ca. 297–294 d. of
 Lysimachus

1. GREECE AND IONIA

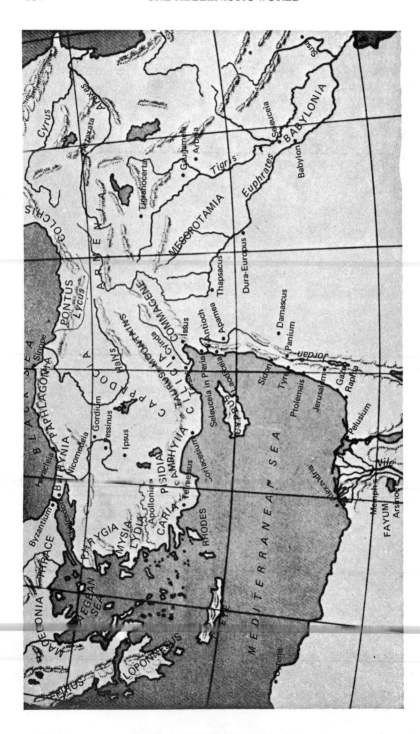

2. THE NEAR EAST

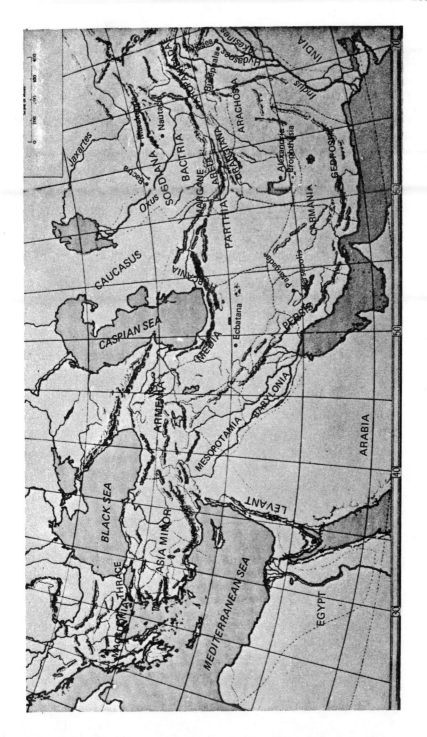

3. ALEXANDER'S EMPIRE